12-22-76

Presidential Power
and Politics

WILLIAM F. MULLEN

Presidential Power and Politics

St. Martin's Press • New York

To Marty

Library of Congress Catalog Card Number: 75-29941
Copyright © 1976 by St. Martin's Press, Inc.
All Rights Reserved.
Manufactured in the United States of America.
09876
FEDCBA
For information, write: St. Martin's Press, Inc.,
175 Fifth Avenue, New York, N.Y.   10010

Preface

Any discussion of the modern American presidency of necessity focuses on the power of the chief executive—its extent, form, sources, exercise, and limits. One of the vital questions facing Americans—indeed, citizens of every nation in the world—is what the president of the United States will do with the vast authority placed in his hands.

For many years authors lamented the restraints on the office and the lack of resources needed to achieve the goals of the "leaders of the free world." Experience in the last decade, however, has called for a reexamination of the unquestioning attitude that has allowed men of modest political talents and even more modest judgment to be placed in a position approaching divine right power. The culmination of the postwar trend toward presidential government is an office exaggerated in size, glorified in the popular imagination, and, when it fails to live up to its promise, vilified for its mistakes. Such a system is obviously in need of reform.

This book concentrates essentially on the powers of the office of the presidency and the dangers inherent in them. How did the powers of the presidency develop? Why have the American people's expectations increasingly come to focus on this office? What role do the media play in perpetuating the dominant presidency? Why has the White House staff swollen in importance since the Second World War? What factors help account for seemingly inexplicable lapses of presidential judgment? And finally, what reforms have been proposed to cut the "imperial" presidency down to size? These are some of the questions that constitute the subject of this book.

The position advanced is that one does not have to support a weak presidency in order to seek some limitation, some alteration in the present condition of the office. Logically there must be some outer limit on power beyond which even elected officials motivated by the best intentions come to resemble, if not dictators, then at least benevolent despots. If power were to continue to flow to the presidency, then the oldest fear in the republic would be realized. America would be governed by a monarch, even though an elected one.

While any errors in this work are of course mine alone, credit for what value it may possess must be shared more broadly. I owe a special debt of gratitude to Professor John C. Pierce, who read an earlier version of the manuscript and offered invaluable suggestions for improvements. Likewise, Professor Max J. Skidmore contributed significantly to the final product, both in form and substance. At St. Martin's I have benefited greatly from the advice and help of Barry Rossinoff and Nancy Perry. A special and personal word of thanks is due Dell Day, Joyce Lynd, Sue Fogarty, and Bobbie Noble, who typed the manuscript.

Finally, without the encouragement, understanding, patience, and love of my wife, Marty, I would not have been able to complete this work. It is to her that this book is dedicated.

WILLIAM F. MULLEN

Contents

Introduction   1

1 *The Need for a Dominant Presidency*   8
   Constitutional Provisions   9
   Historical Growth of the Office   12
   Presidential Greatness   28
   The Traditional View of Why We Need Strong
      Presidents   31
   Summary   50

2 *Sources of Presidential Power*   54
   Legislative Clearance   54
   The Budget   61
   Impoundment   64
   Contingency Funds, Reprogramming, Transfers,
      and Full Funding   70
   The Veto   73
   Patronage   74
   Legislative Liaison and Control of Information   77
   Secrecy and Classification   80
   Executive Privilege   88
   Emergency Powers   93
   War Making   98

3 *The People and Presidential Power*   110
   Political Socialization   111
   The President and the News Media   126
   The Effects of Vietnam and Watergate   144

4 *Elevation and Isolation in the White House* 156
   The Sun King 158
   Isolation 172
   The White House Staff System and the Decline of
      the Cabinet 181
   Growth of the Staff 192
   Problems with the Staff System 216

5 *Reforms* 222
   Change in the Term of Office 223
   A Plural Executive 226
   Bringing Congress into the Cabinet 230
   Revitalization of the Cabinet and Limitation of
      Staff 232
   Reform in Justice 239
   The Strengthening of Congress 245
   Demythologizing the Presidency 251
   Conclusion 263

Appendix A *Presidents of the United States* 269

Appendix B *Constitutional Provisions Pertaining
to the President* 271

Bibliography 278

Index 287

Presidential Power
and Politics

Introduction

Presidents have intrigued the American people since George Washington agreed to become the nation's first chief executive. Political history generally has been written in terms of presidential administrations rather than congressional eras or Supreme Court chief justiceships. Schoolchildren are required to memorize the list of illustrious men who have held the office, even when they cannot remember the specific achievements of a Tyler, Taylor, Pierce, or Arthur. To know that a person was president is to know that he was important. The privilege of holding the office is so great that Gerald Ford claimed that former President Nixon had suffered enough merely by being forced to resign. Like the Christian belief that hell is the denial of access to the presence of God, the denial of tenure is deemed insufferable punishment for chief executives.

Today the president *is* the government for millions of Americans. Many among them may not like the incumbent personally, or approve of his policies, but they want him to succeed and in most areas to be left alone by Congress and others who would interfere with his conduct of the office. The people don't want carping critics, intellectuals, or student demonstrators belittling their government and its symbol, which the president has become. Although some may not trust him, "he's all we've got." Since most people pay little attention to politics, the majesty and pageantry of his office capture the public imagination, while political parties, the bureaucracy, Congress, the judicial system, pressure groups, and social movements either are condemned or go unnoticed. The president's individual status enables him to

1

personalize the complexities of government. He thus becomes the subject of magnified reverence as well as of love and hatred. He is the target not only of the hopes and aspirations of the people but also of their frustrations. In the latter instance, he may also become the target for assassins' bullets.

It may be that public dissatisfaction with the administrations of Lyndon Johnson (because of the Vietnam War) and Richard Nixon (because of both that war and Watergate) has led to a more realistic, less idealized version of the presidency. More likely, however, is the belief that the institution was perverted by two men not worthy of holding the office. Since many of the people felt betrayed, their contempt for these men became acute. If the right person could just be elected, some continue to believe, all would be well again. Beliefs about the heroic cast of previous incumbents were not wrong, but the corrupted political parties have recently forced the electorate to choose among such candidates as Lyndon Johnson, Hubert Humphrey, George McGovern, Barry Goldwater, and Richard Nixon. If the people could vote for another Jackson, Lincoln, Roosevelt, or Kennedy, then the restoration could be accomplished. The office has been a gallery of the nation's most revered patriots; the civic religion of American nationalism has nearly deified its former occupants. If not quite divine himself, a newly elected president is at least the successor to that heroic tradition. Like the popes for Catholics, a president is the direct spiritual descendant of America's venerated saints. The office was founded on the rock of Washington, tested through the martyrdom of Lincoln, and made relevant to legions of supplicants by Jackson, Wilson, and the two Roosevelts. The recently inaugurated politician inherits the mantle of office from those enshrined on Mt. Rushmore.

Just as his predecessors were able to achieve miracles of democracy, so the new chief executive is expected to find solutions to all of the problems facing the nation today. A mysterious process begins to take place as soon as it is clear that one of the aspirants to the office has been elected. His defeated opponent wires his congratulations, promises support, and wishes the president-elect every success. The press points to fresh opportunities and the dawning of a new era. Polls conducted after the election find far more people saying they voted for the victorious nominee than the ballots indicate actually did. Many of those who voted against the man as a candidate begin to view him in a different light. Support increases among the population at large as the magic of the office begins to lend its coloration to the next chief executive. By inauguration day, a large majority will say they support the president, regardless of how slim his electoral margin may have been. With such an auspicious beginning, it may appear at first glance that the new president would almost be guaranteed of success. But because so much is expected, because so many of the hopes of the nation are centered on the actions of a single man, problems that do not yield to ready solutions are soon blamed on him. The danger in presidential government is that when confidence in the man is shaken (over Vietnam, civil rights, Watergate, the economy) trust in government is shattered as well. The result in recent years has been added cynicism and alienation.

Presidents know they are at the center of the political system. They are also aware of the expectations that the public has of the office. And they know which of their predecessors have been singled out for greatness—those who strengthened the office at the expense of Congress, the states, or private interests. The chances are that any new incumbent will feel that the only way to live up to these responsibilities—to be a successful president—is to gain as much control over the vital decisions of government as possible. When this is coupled with the unwillingness or inability of other institutions to fill the leadership role required in a democracy, the trend toward ever increasing presidential power becomes understandable.

Until recent years, this trend went largely unquestioned by scholars, journalists, and other observers of the presidency. In fact, it was applauded as a necessary and desirable manifestation of the adaptability of American political institutions to meet the needs of the twentieth century. "Strong" presidents had always been good for the United States: they had launched the republic, helped democratize it, saved the Union, sided with the common people against established privilege, rescued the nation from economic collapse, and helped defend the world against absolutism. Although the picture here is overdrawn, it is true that presidents such as Washington, Jackson, Lincoln, Wilson, and the two Roosevelts were truly outstanding leaders who contributed significantly to the success of the American democratic experiment. When compared to their less dynamic colleagues (such as Buchanan, Grant, Taft, or Harding), the need for vigorous presidents seemed obvious. Strong presidents in the past had generally served during periods of upheaval. Now permanent crisis required a permanently strong and active chief executive at the helm of state.

To those who expressed fears about the potential dangers of concentrating so much power in the presidency, the defenders of the institution pointed to history. Instead of suppressing freedom and liberty, presidents had been their chief protectors. While the states, Congress, and economic interests had engaged in or condoned exploitation and discrimination, not so the strong presidents. As for the possibility that some future unworthy cloaked in the mantle of Lincoln would abuse his trust, this too was rejected. As James MacGregor Burns wrote: "The party and electoral systems have their own checks and balances that operate to exclude adventurers from high office." "The whole presidential selection system is almost ideally suited for the selection of men who can become great in the White House."[1] To a generation of scholars steeped in admiration for Franklin Roosevelt, these truths seemed self-evident.

With Lyndon Johnson began the first glimmerings of a rethinking of the wisdom of entrusting so much power to the presidency. By the time Richard Nixon was forced to resign from office, wholesale doubts were being expressed about the desirability of presidential domination. Although hindsight is always more accurate than foresight, Franklin Roosevelt's warning should perhaps have been taken more seriously:

> We have built up new instruments of public power. In the hands of a people's Government this power is wholesome and proper. But in the hands of political puppets of an economic autocracy such power would provide shackles for the liberties of the people. Give them their way and they will take the course of every autocracy of the past— power for themselves, enslavement for the public.[2]

As events were to demonstrate, economic autocracy was not the only danger to fear from an unchecked concentration of power.

Perhaps more fundamental was the threat to political and civil liberties. The Nixon administration was not responsible for the current push toward executive rule. That had begun under a line of Democratic presidents. What called attention to the trend was not only the clear illegality of many of the activities that took place in Nixon's administration (unique among presidencies) but also his manner and style. Where others—including Johnson—had bargained, soothed egos, and sought consensus, Nixon openly displayed his contempt. He ignored Congress or treated it with ridicule. The federal bureaucracy was pictured as an alien enemy of the people and their president rather than as a group of civil servants implementing the policy of the government. Most of the members of the cabinet were reduced to carrying out the orders of White House aides. Nixon held fewer press conferences than any other modern president, and he and his aides accused reporters and television anchormen of being part of a liberal conspiracy bent on destroying a conservative administration. Thus the traditional checks on the president were seriously eroded. Even the people were patronized by appeals to their fears rather than to their better instincts. The president revealed what he thought about the electorate in an interview given on the eve of his landslide reelection victory in 1972: "The average American is just like the child in the family. You give him some responsibility and he is going to amount to something. . . . If, on the other hand, you . . . pamper him and cater to him too much, you are going to make him soft, spoiled and eventually a very weak individual."³

Nixon's self-imposed isolation from Congress, the press, the people, and even most of his own government brought into question the idea that the "institutionalized" presidency had safeguards built into it that would insure against unilateral decisions inimical to the public interest. The secret bombing of Cambodia, the unleashing of *schrecklichkeit* against North Vietnam, the activities of the White House "plumbers," the arrogant nomination of unqualified judges to the courts, the misuse or attempted misuse of governmental agencies, the plans for a secret police force, the attempts at political espionage and sabotage—all illustrated what could be done with the office. Giving the president power to achieve unlimited good means that, in the wrong hands, power can be used for unlimited evil. But one does not have to presuppose evil men to believe that power can be corrupted. Perhaps more dangerous is the well-intentioned but misguided patriot who believes that he must act to suppress "threats" to the nation in the form of citizens exercising their freedoms.

It would be tempting to write off Watergate and the Nixon administration as temporary aberrations in the otherwise long and successful history of the presidency. It is probably true that for the next fifty years politicians will remember what happened to Nixon and his men and strive to avoid their mistakes. In that sense, Watergate provided a valuable learning experience. An examination of past administrations, however, has raised the question of whether institutional factors may now predispose all presidents to serious mistakes in office, if not of the criminal variety, at least of a judgmental nature. Examples abound of chief executives badly miscalculating problems and suffering the consequences. Franklin Roosevelt tried to pack the Supreme Court; Harry Truman seized the steel industry; Dwight Eisenhower failed to see the danger in not calling off U-2 flights before the summit meeting with Khrushchev; John Kennedy ordered the Bay of Pigs invasion; and Lyndon Johnson dragged the nation deeper into the bottomless pit of Vietnam.

Contrary to what some may believe, the removal of Richard Nixon did not automatically signal a rebirth of Congress and the establishment of a full partnership between the political branches of government. Long before his resignation, Congress—through its abdication—had allowed the president to dominate almost all controversial issues. Thus, even though it had the power to establish by law a policy concerning Vietnam War resisters, Congress had allowed Nixon's policy of "no amnesty" to be decisive. Similarly, it allowed Gerald Ford to decree his own preferences on this subject. The same is true of the inflationary crisis in the United States. Although the idea for an "economic summit" originated in the Senate, and Congress could have called one on its own, it let Ford summon, organize, and dominate "his" conference and then awaited recommendations from the executive branch. On many controversial topics, Congress would rather let the president make tough or unpopular decisions. If they don't work out, or if they raise the ire of the citizens, Congress can put the blame on the president. In other cases, a committed majority cannot muster the two-thirds vote to override a presidential veto.

In order to understand how we came to the present state of affairs, it is necessary to probe the reasons for the development of presidential government in the United States. Chapter 1 begins this examination.

NOTES

1. James MacGregor Burns, *Presidential Government* (Boston: Houghton Mifflin, 1973), pp. 305, 304.
2. *The Public Papers and Addresses of Franklin D. Roosevelt*, V (New York: Random House, 1938), 16.
3. *Washington Star-News*, 9 November 1972.

1

The Need for a
Dominant Presidency

The proper shape and scope of the presidency has been one of the perennial questions confronting American constitutional scholars, politicians, and the general public. Even before George Washington's inauguration, there was intense debate over the power he and his successors should be allowed. Since almost everyone at the Constitutional Convention assumed that the presiding officer, the most trusted and revered of the newly independent nation's heroes, would be the first to occupy the office, few worried that power might be abused in the immediate future. But possessed of some measure of foresight, plus a healthy skepticism about the nature of man, the men of the convention could see that such worthy candidates might not always be available to fill the role of chief magistrate for the fledgling nation.

Their recent experience under the British monarchy had made the convention delegates fearful of executive tyranny, while their unsatisfactory government during the revolutionary period had soured them on legislative dominance. Part of their solution was to separate power among three branches of government—in effect checking power and ambition with power and ambition. Thus the creation of "separated institutions sharing power" would safeguard the people from the danger of a single man, or even a temporary popular majority, seizing all power and destroying the liberties of the people. As Madison wrote in *The Federalist*, number 47: "The accumulation of all powers, legislative, execu-

8

tive, and judiciary, in the same hands, whether of one, a few, or many, and whether hereditary, self-appointed, or elective, may justly be pronounced the very definition of tyranny." Similarly, many delegates shared Jefferson's belief that although executive despotism was the ultimate threat to the citizen's liberties, legislative tyranny was the more immediate danger.

Constitutional Provisions

The final product of the Constitutional Convention's deliberations was an executive article—Article II—rather short in length but broad in compass. "The executive power shall be vested in a President of the United States of America," it begins. (Compare this with Article I's "all legislative powers *herein granted* shall be vested in a Congress of the United States.") It makes the president commander in chief of the army and navy and of the militia when called into the service of the United States. It gives him power to require the opinion, in writing, of the principal officers of each of the executive departments; to grant reprieves and pardons in federal cases (except in cases of impeachment); and to make treaties by and with the advice and consent of the Senate.

Further, Article II confers on the president the power to nominate and, by and with the advice and consent of the Senate, to appoint ambassadors, other public ministers and consuls, judges of the Supreme Court, and all other officers of the United States not covered by some other means of selection. (However, Congress was given power to vest by law the appointment of inferior officers in the president alone, in the courts, or in the heads of departments.) He receives ambassadors and other public ministers and commissions all officers of the military. He is required to give Congress information on the state of the Union and may recommend measures to them, convene extraordinary sessions, adjourn both houses when they disagree on the proper time of adjournment, and veto bills passed by Congress (subject to repassage by two-thirds majorities in each House). Finally, the president is responsible for taking care that the laws are faithfully executed. These then are the gossamer constitutional threads from which the fabric of the modern American presidency has been woven.

Many who opposed the adoption of the Constitution did so because they agreed with Patrick Henry's conclusion that the presidency created "squints toward monarchy," and monarchy of the worst kind—an elective kingship. The president's powers as commander in chief were opposed by George Mason, who had been a delegate to the convention. James Monroe feared that the office would become a matrix for treason for some future usurper. Governor George Clinton of New York, writing a series of Anti-Federalist attacks under the pen name Cato, cited numerous opportunities for an ambitious president to ruin his country. Jefferson opposed the provision for unlimited reelection on the grounds that it would mean incumbency for life and thus intense power struggles and even foreign intervention to determine who would occupy the office.

The most notable early defense of presidential power (as well as of the other provisions of the Constitution, of course) is to be found in *The Federalist* Papers. Hamilton's eleven papers, beginning with number 67, comprise a brilliant and oft-cited explication of why the dangers seen by the Anti-Federalists were unlikely to come about and why, to the contrary, a strong and vigorous executive was a requisite for the new republic.

As for the fear that ambitious, base men would be selected, Hamilton wrote:

> This process of election affords a moral certainty that the office of President will seldom fall to the lot of any man who is not in an eminent degree endowed with the requisite qualifications. Talents for low intrigue, and the little arts of popularity, may alone suffice to elevate a man to the first honors in a single state; but it will require other talents, and a different kind of merit, to establish him in the esteem and confidence of the whole Union. . . . It will not be too strong to say that there will be a constant probability of seeing the station filled by characters preeminent for ability and virtue. [No. 68]

Nor is the danger of a president misusing the armed forces of the United States a serious one.

> The President is to be commander-in-chief of the army and navy of the United States. In this respect his authority would be nominally the same with that of the king of Great Britain, but in substance much

inferior to it. It would amount to nothing more than the supreme command and direction of the military and naval forces, or first general and admiral of the Confederacy; while that of the British king extends to the *declaring* of war and to the *raising* and *regulating* of fleets and armies—all which, by the Constitution under consideration, would appertain to the legislature. [No. 69]

To make obvious the myriad other distinctions between the proposed presidency and the British monarchy, Hamilton set forth a long list of contrasts:

The President of the United States would be an officer elected by the people for *four* years; the king of Great Britain is a *perpetual* and *hereditary* prince. The one would be amenable to personal punishment and disgrace; the person of the other is sacred and inviolable. The one would have a *qualified* negation upon the acts of the legislative body; the other has an *absolute* negative. . . . The one would have a concurrent power with a branch of the legislature in the formation of treaties; the other is the *sole possessor* of the power of making treaties. The one would have a like concurrent authority in appointing to offices, the other is the sole author of all appointments. The one can confer no privileges whatever, the other can make denizens of aliens, noblemen of commoners; can erect corporations with all the rights incident to corporations. The one can prescribe no rules concerning the commerce or currency of the nation; the other is in several respects the arbiter of commerce, and in this capacity can establish markets and fairs, can regulate weights and measures, can lay embargoes for a limited time, can coin money, can authorize or prohibit the circulation of foreign coin. The one has no particle of spiritual jurisdiction; the other is the supreme head and governor of the national church. [No. 69]

At the same time that limitations on executive authority would prevent abuses to the liberties of the people, substantial powers for the office were necessary to provide for the kind of government that a free people needed to protect their interests.

Energy in the executive is a leading character in the definition of good government. It is essential to the protection of the community against foreign attacks; it is not less essential to the steady administration of the laws; to the protection of property against those irregular and high-handed combinations which sometimes interrupt the ordinary course of justice; to the security of liberty against the enterprises and assaults of ambition, of faction, and of anarchy. . . .

The ingredients which constitute energy in the executive are unity; duration; an adequate provision for its support; and competent powers.

The ingredients which constitute safety in the republican sense are a due dependence on the people, and a due responsibility. . . .

That unity is conducive to energy will not be disputed. Decision, activity, secrecy, and dispatch will generally characterize the proceedings of one man in a much more eminent degree than the proceedings of any greater number; and in proportion as the number is increased, these qualities will be diminished. [No. 70]

Though some of these quotations may seem ironic to a generation that has lived through Vietnam and the White House "horrors" associated with Watergate, the purpose for which Hamilton composed those lines must be recalled. Moreover, the Federalist defense of the presidency has been cited at such length because the same points, or enlargements or variations of them, still form the basis of claims made for the office today. The style may not be as eloquent, nor the historiography as erudite, and the checks on the office discussed by Hamilton are likely to be minimized or viewed as unfortunate relics from the past, but the basic outline of the case made for the presidency almost two hundred years ago can still be found in the works of contemporary historians and political scientists (not to mention White House lawyers).

Historical Growth of the Office

Any attempt to understand presidential power must go beyond the skeletal outline laid down by the Philadelphia Convention and the expositions of *The Federalist* papers. The men who filled the office, the conditions in society, the problems the presidents faced, and the policies and practices they adopted are also keys to our understanding.

WASHINGTON

Washington's years as president were crucial for the institution, since the precedents he established and the patterns he set have had a major impact on the political system to this day. He gave the office content and form where only potentiality had existed. The first Congress established the executive departments of State, War, and Treasury and the position of attorney general, to which Washington named Thomas Jefferson, Henry Knox, Alexander Hamilton, and Edmund Randolph, respectively. Washington submitted their names to the Senate for approval, as the Constitution required, but in doing so he established the precedent that the power to give "advice and consent" merely meant that the Senate could vote a nomination up or down, not participate in the proposing of candidates. Similarly, Washington removed executive officers without consulting with the Senate, thereby establishing a firm chain of responsibility that excluded congressional partnership.[1]

The president began meeting more and more frequently with his four advisors for a joint consideration of policy. Often Jefferson and Hamilton were arrayed on opposite sides of the issues. This gave Washington the opportunity to check the advice he received in the internally competitive but private arena of his own office. Thus was established an institution nowhere provided for in the Constitution—the cabinet. (Most modern presidents have allowed the cabinet to become subordinated to other advisory sources—mainly the White House staff—for reasons which will be examined in Chapter 4.) Aware of centrifugal forces in the thirteen new states and the need for a sense of legitimacy for the new government, Washington carefully balanced these important appointments among the geographic regions of the country and in so doing set another important example for his sucessors. Unfortunately, the precedent of appointing the best minds available to these important posts and the practice of insuring the representation of conflicting viewpoints have sometimes been honored more in the breach than in the observance.

Washington's presidency is also notable for its broad interpretation of legislative leadership. Relying on Alexander Hamilton to draw up proposals for legislation as well as to rally Federalist support in Congress for these programs, the executive provided leadership for the legislature. This quickly put to rest the notion that Congress would be the sole source of national policy, since

Washington made much of the constitutional provision that he "shall from time to time give to the Congress information of the state of the union, and recommend to their consideration such measures as he shall judge necessary and expedient." He appeared in person before Congress to deliver his state of the Union address, vetoed legislation deemed unconstitutional or unwise, and fended off what he considered to be unwarranted encroachments by Congress into his sphere of authority. The latter point was made clear in 1796 when the House of Representatives called upon the president for papers, documents, and instructions involved in John Jay's treaty negotiations with Great Britain. Washington refused this demand (primarily sponsored by James Madison) on the grounds that the House was not constitutionally involved with the president and Senate in the treaty-making process and that the documents requested were "of a nature that did not permit of disclosure at this time."[2] This last assertion has been cited by later presidents as the right of "executive privilege" (though not formally labeled such for another 150 years). Although the House fumed, Washington's decision stood.

In other areas of domestic policy, Washington also dominated. When farmers in western Pennsylvania rebelled against a tax on whiskey imposed by the federal government (grain being too bulky to transport, the farmers reduced their crop to a more portable—and potable—commodity), the president mobilized the militia and sent it to crush the uprising. This demonstration of the power of the national government was also an illustration of the power of the presidency, one that would not be soon forgotten. In more mundane matters, Washington also proved his mastery. As Louis Koenig points out:

> With few exceptions he prescribed the duties of his department heads and kept abreast of daily detail. He read incoming and outgoing communications of the executive branch and passed upon important plans and actions that the departments submitted in writing. All loan and debt transactions were subject to his approval. Each use of the seal of the United States required his consent. No lighthouse keeper, customs collector, or captain of a cutter could be appointed without his consideration.[3]

It was, however, in the field of foreign affairs that Washington exerted his greatest leadership. The Constitution here again had divided responsibilities between two branches of government, giving to Congress the power to declare war, grant letters of marque and reprisal (that is, to authorize limited war), appropriate monies to carry out foreign policies, regulate commerce with foreign nations, establish naturalization policies, regulate the value of foreign currency, raise and support armies and navies and furnish rules and regulations for those forces, and provide for the organizing, arming, and disciplining of the militia and for calling it into federal service (this was especially important since no large standing armies were anticipated). The Senate was given the added responsibility of giving the president "advice and consent" on treaties with foreign governments as well as on appointments of ambassadors and consuls who serve as our representatives abroad. It might well have been expected, then, that Congress would have a determining voice in the broad direction of our policy toward other nations. The president's rather limited constitutional claim to the control of foreign policy rested upon his power to make treaties (although it was assumed he would consult with the Senate in so doing), receive ambassadors and other public ministers, and nominate and—by and with the advice and consent of the Senate—appoint ambassadors and consuls.

The president's first attempt to consult with the Senate involved a proposed treaty with several Indian tribes. Appearing before the twenty-six senators in person, he had the treaty read aloud and waited for their approval. After several moments of pained silence, Washington was informed that the Senate would require some time and privacy before making its final decision.[4] Chagrined by this incident, Washington withdrew and except for formal submission of the finished product, never again deigned to involve the Senate in the treaty process directly. Future presidents have copied Washington in this, and some, like Wilson, have paid the price for their independent action.

In other areas Washington also acted alone. In 1793 he issued a Proclamation of Neutrality in the War between France and Great Britain,[5] a prerogative many assumed belonged to Congress. That body, after all, was charged with declaring war, and the ability to assert the opposite state could logically be assumed to inhere in that institution as well. In 1794 Congress officially passed a Neutrality Act of its own, and since that date the subject has largely been conceded to lie within its province (while presidents have more and more come to take on the responsibility for involving us in armed conflict).

Despite Madison's contention that the power to "receive Ambassadors or other public ministers" was purely a ministerial and ceremonial function, one designed to authenticate the credentials of representatives accredited to the United States, Washington acted alone in accepting Citizen Genêt as the envoy of France. Similarly, when the president several months later demanded the recall of Genêt, he acted without consulting Congress, establishing the precedent that the president alone decides when and with which foreign governments the United States will establish and maintain relations.[6]

Thus when Washington retired after two terms (putting to rest the fear that the presidency would become a lifetime possession), he had proved to be a resourceful and innovative expositor of executive authority, one who, along with his chief aide Hamilton, seemed ready to fill the interstices of power inevitably left by the new Constitution. His dignity, authority, and unquestioned integrity launched both the new Constitution and the institution of the presidency on a much needed wave of respect and legitimacy.

JEFFERSON

Among other things, Thomas Jefferson is known as the president who overcame his republican scruples about executive domination and constitutional scruples about strict construction long enough to purchase the Louisiana Territory from France. More important, he was also an extraordinarily skilled party leader.

Jefferson worked with and through the congressional leadership and the party caucus as instruments of majority rule government. He provided the agenda, and he and his aides saw the program thus designed through to final enactment by the legislature. Jefferson made the presidency into a preeminently *political* office, closely tied to the legislature (a fact that was inevitably to have unfortunate consequences for the office when a person of lesser manipulative talents sat in the president's chair). Since Jefferson was a very talented man, most of his successors have suffered by comparison in their leadership of party and Congress. Nevertheless, the Jeffersonian prototype of the presidency, one of majority rule, executive leadership of Congress, and party responsibility, has been one of the most attractive and influential models for political scientists from Woodrow Wilson down to this day.

Washington and Jefferson were responsible for honing two of the major weapons in the presidential arsenal—respect and awe for the office and leadership of party. Not all of their successors were able to wield these mighty weapons as ably as did these two early presidents, but for the twentieth century they form indispensible arms of presidential power.

JACKSON

"The Second American Revolution," "The Democratic Revolution," and "The Rise of the Common Man" have all been rubrics used to summarize the Age of Andrew Jackson and his administration. He was the first president elected under universal white manhood suffrage, and his presidency is primarily noted for his assertions that the president best represented the people. The essentially heretical notion that the president is more of a popular representative of the people than is the Congress was astounding to congressional students of Locke, such as Henry Clay and Daniel Webster. The Whigs' belief in Congresssional supremacy was based on well-established opposition to executive prerogative—the fear of monarchical tyranny. Here was a president claiming that he, because of the way he was elected, was the spokesman for all the people and that leadership in government must spring from his independent judgment. This battle over representativeness and democratic leadership is one that is still being fought between contemporary presidents and Congresses, and one that will be explored in greater detail later in this chapter and in Chapter 5.

The generally accepted interpretation is that Jacksonian democracy represented the frontiersmen, the small farmers, the emerging class of industrial workers—essentially those without substantial property holdings. In the eyes of the Jacksonians, government had been conducted primarily by and for the interests of the "nonproducing" classes—those who received patents and monopolies from the state, whose property was increased through judicious use of federal power, and whose banks and corporations had come to dominate most other American institutions. Thus "human rights" were being trampled in the name of "property rights."[7] The most famous measure taken by Jackson to get government off the side of business was his veto of the bank bill of 1837, which would have extended the charter of the Second Bank of the United States. This bank had a unique relationship with the federal government, acting as its depository and using government funds without interest for its own commercial profit. This, along with other provisions, made the bank highly controversial. In his veto message Jackson complained that "many of our rich men have not been content with equal protection and equal benefits, but have besought us to make them richer by act of Congress." He acknowledged distinctions in society based on talent, industry, thrift, and virtue, but

> . . . when the laws undertake to add to those natural and just advantages artificial distinctions, to grant titles, gratuities, and exclusive privileges, to make the rich richer and the potent more powerful, the humble members of society . . . who have neither the time nor the means of securing like favors to themselves, have a right to complain of the injustice of their Government.[8]

Thus the notion of the presidency fighting for the common man, the dispossessed, the alienated, the despised, stems from Jackson and the forces he brought into and represented in government. If Congress had come to be dominated by narrow considerations of region and economic privilege, the president, elected by all the people, would speak for the little man. Such at least has been the accepted dogma in the literature of presidential worship.

Jackson is also noted for reliance on his "kitchen cabinet" rather than on the heads of departments for advice and aid in policy areas and for speech writing and other services previously exercised by those in formal governmental positions. Unofficial advisors could serve a president with candor and complete loyalty to the president's cause—elements that might be lacking in a cabinet made up of politicians, whether political opponents appointed to placate losing factions of the party or hacks paid off for past services to the candidate.[9]

As for appointments generally, Jackson is given the dubious credit for inaugurating the "spoils system" ("to the victor belongs the spoils of the enemy"), originally intended merely to establish the principle of rotation in office. Whether or not Jackson did initiate this system, he was by no means as ruthless in carrying out the policy as some historians have portrayed him. Only around 10 percent of federal officeholders were replaced during Jackson's tenure.[10] The principle was defended by Jackson in his first annual message with the claim that "the duties of all public officers are, or at least admit of being made, so plain and simple that men of intelligence may readily qualify themselves for their performance; and I cannot but believe that more is lost by the long continuance of men in office than is generally to be gained by their experience." And further that "in a country where offices are created solely for the benefit of the people, no one man has any more intrinsic right to official station than another."[11] It is probably true that almost all government jobs of the day were within the capacity of most citizens of average intelligence, and since our society had not yet become as enamored with "credentials" as it is today, rotation in office made sense to those bent on egalitarian policies.

By the time Jackson retired to the Hermitage after two terms, the office he left behind was one of enhanced power and prestige among the general population. Clinton Rossiter concluded that "the Presidency would surely have become a democratic office had Jackson never held it, but he was the one who presided imperiously over the radical reversal in the roles of President and Congress as instruments of popular power and targets of popular feeling."[12] When added to the other potentialities of the office, this ability to serve as the focus of expectations for democratic leadership immeasureably expanded a president's power to dominate the political process.

LINCOLN

Among those enshrined in the Valhalla that America reserves for its greatest heroes, none is more elevated than Abraham Lincoln. Only Washington rivals Lincoln in our hearts, on our currency, and on our classroom walls. The personal qualities of the man were the stuff from which legends have been created.

Although Lincoln as a congressman had opposed the Mexican War on the grounds that it had been unconstitutionally instigated by President Polk, his actions as president expressed a conception of presidential power unparalleled in scope for the next hundred years. During his first eleven weeks of office—a time when Congress was neither in regular session nor called into special session by Lincoln—he proceeded to blockade Southern ports, enlarge the army and navy beyond the limits set by legislation, spend money from the Treasury unappropriated by Congress, secure a loan by pledging the credit of the United States, authorize the arrest of certain suspected persons, suspend the writ of habeas corpus in parts of the country, and close the mails to "treasonable correspondence." [13] These acts were either unconstitutional, illegal, or at best of highly dubious presidential prerogative (as opposed to resting within the province of Congress), but the authority for all of them he arrogated unto himself in his role as commander in chief with the responsibility of taking care that the "laws be faithfully executed." He defended his actions by citing his solemn oath to "preserve, protect, and defend the Constitution of the United States." Thus were born the war powers of the president.

When Congress convened in special session on July 4, 1861, Lincoln submitted these *faits accomplis* and invited ratification of his actions. In his message he justified the steps he had taken in these words:

> These measures, whether strictly legal or not, were ventured upon, under what appeared to be a popular demand and a public necessity; trusting then as now that Congress would readily ratify them. It is believed that nothing has been done beyond the constitutional competency of Congress.[14]

Congress on August 6, 1861, approved all military action taken up to that date by the president and finally in March 1863 authorized Lincoln to suspend the writ of habeas corpus.

Lincoln's justifications for the actions he took rested on his conception of necessity during the kind of emergency that threatened the continued existence of the Union and its Constitution. He employed the analogy of one trying to protect both life and limb from loss and concluded that, although sometimes a limb must be amputated to save a life, life is never wisely sacrificed to save a limb. So too with the Constitution. Circumstances may demand a provision be stretched, bent, or even broken in order that the whole survive. For what would remain of the Constitution if the Union were destroyed? "Are all the laws but *one* to go unexecuted, and the Government itself go to pieces lest that one be violated? Even in such a case, would not the official oath be broken if the government should be overthrown when it was believed that disregarding the single law would tend to preserve it"?[15] Emergency, then, may make otherwise unconstitutional actions acceptable if those actions contribute to the preservation of the Constitution and the society it represents. Note that the danger must be of such magnitude that the existence of the nation itself is in peril.[16] Furthermore, this ultimate power to protect the nation in its darkest crisis belongs to the president, even if that means exercising legislative powers (Lincoln instituted national conscription and only later requested congressional authorization), judicial powers (the use of special war courts in occupied territories), or powers completely denied to the government (the suspension of civilian courts where no rebellion existed, suppression of newspapers, seizure of property without due process of law, and so on).

After Lincoln's death and the end of the Civil War, congressional reaction to expansive presidential claims of powers was swift and devastating. Congress asserted its supremacy in almost every sphere of contention between itself and the president and impeached Andrew Johnson when he sought to defend what he considered to be the integrity of his office. For the remainder of the century, the American political system could best be described—as indeed that early political scientist Woodrow Wilson did describe it—as "Congressional Government."[17] Nevertheless, Lincoln had established a cardinal principle of American politics: crisis government would essentially be presidential government, and the more severe the crisis, the more Congress, the courts, and the people would defer to the president's judgment. In an age when crises of one sort or another seem to be a permanent condition of society, this has had a profound impact on the way the American people are governed.

THEODORE ROOSEVELT

After consolidating its hold on the continental United States by crushing the last remaining vestiges of independence by native

Americans, the emerging American giant turned its attention abroad. The Spanish-American War of 1898 was to have further profound effects on the United States, as well as on the office of the presidency. Largely at the urging of Congress and the yellow press, President McKinley reversed his previous antiwar policy and sought American intervention in Cuba, then a Spanish possession in revolt against colonial oppression. Ultimately the United States occupied not only that nation but the Philippines, Samoa, Guam, Wake Island, Puerto Rico, and Hawaii as well (with only Cuba given its immediate independence). Consequently, the United States became a world power with an overseas empire to look after and, at the same time, gained a new raison d'être for the existence of a large navy and an expanded role for the commander in chief of its armed services. However, it was Theodore Roosevelt, not McKinley, who was the first to take advantage of the possibilities inherent in the situation.

Every schoolchild can recount how in 1907 Teddy Roosevelt faced down congressional opposition to a proposed trip around the world by the Great White Fleet by reminding the legislators that he had enough money to get the ships halfway round, and if Congress did not want the fleet stranded there, it would have to appropriate the funds to get them back again. Furthermore, Roosevelt announced it would henceforth be the policy of the United States to intervene in Latin American countries whenever he felt them incapable of protecting the lives of American citizens or American business interests. Even before the announcement of this Roosevelt Corollary to the Monroe Doctrine, the president had manufactured a revolt in Colombia in order to establish a new republic in Panama favorable to the U.S. construction of, and sovereignty over, a Panama isthmus canal.

These things Roosevelt did during an era when mass circulation newspapers and magazines were beginning to have a nationwide impact on the American reading public. His colorful past as a cowboy, Rough Rider, and cop, combined with his lifelong participation in numerous sports, enabled him to personify the ideal rugged individualist so admired in the popular imagination of the day. Along with his similarly active family, he put the presidency and all its activities on the front page of the daily newspapers—where it has remained to this day, regardless of the habits and hobbies of the incumbents. What the president did was news. Even what the president said was news, especially when he had a flair for the dramatic and a talent for a well-turned phrase. Roosevelt is credited with many expressions which have entered the American lexicon, including "square deal," "speak softly and carry a big stick," "muckraker," and "lunatic fringe." Roosevelt also realized the emerging importance of the press in molding public opinion and the ways in which a president could use the press for his own purposes. He originated the modern presidential press conference and employed it to build popular support for programs he favored in Congress.[18] The first Roosevelt was thus able to convert the office into the "bully pulpit" which would dominate the attention of those attuned to the political arena.

Teddy Roosevelt is also credited with one of the most articulate presidential expositions of executive authority. His oft cited "stewardship" theory of presidential power has seemingly become the credo of all strong twentieth-century presidents:

> The most important factor in getting the right spirit in my administration, next to the insistence upon courage, honesty, and a genuine democracy of desire to serve the plain people, was my insistence upon the theory that the executive power was limited only by specific restrictions and prohibitions appearing in the Constitution or imposed by the Congress under its constitutional powers.
>
> My view was that every executive officer, and above all every executive officer in high position, was a steward of the people bound actively and affirmatively to do all he could for the people, and not to content himself with the negative merit of keeping his talents undamaged in a napkin. I declined to adopt the view that what was imperatively necessary for the nation could not be done by the President unless he could find some specific authorization to do it. *My belief was that it was not only his right but his duty to do anything that the needs of the nation demanded, unless such action was forbidden by the Constitution or by the laws.* Under this interpretation of executive power I did and caused to be done many things not previously done by the President and the heads of the departments. I did not usurp power, but I did greatly broaden the use of executive power. In other words, I acted for the public welfare, I acted for the common well-being of all our people, whenever and in whatever manner was necessary, unless prevented by direct constitutional or legislative prohibition. . . .

... I ... refused to recognize the right of Congress to interfere with me excepting by impeachment or in other constitutional manner. [Emphasis added.] [19]

WILSON

Woodrow Wilson combined a theoretical conceptualization of the possibilities of presidential leadership with astute practical political maneuvering. The combination enabled him to enjoy an immensely successful period as president. As a political scientist, he had written two scholarly treatises on the American political system, noting both the limitations [20] and the potentialities of the office. [21] A moralistic and spellbinding orator, he made much of his ability to lead public opinion and generate support for his positions.

During the second decade of the twentieth century, the party system was in flux, the Progressive movement was gaining increasing influence over public thinking, and circumstances were such that nearly half of the Democratic congressmen who faced Wilson in 1913 were first termers. Into this maelstrom of opportunity Wilson plunged vigorously, anxious to serve as the nexus of political leadership. His personal appearance before Congress— something no president since John Adams had done—was an act that captured the imagination of both the public and political leaders. His operating style was to intervene personally at each stage of legislative activity. He carefully nursed his program from introduction to committee to final passage, attempting along the way to reconcile divergent points of view so as to end up with the maximum amount of consensus possible on a particular measure. In this way Wilson was able to achieve a remarkable legislative record in his first administration. Perhaps no president since Jefferson had been so successful with Congress. Among the progressive achievements were a lowered tariff, an income tax on the wealthy, the establishment of the Federal Reserve System and the Federal Trade Commission, and the Clayton Antitrust Law. [22] As one of Wilson's major biographers has written: "What made him irresistible was his fusion of the powers of the Preisdency with those of party leader, along with intense moral purpose." [23] The tools forged by his predecessors were thus combined in his administration.

That Wilson was consciously carrying out his own acute observations on the functioning of the office can scarcely be doubted. In one of the most enduring classics of American political science, he laid out the scope of presidential powers and the reasons for executive predominance in the political arena:

> He can dominate his party by being spokesman for the real sentiment and purpose of the country, by giving direction to opinion, by giving the country at once the information and the statement of policy which will enable it to form its judgments alike of parties and of men.
>
> For he is also the political leader of the nation, or has it in his choice to be. The nation as a whole has chosen him, and he is conscious that it has no other political spokesman. His is the only national voice in affairs. Let him once win the admiration and confidence of the country, and no other single force can withstand him, no combination of forces will easily overpower him. His position takes the imagination of the country. He is the representative of no constituency, but of the whole people. When he speaks in his true character, he speaks for no special interest. If he rightly interpret the national thought and boldly insist upon it, he is irresistible; and the country never feels the zest of action so much as when its President is of such insight and calibre. Its instinct is for unified action, and it craves a single leader. It is for this reason that it will often prefer to chose a man rather than a party. A President whom it trusts can not only lead it, but form it to his own views.
>
> . . . The President is at liberty, both in law and conscience, to be as big a man as he can. His capacity will set the limit, and if Congress be overborne by him, it will be no fault of the makers of the Constitution—it will be from no lack of constitutional powers on its part, but only because the President has the nation behind him, and Congress has not.[24]

It was in the crisis of the First World War and its aftermath that Wilson was to reach the zenith of power—and also of frustration. Although Wilson was reelected in 1916 on the slogan "he kept us out of war," the United States was eventually drawn into the conflict raging in Europe. After some hesitant starts and stops, the president realized that his hopes for voluntary programs for war preparation would not suffice. Nor could the American contribution to the Allies' effort be limited to money and supplies, he believed. A vast army would have to be created, industry converted to armament manufacture, agriculture stimulated to compensate for interrupted production elsewhere, transportation mobilized to tie the whole war effort together, and public opinion molded into a cohesive and somewhat fanatical bulwark for whatever policies be deemed necessary to do the job.[25]

Unlike Lincoln, who often acted first and then submitted his *faits accomplis* to the Congress for acceptance or ex post facto ratification, Wilson almost always sought congressional authorization for the steps he considered necessary. For instance, when congressional criticism of the war effort grew into demands for a coalition war cabinet, with Wilson reduced to a position of relative powerlessness, he countered by authoring a measure granting himself total power to organize and manage all the war-related agencies. This proposal, embodied in the Overman Act, became law in April 1918 and conferred almost dictatorial authority over the domestic economy on Wilson. In one area, however, Wilson did not wait for the Congress to act but rather initiated action on his own. By executive order he created the Committee on Public Information (the Creel Committee) shortly after the war began. This body was responsible for some of the most noxious abuses of the entire period, fanning the flames of war hysteria by painting Germany and all things German as monstrous enemies of civilized society. German music and the German language were banned from many concert halls and schools. Citizens of German extraction were harassed and sometimes driven from their property by overzealous "patriots" venting their Creel-heightened hatred.[26] (Generally Americans, like other peoples, need no officially inspired program to generate sufficient moral outrage against their perceived enemies. When their governments seem to sanction these sentiments, abuses are almost certain to occur.) Unfortunately, Wilson was never very interested in expending time or energy in cooling the xenophobia which he had allowed the governmental propaganda apparatus to stimulate.

In a related area, Wilson was also guilty of contributing to the attack on civil liberties. In 1917 he signed into law the Espionage Act, which provided for penalties of up to twenty years in prison for aiding the enemy, obstructing recruiting, or causing insubordination, disloyalty, or refusal of duty in the armed services. The postmaster general was given the power to exclude books, magazines, newspapers, and other materials from the mail if he found them to be treasonable or seditious. (This statute was primarily used against Socialists and the foreign language press.) The very next year Congress passed an even tougher measure in an amendment to the Espionage Act. The Sedition Act of 1918 was the first such law since the infamous Alien and Sedition Acts of 1798 and provided for severe punishment for those making false statements that interfered with the prosecution of the war; employing disloyal, profane, scurrilous, or abusive language about the American form of government, the Constitution, the flag, or the military and naval forces; urging the curtailed production of war materials; or advocating, teaching, defending, or suggesting any such acts. It was under this measure that the Wobblies (the IWW) and other leftists, including such leaders as Eugene V. Debs and Victor Berger, were prosecuted and jailed. Thus "national security" (although that euphemism was not generally applied as yet) came to serve as a rationale for persecuting groups and organizations unpopular with those in power.

It is impossible to say whether a more flexible, less moralistic president would have escaped the aftermath of the war unscathed from congressional and popular reaction to such a period of presidential aggrandizement (although it seems unlikely). In any case, the story of Wilson and his failure to win senatorial approval for American entry into the League of Nations is well known. Historically, the successors to almost all "strong" presidents have suffered for the aggressiveness of their predecessors, as the public grows wary (usually after a crisis) of an individual entrusted with so much power, and as Congress reasserts what it considers to be its rightful role in the American political system.

Woodrow Wilson brings to a close this brief historical section describing some of the accomplishments of the more prominent "early" presidents. The modern presidency really dates from the administration of Franklin Roosevelt, and no chief executive since has been able to operate a totally passive presidency. Each has contributed significantly to the expansion of executive control over the political system (with the Eisenhower administration serving perhaps as an eight-year partial hiatus in some areas). Discussion of their activities and innovations will comprise the substance of much of the rest of this book.

Presidential Greatness

The ranking of presidents is an enterprise engaged in either explicitly or implicitly by virtually every book on the presidency. Arthur Schlesinger, Sr., in an early attempt to get the collective judgment of students of the subject, polled fifty-five historians and political scientists throughout the country for an "authoritative opinion" on presidential greatness.[27] Although he noted that his subjects did not always inform him what the bases of their judgments were, their collective ratings were remarkably uniform, especially concerning which presidents fitted into the "great" and "failure" categories. Lincoln was the only unanimous choice for his position, with Washington and Franklin Roosevelt following closely behind.[28]

Great

1. Abraham Lincoln
2. George Washington
3. Franklin Roosevelt
4. Woodrow Wilson
5. Thomas Jefferson
6. Andrew Jackson

Near Great

7. Theodore Roosevelt
8. Grover Cleveland
9. John Adams
10. James K. Polk

Average

11. John Quincy Adams
12. James Monroe
13. Rutherford B. Hayes
14. James Madison
15. Martin Van Buren
16. William Howard Taft
17. Chester A. Arthur
18. William McKinley
19. Andrew Johnson
20. Herbert Hoover
21. Benjamin Harrison

Below the Average

22. John Tyler
23. Calvin Coolidge
24. Millard Fillmore
25. Zachary Taylor
26. James Buchanan
27. Franklin Pierce

Failures

28. Ulysses S. Grant
29. Warren G. Harding

William Henry Harrison and James Garfield, both of whom served in the office for less than a year, were excluded from the survey. Harry Truman, who was president at the time, also was not ranked. When Schlesinger repeated his ratings in 1962, he found that Truman was then considered to be one of the "near greats" by his panel, while Eisenhower was judged only an "average" president.[29]

What sets the "great" presidents off from their brothers? Schlesinger suggested that each was identified with some momentous development in the nation's history, revolutions under the law that led to new conceptions of America's destiny. "All of them, moreover, took the side of progressivism and human betterment as understood in their day. However much is to be said for preserving the status quo, the men whom Clio has canonized were those who gambled on the future rather than the past."[30] In addition to being men who were ahead of their times, they excelled at the game of political maneuver and management; they were adept in the art of give and take and the trading of advantage. Those most likely to fit into the mold came to office from elevated stations in life, motivated by a sense of noblesse oblige to further the interests of those less favorably situated than themselves.[31] Finally, these great presidents "were also strong Presidents, magnifying the executive branch at the expense of the other branches of the government. . . . From Washington's time onward, each conceived of the office in heroic proportions, and each left it more powerful and influential than he found it."[32] This assertion of authority naturally led to clashes with Congress, political parties, and the courts, and the press frequently joined in the denunciation of the "usurpers." President Nixon, in an appearance at the Lincoln Memorial in 1974, said, in what some have contended was an attempt to draw a parallel between himself and Lincoln,

It is quite clear that no President in history has been more vilified or was more vilified during the time he was President than Lincoln. Those who knew him, his secretaries, have written that he was very deeply hurt by what was said about him and drawn about him, but on the other hand, Lincoln had that great strength of character never to display it, always to stand tall and strong and firm no matter how harsh or unfair the criticism might be. These elements of greatness, of course, inspire us all today.[33]

Other rankers of presidents have come to conclusions similar to those of Schlesinger, both in terms of the preeminence of those they chose and their standards of judgment. Harold Laski concluded that at least eleven Presidents were "extraordinary men," a number he found comparable to the number of outstanding prime ministers in England during the same time period.[34] Clinton Rossiter, in a content analysis of more than one hundred presidential biographies, discovered the criteria for greatness to include the following:

1. The times in which the president served. To be remembered as a great president, he must serve during periods of upheaval, turmoil, war, or crisis.
2. The imagination and bravery with which the president bore the responsibility of office. He must be the leader of Congress and the people. He must be decisive and intelligent and be fortunate in having his decisions judged as the correct ones by history.
3. His philosophy of presidential power. He must follow the precepts of Teddy Roosevelt's stewardship theory, doing what needs to be done rather than merely what the law says he can do. If he is not considered a dictator during his own term, he has little chance for being considered great by future generations.
4. Technical skill at organization and administration. The times have come to demand this quality, which some notable occupants of the office did not manifest. The size and complexity of modern government make it unlikely that an inefficient manager will be successful in making staff, cabinet, and bureaucracy bend to his will.
5. The quality of his lieutenants. So much of the office has become institutionalized and so many burdens placed upon the president that he must delegate a considerable amount of discretionary power to those around him. He also perforce relies on these people for technical, policy, and political advice. They must be the very best minds available in the country.

6. The kind of person he was beneath the mantle of office. The characteristics of warmth, honesty, integrity, compassion, humor, and vigor make for the personal qualities that our heroes in office possess. He must be the kind of person who generates legends about himself.

7. His influence on the presidency. He must strengthen the office and set the kinds of precedents that future strong presidents can build upon in their times of crisis.

8. His influence on history. The great presidents inspired, symbolized, or led the country during periods of "earth-shaking readjustments" and are considered to have furthered the true interest of the American people.[35]

Emmet John Hughes, an adviser to Eisenhower, largely concurs with other scholars about what constitutes greatness in our presidents. Superior intellectual ability, he finds, is not one of the requisites, for brainpower can always be hired. Rather, what is needed is fortitude, intuition, and "a near passion for pragmatism." Those who would be great must possess a gusto for action, an impelling need to be at the center of the political maelstrom. Activism and pragmatism alone do not guarantee historical accolades, of course. These qualities must be put to the service of humanity, and the president who would succeed must exercise moral leadership in its name.[36] Until the Johnson and Nixon administrations, it was almost universally assumed that the strong presidents would exert such leadership. After all, had not the giants in office always done so? Whatever the detractors of the day found to criticize in Washington, Lincoln, and the others, history surely had demonstrated conclusively that American interests were best served by those who expanded the office.[37]

The Traditional View of Why We Need Strong Presidents

The second part of this chapter will outline the conventional scholarly wisdom of the last forty years concerning the need for a dominant presidency—what Thomas Cronin has referred to as the "textbook presidency." The explanations that have been offered for the growth of the office are varied. Some emphasize the historical factors in the development of the United States into a modern industrialized society with a need for a large measure of control over its productive and economic institutions. Others stress the rise of the welfare state and its attendant governmental bureaucracies; the many crises, domestic and foreign; the special characteristics of the office which uniquely suit the presidency for leadership in the twentieth century; or the incapacity of other governmental institutions to cope effectively with the problems of the modern world.

GROWTH OF THE POSITIVE STATE

A brief historical sketch is necessary to understand the conditions under which the modern presidency flourished. The period following the Civil War was one of rapid expansion in the United States in terms of population growth, urbanization, industrialization, and concentration of resources. Between 1860 and 1900 our population more than doubled, from 31 million to almost 76 million. Cities such as New York, which had been what today is considered "small," were major recipients of this increase. The large influx of people seeking newly created jobs in the burgeoning industrial centers of the North and Midwest put tremendous pressure on city governments for services largely beyond their capacity to deliver.

The principles of separation of powers and weak government had influenced not only the authors of the federal constitution but those who wrote city charters as well. When these principles were combined with the democratic notion popularized in the Jacksonian era that most public positions should be elective, the result was urban governments with many officeholders, each with a limited measure of power but with little or no responsibility to each other, and almost no coordination of their efforts. The millions of immigrants and others who were pouring into the cities thus were willing to turn to those who could provide the centralized direction necessary to deal with the problems generated by this rapid expansion (and by their own poverty). The political boss and the machine emerged as the entrepreneurs who could fulfill the needs not only of the workers but of business as well. Centralization of control in a few hands enabled those in power to circumvent the formal rigidities built into the structure. As Robert Merton has said, "The lawyer having been permitted to subordinate democracy to the law, the Boss had to be called in to extricate the victim, which he did after a fashion and for a consideration."[38]

Gradually, then, many in the cities came to look more and more to government for aid with their problems. The conclusion that "negative government"—essentially just the preservation of law and order—no longer sufficed for the conditions of "modern" society led to an increased belief that the political system should bear responsibility for the amelioration of conditions beyond the capacity of individual citizens to change. Most frequently those expectations focused on the executive. State legislatures were largely controlled by rural interests with little concern for the problems of the cities, while the national Congress exhibited much the same attitude. United States senators were still selected by state legislatures (ratification of the Seventeenth Amendment, which provided for their popular election, did not take place until 1913), and the wealthy business interests and the trusts effectively controlled many of their decisions.

Meanwhile, in the countryside discontent with laissez-faire government was also on the rise. The steady decline of farm profits because of high interest rates charged by "eastern monied interests," overproduction, foreign competition, and the rates charged by monopolistic railroads led to demands by farmers for the breakup of monopolies, the abandonment of the gold standard, and laws fixing maximum charges for the shipment of freight and passengers. More than 155 million acres of public lands had been granted to railroads to encourage construction. The railroads in turn sold or leased much of this land to farmers, who would then ship the commodities they grew to market by the only means of transportation available to them—the railroads. The outcry over these abuses led in 1887 to the creation of the first regulatory commission in U.S. history. The act creating the Interstate Commerce Commission provided that all rates charged by the railroads be reasonable and just (without granting the commission power to set those rates), prohibited rebates to wealthy customers, made it illegal to charge more for a short haul than a long haul, and prohibited discriminatory rates. Although the Supreme Court soon eviscerated even these modest powers, the trend toward governmental intervention in the economy accelerated, with profound implications for the future of presidential power.

By the turn of the century, it was becoming clear to many that the United States was well on its way to becoming a plutocracy— a government of the wealthy, by the wealthy, and for the wealthy. Beginning with the formation of the Standard Oil Trust in 1879, there rapidly developed a whole series of business combinations designed to promote monopolistic control of basic commodities and services that could guarantee owners huge profits while quashing rivals who might wish to compete with them. Some of the commodities controlled were whiskey, beef, lead, sugar, railroads, and steel. The Populist movement, farmers in near rebellion, and journalist muckrakers attacked these bastions of privilege and demanded that government abandon its promotion of the interests of the wealthy and begin to concern itself with the problems of the average citizen. Frequently people discovered that corrupt officials were in league with the robber barons who preyed upon them. The stage was thus set for the rediscovery of the Jacksonian link between the president and the people.

It is impossible to fix a date, or even an administration, by which time presidents and many citizens alike came to look upon the chief executive as the special protector of the rights of the people. Some elements of this symbiotic relationship were evident in the Cleveland administration, although they did not begin to ripen until Theodore Roosevelt and later Wilson occupied the office. We have already cited at some length Roosevelt's stewardship theory propounding his belief that the president must serve "the plain people." As an example of this determination, he attacked the Northern Securities Company (a railroad holding company) and demanded that it be broken up. The people deserved a "square deal," he said, and implied that in the president they had a dealer who would reshuffle the deck in their behalf. Although Roosevelt was by no means a radical bent on destroying the corporations, millions of people came to believe that at last they had a spokesman in high office whom they could trust to put the needs of nation ahead of those of "the Interests." "Positive" government came then to take on a new meaning. Wilson too felt that the federal government must be an active reforming instrument in the economic life of the country, no longer content just to promote private gain and abdicate responsibility under laissez-faire and states'-rights doctrines. As the embodiment of all the people, the duty to lead naturally fell to the president, he wrote. This assumption increasingly was accepted by the voters as well.

The conversion, of course, was neither unanimous nor continuous among politicians or citizens. After the First World War, the desire to return to "normalcy" meant a retreat not only from the world but from a conception of vigorous presidential leadership in domestic affairs as well. With the prosperity that followed the war and the related prestige of industry, Calvin Coolidge could say in all sincerity, "the business of America is business," and mean thereby that it was the duty of government to interfere as little as possible with its functioning. Coolidge's landslide election in 1924 signified a public acceptance of that philosophy. Herbert Hoover, who followed as president in 1929, campaigned on a platform of "rugged individualism" and free competition as the American way to solve problems. The depression that followed did little to convince him that his basic principles were unsound. Hoover's reluctance to intervene in the economy, except for attempts to stimulate private industry through government loans and the encouragement of voluntary self-help programs, however, signaled the end of an era of chief executives whose conception of the office avoided the direct involvement of the president in furthering the economic welfare of the people. (The Eisenhower years were perhaps a partial qualification to these generalizations.)

Franklin Roosevelt, a distant cousin of Theodore, campaigned in the 1932 election on a platform of social and economic reconstruction aimed at putting America's productive resources back to work. Financial reforms, the regulation of holding companies, aid to farmers, unemployment and old-age insurance, and veterans' pensions, along with reduced spending and a balanced federal budget, would be the prime instruments of recovery. Borrowing from Teddy, he promised the American people "a new deal," especially for the "forgotten man at the bottom of the economic pyramid." His speeches evoked the memories of the active presidents of the past—of Jackson and

Lincoln, of the first Roosevelt and of Wilson—as he sought to educate the nation to the need for dynamic leadership. FDR's first inaugural address was a masterpiece of political rhetoric, calling upon the people to rally behind him as he sought to lead the country out of its economic misfortune. Sacrifice in the name of the common good was as necessary now as it was in war, he said, and the president would be the motive force in the people's ultimate triumph.

First of all let me assert my firm belief that the only thing we have to fear is fear itself—nameless, unreasoning, unjustified terror which paralyzes needed efforts to convert retreat into advance.

In every dark hour of our national life a leadership of frankness and vigor has met with that understanding and support of the people themselves which is essential to victory. I am convinced that you will again give that support to leadership in these critical days. . . .

If I read the temper of our people correctly, we now realize as we have never realized before our interdependence on each other; that we cannot merely take but we must give as well; that if we are to go forward, we must move as a trained and loyal army willing to sacrifice for the good of a common discipline, because without such discipline no progress is made, no leadership becomes effective.

We are, I know, ready and willing to submit our lives and property to such discipline because it makes possible a leadership which aims at a larger good.

This I propose to offer, pledging that the larger purposes will bind upon us all as a sacred obligation with a unity of duty hitherto evoked only in a time of armed strife.

With this pledge taken, I assume unhesitatingly the leadership of this great army of our people, dedicated to a disciplined attack upon our common problems. . . .

It is to be hoped that the normal balance of executive and legislative authority may be wholly adequate to meet the unprecedented task before us. But it may be that an unprecedented demand and need for undelayed action may call for temporary departure from that normal balance of public procedure.

I am prepared under my constitutional duty to recommend the measures that a stricken nation in the midst of a stricken world may require.

These measures, or such other measures as the Congress may build out of its experience and wisdom, I shall seek, within my constitutional authority, to bring to a speedy adoption.

But in the event that the Congress shall fail to take one of these two courses, and in the event that the national emergency is still critical, I shall not evade the clear course of duty that will then confront me.

I shall ask the Congress for the one remaining instrument to meet the crisis—broad executive power that would be given me if we were in fact invaded by a foreign foe. . . . ·

We do not distrust the future of essential democracy. The people of the United States have not failed. In their need they have registered a mandate that they want direct, vigorous action.

They have asked for discipline and direction under leadership. They have made me the present instrument of their wishes. In the spirit of the gift I take it.[39]

The admiration of Roosevelt among scholars and journalists during the last forty years has contributed significantly to the portraits that have filled our textbooks and newspapers. Strong, progressive presidents were always painted as rushing to the rescue of America. These images we all have grown up with color Americans' expectations about what a president can, and should, do. Not only average citizens but members of Congress and even presidential aspirants carry these pictures in their minds. Americans have come to expect, even to demand, that the president solve the country's problems.

There is no doubt that decisive action was necessary in Roosevelt's case. By the time he took office, hunger was stalking the land. Nearly 13 million Americans were unemployed—close to 25 percent of the labor force. More than five thousand banks had collapsed, taking with them the savings of literally thousands of depositors. At the same time, the bottom had dropped out of the market for agricultural products, causing many farmers to lose their land when they were unable to pay their mortgages. It was not at all curious, then, that some began to question whether the economic system, or indeed the political system, was capable of coping with the situation. Admiration for those foreign experiments that seemed to be dealing successfully with the worldwide crisis grew. Fascism in Europe or Communism as practiced in the Soviet Union attracted more and more interest as models for what the United States should perhaps seek to emulate.

A few days after his inauguration, Roosevelt went on nation-wide radio to explain the steps he had taken to staunch the economic wound that was bleeding the nation to death. This first "fireside chat," along with the Emergency Banking Relief Act, seemed to alter the psychology of "nameless, unreasoning, unjustified terror" that had paralyzed so much of the nation. Within a few weeks, the stock market had regained 15 percent of its previous loss. Nor did Roosevelt stop there. What followed was one of the most remarkable periods of legislative leadership in U.S. history. The special session of Congress, later known as the "Hundred Days," proceeded to pass virtually every economic recovery measure which the president and his aides sent up to the Hill. The "alphabet soup" group of federal agencies created by this legislation affected almost every segment of the economy. The Civilian Conservation Corps (CCC) employed as many as five hundred thousand young men between the ages of eighteen and twenty-five in conservation work. The Federal Emergency Relief Act (FERA) provided for direct grants to cities and states for work relief programs. The Agricultural Adjustment Act (AAA) established parity price support levels for farmers and subsidized the reduction of the number of acres in production. The Tennessee Valley Authority (TVA) was established to construct dams and power plants along the Tennessee River to boost the economy of that region. The Federal Securities Act compelled full disclosure of all relevant information about issues of stocks and bonds in order to protect investors. The Home Owners Loan Corporation (HOLC) provided for the refinancing of home mortgages, while the Farm Credit Administration (FCA) did the same thing for farmers. A system to guarantee bank deposits was set up. And finally, on the last day of its special session, Congress passed the National Industrial Recovery Act (NIRA) to stimulate business activity through industrial self-regulation under government supervision. Among its provisions was one guaranteeing labor's right to organize and bargain collectively and another establishing the Public Works Administration (PWA) to put the unemployed to work on government construction projects.

Some of FDR's agencies and programs were subsequently declared unconstitutional by the Supreme Court, and others were abandoned as unworkable by the administration itself, but still more were created in the years that followed. Almost all demonstrated that the president was expected to play a leading role in shaping the decisions that affect the economic well-being of the nation. In the Employment Act of 1946, that responsibility was formalized by the establishment of the Council of Economic Advisers in the Executive Office of the President to advise the chief executive on measures designed to promote competition, avoid economic fluctuations, and maintain employment, production, and purchasing power. The president was made responsible for providing a program to Congress to carry out the mandate of the act. By 1968 even Richard Nixon, the inheritor of the Whig and Eisenhower traditions of the office, would say:

> The days of a passive Presidency belong to a simple past. Let me be very clear about this: The next President must take an activist view of his office. He must articulate the nation's values, define its goals and marshall its will. Under the Nixon Administration, the Presidency will be deeply involved in the entire sweep of America's public concerns.[40]

THE CRISIS PRESIDENCY

Control over the economy and initiatives in domestic affairs have manifestly accounted for great accretions of power in the executive branch. Foreign affairs, wars, preparing for new wars, or dealing with the problems attributable to past wars, however, are responsible for even more of this centralization. Previous pages outlined some of the measures taken by Abraham Lincoln, Theodore Roosevelt, and Woodrow Wilson in dealing with conflict either at home or abroad. It has become a maxim that crisis leadership must be presidential leadership, that the more serious a potential threat, the more power must be entrusted to the chief executive to deal with the problem. In former times, crises only intermittently punctuated the national existence, and periods of respite allowed other institutions in society to exert their dominant influence. In an age when crisis has become perpetual and the everyday condition of life, however, the trend has been toward lodging ever-increasing and permanent authority in the one institution judged capable of a unified response.

Aaron Wildavsky has written of "two presidents": one in domestic affairs, severely dependent upon Congress, pressure groups, and the people for getting his policy preferences approved; and the other in defense and foreign policy questions, much more independent of restraints.[41] Louis Koenig has taken this dichotomy one step further and poses two presidents in foreign affairs as well. One is characterized by reliance on Congress for money to carry out his foreign policy (foreign aid and assistance, for example), for laws (trade expansion and "most favored nation" status), and for votes (approval of treaties and ambassadors and polity officials). The other president largely acts alone, making decisions affecting war and peace, ordering the use of the atomic bomb, invading Cambodia or Cuba, bombing North Vietnam, or following a policy of hostility or détente toward our foreign enemies. This latter presidency is the one that has grown by leaps and bounds in recent years.[42]

It is when war and threats of war dominate the nation's attention that the president's power expands the most rapidly. Since the Second World War, of course, international crisis has been nearly constant. Almost as soon as the fighting was over, the United States was waging a cold war with the Soviet Union and its allies. Fears of domestic subversion coupled with real or imagined threats from abroad led to something of a siege mentality that justified increased control at home and the maintenance, for the first time in the country's history, of a large standing army to do battle with potential aggressors abroad.

The list of events and issues that riveted attention on matters of national security is a long one: the Berlin blockade, the "fall" of China, the McCarthy hearings, the Korean War, the Russian explosion of an atomic bomb, the fear of radioactive fallout, the Suez crisis, the sending of marines to Lebanon, "brinkmanship," the Bay of Pigs, the Cuban missile crisis, the U-2 affair, *sputnik*, the missile gap, Hungary, various Mideast wars, and Vietnam. The existence of large security forces to protect the United States from foreign dangers presented the president with a capacity that no prewar president possessed—he now had at his fingertips command of forces that allowed him to intervene anywhere in the world, almost at his own discretion. Security treaties, executive agreements, and presidential policy declarations put much of the world within the sphere of American "national security," from Europe to the Middle East, from Latin America to Southeast Asia, and from Iceland to Australia. Our national security demanded a form of Pax Americana that guaranteed protection to traditional ally and petty satrapy alike, so long as the United States (or its president) could convince itself that somehow these nations had been the victims of aggression from monolithic communism. Politics must stop at the water's edge, it was believed, and Americans had to support any action of the president that in his judgment was necessary for our security. Although there was room for disagreement on domestic matters, the United States had to speak with one voice abroad—that of the president.

PRESIDENTIAL ADVANTAGES

The idea that the president should dominate foreign affairs is not an invention of postwar presidents, of course. Thomas Jefferson wrote that the transaction of business with foreign nations is executive altogether. It is to the reasons offered for this exclusivity that we now turn our attention. What does the presidency have that other political institutions lack in foreign relations? Unity, decision, activity, secrecy, and dispatch, answered Hamilton. When access to information and representativeness is added to the above list, we get the general outline for executive predominance in the area. It is often argued that Congress possesses none of these attributes.

Five hundred thirty-five senators and representatives, elected from districts and states for generally local reasons, can hardly be expected to oversee the day-to-day conduct of international relations. Thus, as chief executive as well as chief diplomat, the president appoints ambassadors, the secretary of state, and other top echelon State Department officials to conduct American exchanges with foreign countries. In their dealings with one another, nations need a sense of stability and the assurance that there is a single voice speaking which is authoritative in most matters. Nowhere in the world do parliaments or legislatures conduct foreign policy. And when Congress has intervened to take direction away from the president, the consequences have not always been fortunate. As with the Senate's blocking of our entry into the League of Nations and Congress's nearsighted isolationism that prevented adequate American policies to combat the expansion of fascism in Europe, congressional policy almost always proved wrong. As Arthur Schlesinger, Jr., has said:

No one for a long time after would trust Congress with basic foreign policy. Congress did not even trust itself. The grand revival of the Presidential prerogative after Pearl Harbor must be understood as a direct reaction to what happened when Congress tried to seize the guiding reins of foreign policy in the years 1919 to 1939.[43]

The point made in the previous paragraph that members of Congress generally are elected because they are perceived to represent local and state interests is another reason for the preeminience of the president in foreign affairs. Few senators and even fewer representatives make national reputations for themselves because of their expertise in this area. Even when an occasional member is able to achieve such a reputation, such as Senator William Fulbright of Arkansas, the desire to be reelected frequently demands that he convince the electorate that he should be continued in office for what he is able to do for the home folks, not because he is respected for his knowledge or ability in international relations. When the people at home become convinced, as they evidently were in Senator Fulbright's case, that their representative in Washington has not paid sufficient attention to their interests, they frequently retire that person from Congress.

Presidents, on the other hand, benefit from this general lack of interest in foreign policy on the part of the people. It means that in most matters the voters are willing to "leave it to the president" to determine the proper stance that the United States should be taking vis-à-vis the rest of the world. We have come to believe that it is his job to do so. The president can speak with one voice rather than many; he symbolizes the nation in his dealings with other countries. He is the only official who is nationally elected (vice presidents do not count) and as such is expected to articulate the interests of the whole people. While a senator may represent Maine, or a representative Brooklyn, the president represents the entire United States. In addition he is the chief of state, our "Queen of England," and thus commands the respect owed no mere politician, such as a prime minister. This combination of roles as leader of government and head of state makes him doubly effective when he speaks for the national interest.

The Constitution also makes the president commander in chief of the armed forces. During wartime presidents appoint and remove their field commanders to suit their own policies, as Lincoln did with McClellan and Truman did with MacArthur. Decisions about overall strategy and tactics rest with the president, as do questions of the deployment of forces, when and where to attack, and, ultimately, the American terms for settlement of the conflict. By the deployment of armed forces abroad, the president may demonstrate our power and determination in an area; for instance, by sending ships to the Middle East or the Indian Ocean. Or a president may actually manufacture reasons for engaging in conflict with other nations. President Nixon cited the "need to protect American boys" as his rationale for the invasion of Cambodia without congressional authorization. Actually, of course, American boys were in a danger zone precisely because he and other presidents had ordered them there. And President Ford ordered the Marines to evacuate American citizens from Vietnam while Congress was still debating whether to grant him that power. Thus, the president can make foreign military policy while others only talk about it.

One example that is most often cited as a case study for successful presidential action in foreign affairs—the Cuban missile crisis—will serve to illustrate some of these points. On October 14, 1962, the United States discovered that the Soviet Union was installing offensive ballistic missiles on the island of Cuba, whether at Soviet insistence or Cuban request still is not clear. When secret U-2 flights by the CIA revealed that such weapons were indeed being put into position only ninety miles off American shores (and despite Soviet assurances that the military build-up there was purely defensive in nature), President Kennedy decided that the missiles would have to be removed.[44] His first step was to order low-level picture-taking missions to insure that his initial information was correct. Next he called a meeting of some of his top military, intelligence, and policy advisors to inform them of the situation and to seek their collective wisdom in dealing with it. This was the group (called the Ex Comm) that the President was to rely upon for recommendations for the proper American answer to the perceived Soviet threat.

In order to insure secrecy and the appearance of normality, the president and the other members of the committee attempted to maintain most of their usual schedules; the president even undertook a political speaking tour of the West for that year's fall elections.[45] The president did not want to tip off the Russians or Cubans that the United States knew of this new development until the American response could be developed. In addition, he felt that his presence at all of the Ex Comm's meetings might inhibit the free exchange of proposals, ideas, and positions, and this he sought to avoid. According to Robert Kennedy, the early position of most of those at the first meeting was that an air strike to wipe out the missiles was the only course of action available to the president. After a few days of intense debate and changing of minds, however, a different recommendation was to emerge.[46]

The pressure to make a rapid decision was intense. Within a few days the Soviet missiles would become operational, with a capacity to hit many of the major cities in the United States. An air strike had the virtue of removing that threat immediately, without giving the Soviet Union an opportunity to demand a quid pro quo for the withdrawal of their weapons. Advocates of a blockade, on the other hand, pointed out that an air attack would probably kill many Russians and might push the USSR to retaliate. Furthermore, unless the United States broadened the scope of the bombing to include airfields and could be absolutely certain that all missiles were destroyed, the possibility of the United States being hit from Cuba would still exist. Even if the Soviets did not retaliate directly against the United States, it was argued, they had the capacity to move against West Berlin, around which Russian forces were concentrated.

One option had been closed off immediately by the president. That was to take no action at all, to accept Russian missiles pointed at the United States from within its own hemisphere as we pointed missiles at the USSR from Italy and Turkey. This new move was perceived as a deliberate Soviet attempt to alter the balance of power and to test the will of the United States. The president felt that if America were to fail to resist this ploy, Berlin and other sensitive areas would soon be subject to threats as well. In preparation for whatever option was ultimately selected, the President began to marshal American military forces. A world-wide alert was ordered and aircraft readied for an attack on Cuba. Troops were moved into position in the southeastern United States in case an invasion became necessary, while an amphibious landing force of 40,000 marines and 180 ships steamed into position in the Caribbean. Atomic weapons were loaded in strategic bombers, which were kept constantly in the air ready to head for the Soviet Union if the need arose.[47]

In the end, five days after they had begun meeting, a majority of the Ex Comm came to favor a blockade of Cuba; but, in a final meeting with Kennedy, both major options still under consideration—blockade or air strike—were presented to the president for ultimate decision. His choice was for a "quarantine" (since technically a blockade is an act of war) to halt all further shipments of offensive weapons to Cuba. In his speech to the nation publicly announcing for the first time the existence of the crisis, Kennedy warned that missiles launched from Cuba against any nation in this hemisphere would be considered as an attack by the Soviet Union upon the United States, and would immediately require full nuclear retaliation. He called upon Chairman Khrushchev to remove all offensive weapons already stationed in Cuba, cautioned against any hostile move against West Berlin, and urged a peaceful solution to the confrontation.[48]

In the tense days that followed, meetings of the Ex Comm continued. The United Nations Security Council was called into special session, while the Organization of American States unanimously endorsed the U.S. action. Letters and proposals were exchanged between the United States and the Soviet Union. Finally, a negotiated agreement was worked out: the Russians would withdraw their offensive missiles already in Cuba and undertake to send no new ones there, and we would remove the quarantine and give our assurances that we would not invade Cuba. Thus ended the crisis that saw the world move toward the brink of destruction.

The Cuban missile crisis clarifies the powers of the president to act during times of emergency and illustrates the resources at his disposal. We will see in later chapters why these "advantages" may be more apparent than real. First of all, the president has access to a tremendous flow of intelligence. CIA reports from Cuban refugees and from spy flights alerted the United States to the existence of the missiles. In addition, military intelligence offered assessments of both our opponents' and our own military capabilities in the area. Foreign policy and area specialists advised the president of the likely reactions of the participants to whatever moves the United States might undertake, and national security advisers were available for their best judgments on the proper course to follow. The president, then, it is argued, possesses superior information on which to base his decisions. Second, the president may operate in relative secrecy when premature exposure of planning may foreclose necessary flexibility and freedom of action. Kennedy did not want the Soviets and Cubans to know that the United States was aware of the missiles until he had decided what to do and could mobilize the forces necessary to carry out his policy. The small group that comprised the Ex Comm was able to contain the information it had within its own ranks and thereby maintain the secrecy that is seen as essential to national security. Congress, critics of that institution say, leaks like a sieve, and had the CIA report been given to them, the news would have soon been spread throughout the press.

Another point highlighted by the Cuban missile crisis is the dispatch with which the presidency can act in times of crisis. Within a week of the original discovery of the Soviet missiles, President Kennedy had decided upon his course of action and had mobilized the forces to execute it. Although debate in the Ex Comm was long and intense, it was always recognized that the president would have to make the final decision. Congress, bound by rules and traditions, would have had a difficult time in acting as rapidly or in speaking with a unified voice.

After he had made his decision, and shortly before he announced it to the nation, Kennedy called in the leaders of Congress to inform them of a decision that he already had reached. The constitutional balance between the executive and legislative branches in questions of war and peace had obviously tilted all the way over to the executive.

THE DECLINE OF CONGRESS

Congress had been the butt of jokes long before the modern era began. Mark Twain said that you couldn't teach a congressman anything the average flea couldn't learn. Will Rogers quipped that American legislators "were the best politicians money could buy," and that if you did not believe that congressmen were comedians, you should read the bills they passed. Part of Congress's problem rests in its plural nature. It is composed of 535 men and women, each selected from a specific district. Each voter chooses only one representative and two senators among the 535 and thus can blame "Congress" for outrages without reflection on local choices. Charles O. Jones found in a survey of four congressional elections that incumbents running for reelection won between 91 and 96.5 percent of the time.[49] In 1972, 96 percent of the incumbents running won reelection, and even in the Democratic "landslide" year of 1974 that followed Watergate, 88 percent won. Knowledge and interest about Congress as a whole can hardly be underestimated—less than a majority of Miller and Stokes's interviewees could even name which party controlled Congress.[50] Guessing alone should have resulted in 50 percent accuracy. When contrasted with the visibility of a single chief executive, it is no wonder that the public's awareness of Congress is low.

Members of Congress, who are elected from relatively small constituencies, have frequently been beholden to large blocs of local voters, the wealthy interests in their states, or outside financial contributors. If cotton or steel production or organized labor is crucial for a district or state, the representatives from that area generally have to speak for those interests or be thrown out of office. Policies have a way of affecting the various states in different ways; thus although there may be common agreement on the need to reduce military spending, for instance, any particular base closure or phasing out of a weapons system will generate opposition from those whose constituents would be thrown out of work. The general welfare tends to be viewed through the narrow lens of local interest. Thus members of Congress have been willing to delegate to the president many tough decisions that they prefer not to have to make themselves. While ten thousand defense workers or twenty thousand cotton farmers may be crucial to the reelection chances of a congressional candidate from Los Angeles or Mississippi, they are not so crucial for a president, who is able to balance off one interest against another. Thus the president, voted on by all the people, represents a national constituency, while the members of Congress represent only local ones. Since the brokering of individual interests in the legislature does not always add up to the general interest, when presidents began appealing to the masses, starting around the turn of the century, they found a receptive audience. This led many observers to agree with the exaggerated sentiment expressed by Rowland Egger: "The President is the literal embodiment of American mass democracy. Indeed, in his most powerful moments he is the sign and symbol of the pervasive egalitarianism which from the beginning has characterized the emergent forces of the American democratic ideal."[51]

Other factors affect the positions of president and Congress as well. One of these factors is the organization of Congress. Through the seniority system as practiced until recently, positions of leadership in the House and Senate and chairmanships of all-powerful committees were given to those members with one prime qualification—the ability to get reelected. This meant in practice that members from safe, one-party districts and states tended to dominate the national legislature. Since the South has been most persistent in sending the same people to Washington year after year, figures like Sam Rayburn, Mendel Rivers, Wilbur Mills, John Stennis, F. Edward Hebert, Richard Russell, Harry Byrd, Howard Smith, and James Eastland exercised power all out of proportion to their numbers. Younger members and members from competitive two-party states rarely got a chance to shape significant legislation. This "gerontocracy" resisted many of the progressive proposals put forth by reform-minded presidents, who, dependent as they tend to be on the large blocks of electoral votes in the urban areas of the North and East, responded to a more liberal electorate. Thus progressives historically favored increasing the power of the executive as an antidote to the conservative domination of the legislature.

A congressional revolt against automatically granting chairmanships to the majority party member with the longest service on each committee came in 1975. This reform was spurred by the addition to the House of seventy-five freshmen Democratic representatives determined to play a significant role in shaping legislation and in the operation of Congress. Three senior chairmen were deposed and a fourth, Wilbur Mills, stepped down for other reasons. This gave new hope to those who would like to see a reinvigorated legislative branch deal with presidents on the basis of equality. Since Congress had also become more liberal than recent presidents on many issues, the change was doubly pleasing to progressives. Many early hopes were soon dashed by the power of the presidency, however.

An example of the quandary in which liberal members of Congress found themselves in the past was their attempt to regain a measure of control over the federal budget. Angered at President Nixon's repeated impoundment of appropriated funds for domestic programs, they sought to create a mechanism to insure that they could deal with the overall budget in one piece rather than dividing it up for consideration by dozens of authorizing and appropriating subcommittees, as had been the practice. Since none of the individual committees saw more than a relatively small piece of the budget, there had been no setting of priorities among programs, no attempt to keep spending within a specified ceiling. This system had allowed the president to charge Congress with fiscal irresponsibility, with spending the country into inflation or bankruptcy, and made him seem able to justify impoundments. The super budget committee that emerged in Congress as a result of this concern has the power to set a total spending level for the year, with a breakdown for major categories. The problem is that this powerful new committee will include many of the senior oligarchs from the old committee structure, people who themselves tend to oppose funding for liberal domestic programs.

The committee structure is also largely responsible for the difficulty Congress has in dealing with other problems that confront the country. On an issue such as the environment, many different committees and subcommittees in each house have jurisdiction over various bills. On one piece of legislation the Senate Committee on Agriculture and Forestry and its subcommittees on environment, soil conservation, and forestry may have the bill; on another measure the Commerce Committee's Subcommittee on the Environment, or the Interior and Insular Affairs Subcommittee on Minerals, Materials, and Fuels; or Parks and Recreation; or Public Lands; or Water and Power Resources may bear major responsibility. Also involved might be the Public Works Committee's subcommittees on water resources; air and water pollution; and environmental science and technology. The president, if he chooses, can cut across departmental and agency boundaries and set up an entirely new institution to deal with the complexities of major problems that affect several areas of society. Congress has generally gone along with the executive in these reorganizations. Thus the Environmental Protection Agency under Russell Train was charged with developing policies across the whole range of environmental concerns. The unity and coordinating ability of the White House in comparison with Congress is manifest.

Summary

Scholars of the last forty years have viewed the American presidency as an enormously successful institution. The strong presidents in our history have been pictured as doing what needed doing at the time, while Congress and the states have largely been seen as failures. According to this view, the creation of the positive state, the concomitant swelling of the federal government, and perpetual crises, both domestic and foreign, all demanded a permanently vigorous presidency. The president is at the center of the political system; only he can make it work. The qualities of secrecy, dispatch, unity, information, and representativeness all adhere to his office. Most authors wrote that the president can act, while Congress finds it difficult to do anything but react. The chief executive can define situations for both Congress and the people through his access to the media; consequently he largely determines the agenda before the nation. His combination of roles makes him commander in chief of the armed forces, head of his political party, chief diplomat, the embodiment of mass democracy, chief executive, head of state, chief legislator, the major articulator of the general interest, and the protector of economic prosperity.[52] It seemed a truism that the ship of state could no longer sail smoothly without a strong, active president at the helm. These generally accepted beliefs led most scholars of the presidency to agree with the sentiment expressed by Louis Koenig: "More power to the president (not less)." Vietnam and Watergate revelations brought these comfortable views into question.

NOTES

1. Marcus Cunliffe, *American Presidents and the Presidency* (New York: American Heritage, 1968), p. 52.

2. Edward S. Corwin, *The President: Office and Powers,* 4th rev. ed. (New York: New York University Press, 1957), pp. 182–183.

3. Louis W. Koenig, *The Chief Executive,* rev. ed. (New York: Harcourt, Brace & World, 1968), pp. 26–27.

4. Cunliffe, p. 48.

5. See Hamilton's defense for Washington's action, "The First Letter of 'Pacificus,'" originally published in *The Gazette of the United States,* 29 June 1793 and reprinted in Robert Hirschfield, *The Power of the Presidency,* 2nd ed. (Chicago: Aldine, 1973), pp. 49–54.

6. Corwin, pp. 181–182.

7. Arthur M. Schlesinger, Jr., *The Age of Jackson* (Boston: Little, Brown, 1950), *passim,* esp. chap. XXIV.

8. "The Veto of the Bank Bill," reprinted in *Andrew Jackson,* ed. Ronald E. Shaw (Dobbs Ferry, New York: Oceana, 1969), p. 52.

9. See Richard F. Fenno, Jr., *The President's Cabinet* (New York: Vintage, 1959), esp. pp. 118–119.

10. Edward Pessen, *Jacksonian America: Society, Personality, and Politics* (Homewood, Ill.: Dorsey, 1969), pp. 336–337.

11. Reprinted in *The Age of Jackson,* ed. Robert V. Remini (Columbia: University of South Carolina Press, 1972), p. 44.

12. Clinton Rossiter, *The American Presidency* (New York: Harvest, 1956), p. 97.

13. J. G. Randall, *Constitutional Problems under Lincoln,* rev. ed. (Gloucester, Mass: Peter Smith, 1963), *passim,* esp. pp. 36–37, 513–514.

14. Lincoln's message to Congress, 4 July 1861, reprinted in Randall, p. 58.

15. Cited in Rossiter, p. 100.

16. For an excellent recent treatment of the war powers see Arthur M. Schlesinger, Jr., *The Imperial Presidency* (Boston: Houghton Mifflin, 1973). The classic study remains Corwin, previously cited.

17. Woodrow Wilson, *Congressional Government* (Boston: Houghton Mifflin, 1885).

18. Erwin C. Hargrove, *Presidential Leadership: Personality and Political Style* (New York: Macmillan, 1966), pp. 11–31.

19. *The Autobiography of Theodore Roosevelt,* ed. Wayne Andrews (New York: Scribner, 1958), pp. 197–200.

20. Wilson, *Congressional Government.*

21. Woodrow Wilson, *Constitutional Government in the United States*

(New York: Columbia University Press, 1908).

22. Arthur S. Link, *Woodrow Wilson* (Chicago: Quadrangle, 1963), pp. 70–80.

23. Link, p. 70.

24. Wilson, *Constitutional Government*, pp. 68, 69, 70.

25. John Morton Blum, *Woodrow Wilson and the Politics of Morality* (Boston: Little, Brown, 1956), pp. 132–140.

26. Link, pp. 117–118.

27. Arthur M. Schlesinger, Sr., *Paths to the Present* (New York: Macmillan, 1949), pp. 94–99.

28. *Ibid.*, p. 96.

29. Arthur M. Schlesinger, Sr., "Our Presidents: A Rating by 75 Historians," *New York Times Magazine*, 29 July 1962.

30. Schlesinger, Sr., *Paths to the Present*, p. 101.

31. *Ibid.*, pp. 102–103.

32. *Ibid.*, p. 105.

33. Richard Nixon, "Remarks at Wreath-Laying Ceremony at the Lincoln Memorial, February 12, 1974," *Weekly Compilation of Presidential Documents*, 10, no. 7 (February 18, 1974), 204.

34. Harold J. Laski, *The American Presidency* (New York: Grosset & Dunlap, 1940), p. 8.

35. Rossiter, pp. 142–145.

36. Emmet John Hughes, *The Living Presidency* (Baltimore: Penguin, 1974), pp. 275–280.

37. It should be noted that some authors on the subject have rejected the rating game. "To say, in the absence of standardized criteria, that a particular Executive was average or poor or near-great is to reason speciously, the difficulty being that in making evaluative judgments each author reveals, consciously or unconsciously, his own emotional responses." Curtis Arthur Amlund, *New Perspectives on the Presidency* (New York: Philosophical Library, 1969), p. 3.

38. Robert K. Merton, *Social Theory and Social Structure*, rev. ed. (New York: Free Press, 1957), pp. 72–82.

39. Inaugural address of Franklin D. Roosevelt, 4 March 1933, in *Senate Documents*, 73rd Cong., 1st Sess., 1933, Senate Document No. 1, pp. 1–4.

40. Richard M. Nixon, campaign speech delivered on radio, 19 September 1968.

41. Aaron Wildavsky, "The Two Presidencies," *Trans-Action*, December 1966, pp. 7–14.

42. Koenig, pp. 209–211.

43. Schlesinger, Jr., *The Imperial Presidency*, p. 99.

44. Arthur M. Schlesinger, Jr., *A Thousand Days* (Greenwich: Fawcett, 1965), p. 733.

45. Pierre Salinger, *With Kennedy* (New York: Avon, 1966), pp. 318–319.

46. Robert F. Kennedy, *Thirteen Days* (New York: Norton, 1969), p. 31.

47. *Ibid.*, pp. 47, 52; Schlesinger, Jr., *A Thousand Days,* p. 735.

48. Radio and TV address by President Kennedy, 22 Oct. 1962, in Kennedy, pp. 163–171.

49. Charles O. Jones, "The Role of the Campaign in Congressional Politics," in *The Electoral Process,* ed. M. Kent Jennings and L. Harmon Ziegler (Englewood Cliffs, N.J.: Prentice-Hall, 1966), p. 24.

50. Donald Stokes and Warren Miller, "Party Government and the Saliency of Congress," *Public Opinion Quarterly,* 26 (Winter 1962), 536.

51. Rowland Egger, *The President of the United States,* 2nd ed. (New York: McGraw-Hill, 1972), p. 4.

52. See, for example, Rossiter, pp. 15–43.

2

Sources of
Presidential Power

Not each precedent, each crisis action taken by the presidents discussed in the last chapter was used or followed by all their successors. Some were even reversed for a time during certain administrations. The "strong" or expanding presidencies, however, have frequently sought to justify their activities by whatever historical precedents they could find. Sometimes what Washington or Jackson had done in a specific instance lay dormant or forgotten until a vigorous president needed or wanted to do something. Then the actions of those energetic predecessors were cited as a habitual practice—almost a principle of government—legitimizing whatever the current incumbent sought to do. Thus, for instance, many of the steps Wilson took during the crisis of world war have almost been turned into routine in the late twentieth century. Although the growth of presidential power has not been a straight-line progression, the long-range trend line of presidential control has been steadily upward. This chapter examines several of the modern devices used by presidents to shape the policy of the United States.

Legislative Clearance

Many of a president's goals depend upon legislation for their enactment, whether those goals aim at breaking up monopolistic control of basic commodities, creating public employment in times of depression, or turning back to the states monies collected at the federal level. As we have already seen, the Constitution, in setting up a system of "separated institutions sharing power," gave the chief executive a role in the legislative process. Presidents such as Jefferson, Wilson, and Franklin Roosevelt made much of this power by urging legislative programs designed to carry out their policy preferences. Roosevelt vetoed 631 bills during his twelve years in office and often urged his aides to "bring me something I can veto" as a reminder that legislation that did not conform to his program would not be allowed to become law. Only nine of those vetoes were overridden.

Since it has now become standard to assign the role of chief legislator to the president, it may falsely be assumed that this was always the way things were, that all past presidents sent detailed legislative packages up to Congress setting forth the proposals of the various executive departments and agencies which they approved and established priorities on important bills. Such is not the case. Prior to 1921 each federal agency was free to request from Congress the budget it thought necessary for its operations or that it believed it could get from the appropriating committees in each house.[1] In that year, however, Congress passed a landmark law that put all requests for money solely in the hands of the president, who would be aided by the newly created Bureau of the Budget. That Congress passed this bill as an economy measure designed to cut down on the number of both requesting agencies in the executive branch and appropriating committees in Congress is immaterial to the outcome. The result was that for the first time the president was given an instrument to oversee the submission of legislative proposals to Congress and a powerful new tool to set his own budgetary priorities. As Wildavsky has said, "If politics is regarded in part as conflict over whose preferences shall prevail in the determination of national policy, then the budget records the outcomes of this struggle."[2]

Enacted in Harding's time, the Budget and Accounting Act of 1921 first had a major impact in Calvin Coolidge's administration. Congress had proven its inability to formulate a comprehensive budget and so had turned the duty over to the executive. Coolidge, with his penchant for budget cutting and his opposition to new programs that could ultimately cost the Treasury money, readily seized upon this opportunity. All departmental proposals that would incur financial obligation had to be cleared with the Bureau of the Budget before submission to the president. The bureau would scrutinize the proposals for congruence with the president's program and make recommendations to him either for his sponsorship of the bill in Congress or his rejection. Only if the chief executive approved would the measure be sent on.

In this, as in most other matters, profound changes took place with the advent of the Roosevelt administration. A newly strengthened bureau was given the mandate to clear all agency proposals for legislation or testimony before Congress to make sure such action was in line with the president's wishes. At first the Bureau of the Budget was located in the Treasury Department, but as a result of recommendations in 1937 by the Brownlow Committee, it was greatly expanded and incorporated into the Executive Office of the President. Here a full-time staff was set to work reviewing agency proposals for legislation and inquiring of other departments how such proposals would affect their interests. A measure of coordination was thus introduced into the burgeoning executive branch. Once Congress had passed a bill, the bureau was in charge of soliciting agency recommendations for presidential signature or veto, a summary of which was then sent to Roosevelt for his ultimate decision. All of this, of course, greatly expanded the president's ability to control his own administration and at the same time led to his increased influence over legislation in Congress.

With Truman the bureau was made even more powerful, actively assisting the president in the development of legislation, rather than merely reacting to the proposals of others. In its coordinating role, the departments, agencies, and White House staff members involved were called together to hammer out administration proposals. On minor matters the bureau itself would sometimes write the legislation for submission to Congress.[3] This meant that the president's program could be planned in advance, that surprises would not be sprung from below, and that timing of messages and bills sent to Congress could be coordinated with the demands of legislative scheduling. For the first time a comprehensive package of detailed proposals was sent by the president to Congress for its consideration at the opening of its session.[4]

Since it is important for Congress to know how the president will react to the measures it passes, in the 1940s some committees began to request that information directly from the bureau at the same time that they were calling for testimony from the agencies involved. This practice grew and served as an additional presidential input into the legislative process at a very early stage of the deliberations (as well as a check on independent requests of the agencies). Contacts were maintained as bills progressed to see if there had been any change in the president's views because of the altered shape of the measures as they emerged from committees. After a bill was passed, Truman would call upon the bureau for recommendations on signing or vetoing the measure, for advice on how the new law would affect his general policies, and for proposals of alternative legislation should he decide the measure in its present form should not become law.

For a while in 1953, it appeared that Truman's heir would abjure sending the kind of itemized program to Congress that had become standard practice since the Second World War. Whiggish tendencies to "let the legislative branch legislate" clashed with the realities that Eisenhower's people were rapidly discovering. But by 1954 the new president and his people were as deeply involved in drawing up proposals for congressional consideration as Truman had ever been, and central clearance of legislation had become an institutionalized feature of the executive branch. In the 1960s and 1970s, this function for major policy initiatives was increasingly performed by White House staff members rather than the Bureau of the Budget (or the successor to that agency, the Office of Management and Budget), but with the presidency it remained.

Here is how the process has worked in recent years. On the vast majority of proposals that originate in the departments themselves, the process of negotiation between interested agencies and ultimate clearance with the Office of Management and Budget (OMB) continues as before. Once a request reaches OMB, the legislative reference staff attaches one of several notations: the bill is "in accord with the Program of the President," is "consistent with the objectives of the Administration," raises "no objection from the standpoint of the Administration's program," or is "not in accord with the President's program."[5] Measures with the latter designation do not proceed. Those that do receive clearance may be the subject of redrafting for inclusion in one of the presidential messages to Congress. Annually OMB routinely processes thousands of bills that spring from within the bureaucracy itself, most of which are minor or technical adjustments to existing law and hold no great interest for the president and his chief policy advisers. The OMB's professional staff is thus able to deal with routine matters without using up a great deal of the president's time. It also has increasingly come to play a major role in supervising and overseeing the departments for the president.

Kennedy, Johnson, and Nixon found this machinery lacking for the development of major legislative thrusts. In the first place there was no guarantee that the kinds of initiatives that they favored would come bubbling up through the departments. In many cases the "bureaucracy" was viewed as an inert, entrenched, conservative force (for Nixon a liberal force) that had to be circumvented to be sure that government would move in the directions favored by the chief executive. Kennedy wanted to lead us to a New Frontier, Johnson to the Great Society, and Nixon through the New American Revolution to restore power to the states. Although specific ideas for these programs did eventually come from within the agencies, the philosophical and policy guidelines had to be imposed from without. Thus, ever increasingly presidents have turned to special study groups, task forces, and White House policy staffs for their ideas and major programs. President Nixon formalized this trend by an executive order in 1970 that converted the Bureau of the Budget into the Office of Management and Budget and gave it prime responsibility for carrying out the policy initiatives that were generated in the newly created Domestic Council under John Ehrlichman.[6] Gerald Ford, early in his administration, indicated that he intended to use his cabinet for policy advice more than had his predecessors. The OMB lost some of its power because cabinet officials once again had a measure of direct access to the president, something they lacked under Nixon.

What the departure of Ehrlichman and the resulting decline of the Domestic Council's role as policy initiator and clearing house did not signify was a return to congressional leadership in most areas of legislation. Even Watergate and the attendant distrust of President Nixon did not accomplish that. To be sure, in the last fifty years Congress has been able to seize the reins from the executive from time to time over specific issues, even overriding presidential vetoes on occasion. The Taft-Hartley Act is an example of what Congress is able to achieve on its own initiative. Congress was also ahead of the Nixon administration on environmental protection legislation, with Nixon impounding funds authorized to clean up the nation's waters. These accomplishments were frequently overlooked by those proponents of the dominant presidency discussed in the preceding chapter. But on most matters any president is still able to get his way (at least in the negative sense of keeping off the statute books laws that he opposes). In 1973, with almost daily revelations about administration involvement in illegal activities filling the air waves and the front pages of our newspapers, with suspicion growing that Nixon himself was implicated, Congress was able to override only one of the ten bills that the president vetoed that year. The only measure on which Congress could muster the necessary two-thirds vote was the War Powers Act, a bill that had grown out of popular and congressional frustration with presidential war. Gerald Ford had four of his first fifteen vetoes overridden, a record unmatched since the administration of Franklin Pierce. This almost equaled the total number of overrides (five) in Nixon's entire presidency. The president's batting average improved over the months, however, as Congress proved unable to override most of Ford's important vetoes. He became so adept at its use that he was accused of "government by veto." The record for his first full year in office was five out of thirty-six vetoes overridden.

It is now time to return to the question of why Congress has largely been reduced to the role of delaying and tinkering in a minor way with the bills sent to it by the administration. Some analysts estimate that at least 80 percent of the public laws enacted originate in the executive branch. Samuel P. Huntington argues that Congress is simply ill-equipped to meet the demands of a complex society, that although the committee structure allows for needed specialization, its concomitant division of power negates the coordinating and integrating ability of Congress as a governing institution.[7] It is argued by those who support this conventional wisdom that only the specialists in the administration and bureaucracy, integrated under the political guidance of the president, are capable of devising the national programs we must have to meet the demands of the twentieth century.

Much congressional activity is in response to requests from the executive agencies that the president has sent along. In this sense the executive branch is the largest "consumer" of legislative services, and it is not surprising that Congress is interested in what the departments have to propose. Congress has come to depend upon the administration for submission of an agenda and for working drafts of legislation that it can react to. Richard Neustadt's oft-cited quotation from a House committee chairman in 1953 is illustrative of how far this situation has progressed: "Don't expect us to start from scratch on what you people want. That's not the way we do things here—*you* draft the bills and *we* work them over."[8] Eisenhower's people soon got the message.

Once the draft of a bill has been submitted, committees need expert witnesses on the proposed legislation. While "outside" specialists are often invited in, most frequently the committees turn to the executive branch for expertise. The testimony of these officials is cleared with OMB to insure that a unified administration position will be presented. To be sure, divergent views are elicited by the questioning of senators and representatives, sometimes even from members of the administration itself. But an official who finds himself too often disagreeing with the president probably will soon be looking for another job. Thus Congress starts with a draft bill from the administration and then relies heavily upon the same people for the information and advice it receives on the measure. Such a system is guaranteed to assure a dominant role for the executive in the passage of legislation.

When the headlines tell of a major setback for the president in the defeat of one or more of his "must" bills in Congress, one may be lead to believe that an independent legislative branch alone is writing the laws. (Most probably, the Congress will be viewed as obstructionist for thwarting the will of the people.) What such headlines obscure is the fact that the overwhelming number of laws that are passed originated in the administration. Most of these bills do not have dramatic appeal either for Congress or the president; they are routine or technical modifications of existing programs. Without the convenient cues provided by the executive as to which of the thousands of measures introduced each year are likely to be signed and which vetoed, which merit consideration and which do not, Congress would have difficulty in getting through its session. In addition, having the presidential seal of approval on a measure is likely to make it seem more important than the proposals of a mere legislator. On the other hand, during periods when Congress is attempting to reassert its authority, it is also crucial to know which measures can be used to hit back at the president.[9]

The Budget

The struggle to control the money that the government has to spend is essentially a question of who exercises power. When the English Parliament finally wrested the right to originate all bills for raising or disbursing revenue from the monarchy in 1689, it was well on its way to limiting the ability of the king to wage war on his own initiative. By the same token, the authors of the American Constitution sought to restrain independent activities of the president by making him dependent upon Congress for the money needed to carry out the duties of his office. The system would not work as the founders intended without comity on both sides, without mutual respect and cooperation on the part of the legislative and executive branches. Each has to act responsibly in carrying out its functions. Over the years, as the problems faced by government became larger and more complex, presidents have moved increasingly to dominate the political and budgetary processes. In many cases Congress willingly went along, delegating to the chief executive the authority and resources that had been requested. Whether one sees this as a total abdication of responsibility or as an intelligent acceptance of the inevitable swing to executive control that is occuring everywhere in the world largely depends upon how one views the results of this profound alteration. What seemed so right to liberals in the forties, fifties, and early sixties, when Roosevelt, Truman, Kennedy, and Johnson were recommending money for social programs, no longer appeared so attractive when Johnson and Nixon shifted monetary priorities to an unpopular war in Vietnam. When Nixon and later Ford seemed determined to gut the domestic legacy of liberal programs, the call for reexamination of the trend greatly intensified. Conversely, the former opponents of a dominant presidency, the conservatives, have switched to support for the president against a Congress bent on what they consider "fiscal irresponsibility."

The handling of the more than $300 billion budget is an instructive example of how the president and the executive branch are able to dominate Congress. As we have seen, the budget largely determines "who gets what, when, and how" from the federal government. The process is a long one, with almost all of the early stages taking place solely within the executive. Months before the budget is sent to Congress, experts in OMB, the Treasury, and the Council of Economic Advisers set to work forecasting economic conditions for the coming year. Although these estimates are not always totally accurate, they at least partially determine the decisions the president and his policy advisers make about the spending and tax levels that they will recommend. They decide whether they will try for a balanced budget, whether they will seek to stimulate the economy through tax cuts and deficit spending, or whether they will go for major new programs with high price tags. All agencies of the federal government are canvassed for their financial needs. Once all this information is collected, planning levels are set and sent back to the departments, which then work out detailed budgets with justifications for their requests.

In about October, OMB begins reviewing the developing budget, usually making cuts in the requests it has received. These are the subject of negotiations between OMB, the departments, and sometimes the White House. If the president overrules his budget director too frequently after they have agreed on guidelines, he runs the risk of having all the agencies try to end run the OMB and thus destroy its utility for him. Although last minute changes are always possible, usually the budget has taken its final form by December or early January. Toward the end of the latter month, the budget, accompanied by a presidential message, is sent to Congress. After ten months of work on it in the administration, the legislature finally gets its first look at a document that will set the priorities for the next fiscal year. Since the new fiscal year begins July 1, Congress has less than five months to hold hearings, take testimony from agencies and affected groups, and try to reach a conclusion of its own. Appropriation measures by custom originate in the House, and the Senate must await the representatives' determination before even beginning the process. It is small wonder then that Congress in recent years has rarely passed a new budget by the end of June. (Continuing resolutions allow the departments to go on spending money at the previous year's level.)

Once in the House, the budget is divided up among the thirteen subcommittees of the Appropriations Committee. Each segment is acted upon independently, without an overall review of the total proposed spending level.

Angered over President Nixon's refusal to spend money that they had appropriated, frustrated at their own disorganization and lack of control, and perhaps spurred on by Watergate, Congress finally moved to reassert its "power of the purse." In the summer of 1974, it passed a far-reaching measure of reform designed to make the Congress an equal partner with the president in setting budgetary priorities. Under the new plan, the president will have to submit his proposed budget within fifteen days of the convening of Congress each year. By April 15 each house, through new Budget Committees of its own, will recommend total spending levels to the Appropriations Committees with a breakdown by major category. By May 15 the houses will have to agree on a common sum to be spent in the coming fiscal year. Using the guidelines set out by the Budget Committees, the Appropriations Committees will take over and perform their functions much as they do now. However, they will be assisted by a newly created congressional Budget Office staffed by professionals who can give them the same kind of service provided the president by OMB. Revenues can be adjusted to proposed spending as the year progresses. Finally, Congress will have to complete action on appropriations bills by September 25. (Under the new law, the fiscal year will begin on October 1, rather than July 1 as under the old system.) All presidential proposals for new legislation which will require financial support will have to be submitted at least a full year in advance. This new arrangement, set to go into effect in 1976, may finally begin to restore the balance that in recent years has shifted (so many believe) dangerously to the president. Final judgment will have to wait. It may be that this too will prove to be merely a temporary brake on the long slide toward presidential government. If Congress cannot reform its own machinery, generate its own independent expertise, and act responsibly to meet the demands which face government today, the nation may find itself worse off than before.

Impoundment

One of the frustrations of Congress that ultimately led to the budgetary reform of 1974 was President Nixon's impoundment of appropriated funds. According to the Constitution, "no Money shall be drawn from the Treasury, but in Consequence of Appropriations made by Law." This provision clearly meant to give Congress the power of the purse, with the president retaining his prerogative either to sign the entire measure or veto it. No item veto allowing him to strike out individual sections of the law was provided for. If because of dissatisfaction with certain provisions, he feels the bill unwise and exercises his veto power, Congress by a super majority of two-thirds can pass the measure over his veto. It then becomes the law of the land, which the president has a constitutional duty to enforce. Thus in cases of conflict between the executive and legislative branches, ultimate decision-making power rests with two-thirds of Congress. With impoundment, however, the president refused to spend money for projects he disliked, even if the appropriations measure was passed over his veto. This reversed the intention of the framers of the Constitution and gave final power to determine which programs would be funded to the president.

President Nixon, in this as in many other areas, did not originate the practice; he merely carried it far beyond what any of his predecessors had ever attempted. Usually the precedent cited for declining to spend money is Thomas Jefferson's 1803 refusal to spend $50,000 appropriated by Congress for gunboats on the Mississippi River. The Louisiana Purchase had just been negotiated with France, and in Jefferson's opinion America no longer needed to build up defenses there. In a message to Congress he informed the legislators: "The favorable and peaceful turn of affairs on the Mississippi rendered an immediate execution of that law unnecessary, and time was desirable in order that the institution of that branch of our forces might begin on models the most approved by experience."[10] Schlesinger points out that Jefferson did not refuse to spend the money; he merely delayed the ship construction a few months because the situation on the Mississippi had changed, and he wanted to wait until new and improved gunboats could be built for use elsewhere.[11] The corruption of precedent in this case is an example of how recent presidents and their advisers have interpreted the facts to fit their own policy preferences and justify activities for which there may be no clear legal or constitutional foundation.

During the nineteenth century, presidents rarely withheld funds. Grant refused to spend a portion of the money provided for river and harbor improvements on the grounds that they were purely local projects, but beyond that instances are few and far between. The first legal authority for the practice appears in the Antideficiency Acts of 1905 and 1906, which were designed to insure against a department using up all of its funds before the end of the fiscal year. Under these laws the executive can withhold portions of the appropriations for each agency for a period of months to prevent deficiencies from occurring. In 1921 an additional purpose was approved—to effect savings where Congress has provided more money than is necessary to achieve the goals of a program.[12] An example of what Congress had in mind would occur if $10 million were appropriated for snow removal in national parks and then an exceptionally mild winter negated the need for spending the entire amount. It would obviously not be the intent of Congress to have the Park Service drive snowplows up and down bare roads to use up the complete $10 million.

The increasing use of impoundment as a policy and budgetary tool of the president dates from Franklin Roosevelt's administration. In order to allow "Dr. New Deal" and later "Dr. Win the War" sufficient flexibility to cope with the crises of depression and world war, Congress began appropriating funds for programs in lump sums; in effect merely setting a ceiling on how much Roosevelt could spend in a given area. If he did not deem it necessary to spend up to the ceiling, he simply impounded the money. With the war he increasingly used the tool to slash any program that in his opinion had little national security value.

Once the war powers of the president could no longer be relied upon as a justification for failure to fully carry out programs funded by Congress, the executive branch sought new devices. In 1949 President Truman impounded $615 million that Congress had authorized for expansion of the air force from forty-eight to fifty-eight wings; he based his action on "the authority vested in me as president of the United States and Commander in Chief of the Armed Forces."[13] Statutory right to withhold some funds was achieved in 1950 through an amendment to the Antideficiency Act. It provided that:

> In apportioning any appropriation, reserves may be established to provide for contingencies, or to effect savings whenever savings are made possible by or through changes in requirements, greater efficiency of operations, *or other developments subsequent to the date on which such appropriation was made available.* [Emphasis added.]

Although Congress clearly did not intend to give the president power to frustrate its expressed will, that has been the effect in many cases since the law was passed. Eisenhower followed the pattern set by Truman and utilized impoundment primarily in the defense area. Among his impoundments were $137 million for testing Nike-Zeus antimissile missiles, $525 million for manned bombers, and many other millions for submarines and troop level support. Kennedy's impoundments concerned the development of the B-70 bomber; and, at least before the Vietnam War heated up, Johnson also largely confined his refusals to spend to the defense area. A case can be made in defense spending that the president as commander in chief, should be allowed a large measure of scope in determining the adequacy of American protective forces; but even here it is highly questionable whether any "inherent" power to do so resides in the chief executive.

Lyndon Johnson returned to what Roosevelt had practiced during his war: withholding funds from domestic programs. In 1966, just after getting his Great Society program through Congress, the president decided that full funding would be inflationary and ordered a spending cut of $5.3 billion in programs ranging from highway construction to housing and urban development projects. As a result of political pressure, he later released some of these funds.[14] Note that these were not the kind of authorized cuts that Congress from time to time has imposed upon the president to insure compliance with its laws. Examples of this last category are the 1964 Civil Rights Act, which provides for withholding federal funds from segregated programs, and a 1968 law designed to force states to update their welfare programs on the penalty of losing all welfare aid from the national government.[15]

With Richard Nixon came a quantum leap in claims of presidential power to withhold money mandated by Congress. Although there are no accurate figures on exactly how much he refused to spend, the administration admitted to impounding $12.2 billion in 1972. Current estimates range up to more than $28 billion, including more than $9 billion for water pollution control. Among the other recipients of slashes were the Veterans Administration hospital system, food stamps, anticancer research, mass transit, rural environmental assistance, and low-rent public housing construction.[16]

What was new about Nixon's impoundment was not only its unprecedented size and scope but also its use as a device to kill whole programs with which the president disagreed. This occurred despite an early memorandum by Assistant Attorney General William Rehnquist (whom Nixon later elevated to the Supreme Court) stating:

It is in our view extremely difficult to formulate a constitutional theory to justify a refusal by the President to comply with a Congressional directive to spend. It may be argued that the spending of money is inherently an executive function, and it seems an anomalous proposition that because the Executive is bound to execute the laws, it is free to decline to execute them.[17]

President Nixon moved nonetheless to abolish the Office of Economic Opportunity (OEO) by simply not committing any of the funds Congress had appropriated for that agency. The outcry from Congress and an unfavorable lower court decision ultimately forced a compromise that entailed shifting some of OEO's functions to other departments and the retention of a reduced OEO for one more year, but the case is illustrative of just how much power Nixon believed inhered in his office.

The justification most frequently used by Nixon for his use of impoundment was that Congress had been reckless in its spending policies; that it was appropriating the United States into bankruptcy; that the president had to act responsibly to prohibit "budget busting" by the legislature. In a letter to Russell Train, head of the Environmental Protection Agency, Nixon ordered the impoundment of $3 billion appropriated by Congress to help cities construct waste treatment facilities because "the Federal Government must continue its efforts to control spending in order to avoid renewed inflation or a requirement for increased taxes."[18] Citing the testimony of Joseph T. Sneed, deputy attorney general of the United States, Larry Adams discovered these other rationales used by the administration to justify impoundment: Congress has acquiesced in presidential impoundments since the days of Franklin Roosevelt; impoundment allows the president to "harmonize" conflicting laws; "it is necessary to keep total federal spending within the statutory debt limit"; it allows the president to fine tune spending policies for programs "peculiarly within the competence and constitutional authority of the Executive Branch"; and it is needed to prevent waste so the president can faithfully execute the laws.[19] Caspar Weinberger, then Nixon's deputy director of the Office of Management and Budget, rested his defense for impoundment on constitutional as well as legal grounds:

> In addition to the specific statutory authority provided by the Antideficiency Act, authority for the President to establish reserves is derived basically from the Constitutional provisions (Article II, section I) which vest the Executive power in the President. In addition to the President's general responsibility as Chief Executive there may be involved his specific functions as Commander-in-Chief, his responsibilities with respect to the conduct of foreign affairs and the requirement that he "take care that the laws be faithfully executed."[20]

This latter claim, that the president faithfully executes the laws by his failure to spend money that Congress has appropriated, seems a somewhat farfetched twisting of the Constitution to justify imposing the presidential will over that of Congress. "The language of the clause indicates precisely the reverse of this argument: once congressional policy has become law it is the President's duty to execute it whether he agrees with it or not." [21] Perhaps Lewis Carroll explained it best in *Alice in Wonderland:* "When I use a word, Humpty Dumpty said in rather a scornful tone, it means just what I choose it to mean—neither more nor less. The question is, said Alice, whether you can make words mean so many different things. The question is, said Humpty Dumpty, which is to be master—that's all." [22] In fact, even the claim that the president saved the United States from ruinous inflation by failing to spend all the money that Congress appropriated is open to question. Mike Mansfield, the majority leader of the Senate, asserted that Congress had cut President Nixon's first four budgets by $22 billion and that Nixon merely disagreed with the priorities established by the laws enacted by Congress.

Without a large voice in determining "who gets what, when and how," Congress would have been reduced to the status of a debating society by Nixon. Despite that fact the House of Representatives voted in 1972 to allow President Nixon to keep the budget at $250 billion by withholding money from whatever programs he chose—in effect giving him the item veto denied the president by the Constitution. Only the reluctance of the Senate to go along saved Congress from its own abdication of responsibility. As the ire grew over the contemptuous manner with which Nixon treated Congress, movement began to limit his power to impound. Across the country, states and cities that suffered by the withholding of funds instituted law suits. In more than a score of these, district courts ruled that the president had exceeded his authority and ordered the release of impounded funds. In only one of these cases did the president triumph. Finally, in February 1975 the Supreme Court struck down Nixon's refusal to allocate more than $9 billion in water pollution control funds. (Ford also had held on to these funds.) Although this case did not finally settle all impoundment questions, the unanimous vote probably indicated which way the Court would hold in similar cases. Justice White, in the opinion of the Court, reasoned that "we cannot believe that Congress at the last minute scuttled the entire [antipollution] effort by providing the executive with the seemingly limitless power to withhold funds from allotment and obligation."[23]

Congress itself has now been stirred to action. The budget reform legislation of 1974 mentioned earlier includes a provision that allows either house to block the impoundment of funds by the adoption of a simple resolution not subject to presidential veto. Where the withholding of funds would constitute the cancellation of an entire program, the president is required to ask for rescission authority from Congress. If that body fails to give such approval and the president persists in his effort to kill a program, Congress can authorize the controller general to bring suit against the chief executive to force compliance with congressional wishes. That is exactly what happened in the spring of 1975 when President Ford announced that he was refusing to spend $264 million in housing assistance. Ford has sought congressional permission each time he has wanted to defer spending or cut back on money already appropriated, and he released $2 billion of highway funds impounded by his predecessor even before the Supreme Court acted to limit presidential discretion in this area.

Contingency Funds, Reprogramming, Transfers, and Full Funding

Command over preparation and submission of the budget and impoundment of appropriated funds are not the only tools a president has to control spending. We have already mentioned "lump-sum" appropriations allowing a president to spend funds in any way he chooses within a general category and up to a specified ceiling. (These are most common during crisis and wartime.) Contingency funds to cover unexpected events are another device giving the president freedom to spend as he sees fit. Nixon had an annual "Special Projects Fund" of $1.5 million, and the suspicion arose that some of that money was spent to pay E. Howard Hunt for his "plumbers" activities to "stop leaks" and perhaps for other Watergate-related activities as well (although no substantiation has been produced for this suspicion). In addition, the military and other agencies under the president receive contingency funds that the president may order used at his discretion.[24]

Timothy Ingram has described another tool, called reprogramming, used by presidents to circumvent the will of Congress. Essentially this consists of deferring spending on some program Congress has approved—and then spending the money on a project not approved. All that generally needs to be done is to clear the new project informally with the appropriate chairmen of the authorizing committees in House and Senate and then the subcommittee chairmen of the two appropriations committees. The administration in conjunction with four legislators are in this way able to redirect money away from congressionally sanctioned projects to those on which the vote may have been negative. Although the chairmen sometimes hold closed hearings or informally canvass their own members on the new project, this is not always done. There is virtually no opportunity for the rest of the members of the House and Senate to hear of, much less stop, the shifting of funds. Two of Ingram's illustrations will demonstrate how the process works. Congress had by 1971 twice refused to provide money for a new nuclear aircraft carrier. In that year, however, two senators learned that the navy planned to begin construction of it anyway, using $139 million appropriated for an oil tanker and three salvage tugs. The outcry the senators raised forced the navy to back down on this project, but the vast majority of reprogramming efforts are almost routinely carried out. An example is what happened with the F-14 fighter aircraft. Most members of the House Appropriations Committee feared the navy wanted to move into production of this airplane before it had been fully tested, so the committee cut out of the budget $275 million and left only funds for test models. Nine months later, at an informal navy briefing, many members learned to their surprise that the F-14 was now in production, the navy having "reprogrammed" $517 million into the construction of twenty-six production models of the aircraft. Only the members of the Defense Subcommittee of Appropriations had been consulted on this move.[25] The *National Journal* estimates that yearly reprogramming in the Defense Department exceeds $1 billion.[26]

A closely related device is transfer authority. Several statutes permit the president to take money appropriated for one purpose and spend it for a different one. It was under this authority that President Nixon transferred $100 million to Cambodia after the

United States invasion of that country in 1970.[27] The Defense Department is at liberty to transfer up to $600 million a year when it is "important to the security of the United States," without even notifying congressional committees.[28] Congress sometimes finds out about these shifts when the president requests restoration of funds to programs that have had their money transferred out, but almost always after the fact.

One final tool of presidential control over money should be mentioned. This has to do with the timing of the actual spending of the money that Congress appropriates. Most organizations operate on a fiscal-year budget, meaning that, if an agency has not used up all of its funds by July 1, the money is returned to the Treasury. Nobody wants to admit that he requested too much in the first place; agencies fear that if their next budget is reduced to the level actually spent in the current year, unforeseen events or emergencies may leave their organization short of funds. By June, then, agencies of the cities, states, and federal government frequently rush out and use up all the money that is left in their budgets. For some programs, however, Congress has decided that money appropriated in one year may be carried over to the next, or until ultimately expended. These funds are sometimes called "no-year money,"[29] the purpose of which is to let Congress know the full cost of a project over a number of years. The problem with this full funding is that billions of dollars may remain in "the pipeline" for a considerable time period, making it suspectible to various maneuvers such as transfers and reprogramming. Even if Congress votes to terminate a program and refuses to commit any more money to it, sometimes the executive can nevertheless go right along by using past appropriations that have been carried over. By 1972 the Defense Department had an estimated $43 billion in "the pipeline."[30]

What presidential preparation of the budget, expert testimony, impoundment, reprogramming, transfers, full funding, and other devices add up to is that the president has now assumed the major voice in setting budgetary priorities. Most frequently in recent years the congressional role has taken the form of adding pork barrel measures that benefit primarily individual districts and states, increasing funds for pollution control and domestic programs, and trimming the defense and foreign aid budgets. The reforms enacted in 1974 may lead to more responsible behavior on the part of both president and Congress, with the people being the chief beneficiaries.

The Veto

Another powerful tool the president has that he can use to shape legislation is the veto. The Constitution lists three options available to the chief executive once Congress has passed a measure: he may sign it, thus making it law; he may veto it and return it to the house in which it originated along with a meassage stating his objections to the bill in its present form, in which case Congress can override the veto with a two-thirds vote; or he may withhold action completely. In the latter case the bill becomes a law without his signature at the end of ten days if Congress is still in session. However, if Congress has adjourned before the ten days expire, thus preventing the return of the measure, it then has no opportunity to override, and the bill dies by the so-called pocket veto. Since it is very difficult to muster a two-thirds vote against a president when he rallies his party and other supporters behind him, legislators take very seriously the president's desires in passing new laws. Neither Kennedy nor Johnson had a veto overridden. In the exercise of the pocket veto, President Nixon went beyond what any of his predecessors had ever attempted. In the past only adjournments at the end of a congresional session were considered eligible for the use of the pocket veto, but Nixon claimed that he could use it even when Congress only temporarily adjourned for Easter, the Fourth of July, or other short holidays. This meant that he did not return measures he disapproved if Congress had taken a brief recess, and the bill did not become law. Contrary to the Constitution, Nixon attempted to exercise an absolute veto that Congress could not override regardless of how large a vote it could muster. To circumvent this claimed power, Congress began adjourning temporarily subject to call by the leadership so that it could get back into session should the president attempt a pocket veto during Lincoln's birthday or some other brief recess. In addition, Senator Edward Kennedy instituted court action to overturn Nixon's past use of this kind of veto. Both the district court and the court of appeals sided with Kennedy by ruling Nixon's action unconstitutional.

In a step that reminded some people of his predecessor's attitude, President Ford announced that he was using the pocket veto on three bills during the fall congressional recess of 1974. At the same time, the administration refused to appeal the adverse lower court ruling to the Supreme Court, where the issue could finally be settled. As Senator Kennedy pointed out, "Now the Administration is trying to have it both ways. It wants to ignore the Court decision, and it also wants to continue to use the pocket veto."[31]

Patronage

It should not be assumed that the president wins each battle with Congress, or that the legislative branch doesn't have important weapons of its own in the political process. There is an impressive literature on the subject, and the student should be familiar with it if he or she is to get a balanced picture of the dimensions of the relationship between the two.[32] The intent here, however, is primarily to present the weapons the president has in getting the upper hand when there is a disagreement between the chief executive and Congress.

One of the oldest tools at the president's disposal is patronage. Although there are fewer political jobs to hand out than there once were (and even Lincoln is reported to have said that for each position he filled he made nine enemies and one ingrate), patronage can still be an important lever for the ambitious president. There are still federal judgeships, ambassadorships, jobs as United States attorney, and cabinet and subcabinet positions to distribute to the deserving. And in recent years, a whole new category of appointments has become an important resource for playing favorites: the naming of individuals to advisory commissions and panels. For instance, Thomas E. Cronin and Sanford D. Greenberg estimated that under Johnson there were 27 different advisory councils with a membership of around three hundred that reported to the commissioner of the United States Office of Education in the Department of Health, Education and Welfare.[33] No one knows exactly how many of these groups there are scattered throughout the government, but estimates by 1972 ranged from 2,600 to 3,200. The most prestigious of these, of course, are the White House–level advisory commissions, and Johnson had 175 of these alone. But even a position on the less visible panels can be exceedingly attractive to countless persons who would like to "serve" and at the same time receive recognition as being experts worthy of consultation. A local veterinarian who is appointed to the Hoof and Mouth Disease Advisory Commission with the Department of Agriculture may not only impress his fellow vets but his customers as well. Even nonpaying jobs can thus be used as a source of patronage for bargaining with legislators.

Nor should discussion of patronage be restricted to the job market alone. Stanley Kelly, Jr., reminds us that "any action undertaken by an official as a favor may serve as an inducement for the individual who receives that favor to act in accordance with the official's desires."[34] Thus patronage includes all of the discretionary powers at a president's command, and clearly he has more favors to bestow than any other person in politics.

One resource of the president is his almost universal recognition by the people and the comparable obscurity of the average representative. Warren Miller and Donald Stokes in an article published in 1963 found that only 49 percent of the electorate could identify their own congressman.[35] If anything, the record has gotten worse since then. In a 1969–1970 survey of ten thousand young adults, only 39 percent could correctly name their own representative (57 percent could name one senator and 31 percent could name both).[36] Local newspapers rarely cover what the local member of Congress says in Washington, and even if they do it is buried on the back pages. What this means in practice is that the average representative virtually has to engage in self-immolation on the Capitol steps to get noticed—even by his or her own constituents.

On the other hand, almost everyone recognizes the president, and to a degree he can use this fact to persuade reluctant members of Congress to go along with him. Inviting a legislator to a bill-signing ceremony, awarding of presidential pens, and picture-taking sessions with the representative and chief executive smiling at each other all cost the president practically nothing. But these things can be useful to the congressman in gaining recognition back home. The local TV stations may well carry a film clip of Congressman Sludgepump shaking hands with the president, and to locals it appears that he is an important person indeed. Other such cheap favors a president may bestow include invitations to travel on the presidential jet, speaking in a congressman's district, including money for a new local post office in his next budget, or allowing the representative to announce the award of a government contract to a local firm. The president isn't out anything, but the congressman may have increased his visibility and chances for reelection. Perhaps more important, he also owes the president a favor.

Other examples of spreading around loaves and fishes (you get back more than you distribute) have to do with the awarding of governmental contracts or military bases. If a legislator is important enough to bargain with, he may find his district richly rewarded with the pelf of federal largess. It may be unimportant to the president whether Lockheed or Boeing gets a particular contract, but to a representative it may mean thousands of jobs and perhaps votes in Los Angeles or Seattle. Thus decisions in the White House over the location of new bases (or the closure of old ones) and the letting of contracts for the goods and services government must have provide yet another opportunity to reward faithful support.

Even if the president lacks the resources to distribute to a deserving legislator, he may seek to win support in another way—by announcing that he "favors" the pet bill or project of the target representative. This doesn't mean that he actively has to fight for it, but by merely lending presidential prestige to a measure, he may earn the gratitude of the sponsor of the legislation. A word of caution is in order here. Usually the wielding of the patronage weapon in any of its forms is not done blatantly. The patronage market is not quite respectable, and it wouldn't do to let it be known that a legislator's vote can be influenced in this way.[37] So bargaining is generally done tacitly rather than overtly, and this may lead to misunderstanding on the part of both congressman and president as to exactly what constitutes a favor, as well as over how much one party "owes" the other in any particular transaction. The president may view the congressman as an ingrate, while the representative may feel he is not in the slightest debt to the president.

Legislative Liaison and Control of Information

The president is now equipped with a specialized staff that spends almost all of its time attempting to get the president's way with Congress. Among the matters the staff may deal with are conveying patronage requests of legislators, pushing the executive's program, or handling requests for appointments with the president. In earlier days these functions were separated and handled by different members of the staff. In addition, several of the executive departments appoint liaison officials of their own, but until recent administrations, as Estes Kefauver has said, "such efforts at better liaison as have been made by the executive branch have been chiefly informal, often sporadic, frequently personal, and in many cases largely intended to produce or protect appropriations."[38] With Eisenhower and Kennedy came a merger of staff functions in this area; the same people not only acted on questions of patronage but also were given the responsibility of seeing to it that the president's program was pushed through Congress. This procedure has been followed by every president since.[39] Under Kennedy and Johnson the lobbying efforts of the departments were tied together under Larry O'Brien acting for the White House liaison staff. This not only gave increased manpower to the effort but assured the president that a unified administration front would be presented to Congress.

Nixon enlarged on what his predecessors had done and appointed an assistant to the president for congressional relations, plus a deputy assistant for Senate relations and a deputy assistant for congressional relations. Almost all contact between the executive and legislative branches was formalized through this channel. Perhaps this was because of Nixon's distaste for dealing personally with members of Congress and his general lack of interest in what went on up on the Hill. Some part of the bad relations was attributable to the fact that Democrats controlled the Congress and Republicans the White House, but even more of the animosity resulted from the Nixon staffers' failure to understand the workings of the political system. Bryce Harlow (Nixon's first legislative liaison) and his chief lieutenant, William Timmons, did have considerable experience in dealing with Congress; the problem was that Nixon had surrounded himself with public relations men, a former Disneyland guide, lawyers with no political experience, and junior account executives who effectively sabotaged the liaison staff's attempts to work harmoniously with Congress. Harlow and Timmons found Nixon listening primarily to H. R. Haldeman, an advertising executive for J. Walter Thompson before coming to the White House. According to Evans and Novak, Haldeman's approach to Congress vacillated between a "take it or leave it, the-hell-with-them attitude" and an approach he had used on housewives to get them to buy his products—"by using every public-relations and ad-man technique, to go out and *sell.*" [40] The result was that the Nixon administration's relations with Congress were never good—even before Watergate.

Gerald Ford revitalized the congressional relations staff in his first few months in office. Its main purpose for him is to act as an intermediary, transmitting information and opinions between the White House and the Capitol. At the same time, the staff is expected to lobby vigorously for the president's viewpoint. When Congress is in session, Ford meets daily with Max Friedersdorf, the head of the liaison team, and other top policy aides to map legislative strategy. John Marsh, the president's counselor, oversees the daily work of the staff for the president.

Any administration has enormous lobbying resources on its side, despite the fact that Congress has from time to time attempted to protect itself from being unduly influenced by the executive. For instance, a 1913 statute prohibits the use of "publicity experts" by the departments unless money has specifically been appropriated for that purpose. An even tougher measure is the Antilobbying Law, which declares that federal funds can't be used directly or indirectly to influence any member of Congress to cast his vote for or against any measure; only contacts at the request of members of Congress through official channels are sanctioned. [41] How this law is widely circumvented in practice is revealed by this quote from one liaison officer: "I interpret the law that I can answer any requests from a member. So I send out a blanket form stating that I hope I can be of assistance to them and their offices, and, if so, would they please call on us. I've gotten replies from every congressman on the Hill. So I'm fully protected."[42] There are probably at least as many full-time executive lobbyists working on congressmen as there are congressmen themselves. The Center for Political Research in 1970 issued a partial list of these liaison agents: air force, 177; army, 95; navy, 67; Treasury, 28, Post Office, 33; Securities and Exchange Commission, 35; Office of Economic Opportunity, 10; Veterans Administration, 43; Department of Transportation, 28; State Department, 26.[43] By fiscal 1967 the Defense Department's legislative liaison officers were spending more than $3.8 million a year handling congressional inquiries and working for the president's programs. This figure included salaries for 197 civilian and 141 military employees. According to a former member of this team, the Pentagon lobbyists "have Congress organized like a Marine Corps landing."[44]

Legislative liaison thus becomes a powerful tool for the executive by providing information to the legislature that serves as the basis for much of the knowledge that Congress possesses. Rarely do liaison staff lie to representatives.[45] But lying isn't necessary when one side has at its disposal thousands of skilled analysts in the departments, more than four thousand computers, countless advisory commissions and panels of experts, and hundreds of liaison officers. Congress can only act on the information it acquires, and it is ill-equipped in its current state to generate independent information of its own. All of the congressional committees put together have staffs of only around sixteen hundred, many of them clerks and secretaries.[46] As Senator Walter Mondale pointed out when he held hearings on the navy's request to construct a new aircraft carrier, "it was a case of myself and one college kid versus the U.S. Navy and everybody who wanted to build a carrier, or who had a friend who was an ensign or above. We foolishly handicap ourselves by failing to properly staff ourselves."[47] In the age of computers, Congress has equipped itself with fewer than a half dozen, and these are mainly for routine payroll and administrative chores. Charles Jones estimated that its computer capability is roughly equivalent to that of the First National Bank of Kadoka, South Dakota. [48] And Mondale contends, "Whenever I am on the side of the Administration, I am surfeited with computer printouts that come within seconds to prove how right I am. But if I am opposed to the Administration, they always come late, prove the opposite point, or are on some other topic. He who controls the computers controls the Congress."[49]

Control of information and access to expertise thus constitute a major control mechanism for the president. Cronin and Greenberg have listed a number of the advisory channels available to the executive that are not generally accessible to Congress. They include the cabinet, policy and program advisers, political and appointment advisers, speechwriting staffs, special counsels and special consultants, OMB, the Council of Economic Advisers, the National Security Council and staff, the CIA, the Foreign Intelligence Board, the National Security Agency, the Office of Science and Technology, the Office of Emergency Planning, the Federal Energy Office, the Office of Telecommunications Policy, White House advisory commissions, councils, or boards, White House conferences, White House task forces, White House special study commissions, White House consultants, interagency committees, and White House contracted studies from various think tanks and universities.[50] Information garnered from these sources that lends support to the president's policies may be passed on to Congress; if not, it likely will be buried. (For reasons to be discussed in Chapter 4, the president may in reality have less accurate information than members of Congress.)

Secrecy and Classification

Besides being dependent on the executive for much that it does receive, Congress has frequently been deprived of material necessary for the intelligent exercise of its duties. The simplest device for keeping information from members of Congress is the classification system, the stamping of documents as CONFIDENTIAL, SECRET, or TOP SECRET. The rationale for this is that even in a democracy certain matters must be kept secret for the security and well-being of the country. For instance, the argument goes, diplomacy cannot be carried out in public—negotiating stances change, bargains are struck, and compromises are reached. To the unsophisticated, it may appear that our diplomats are sacrificing principle if their original position is known and compared with what they finally accept. Thus the Nixon administration was able to claim "peace with honor" for Henry Kissinger's agreement with the North Vietnamese, a settlement no doubt far from the original bargaining position. In addition, military strategy, intelligence reports, and weapons specifications must remain classified if sources are to be protected and weapons unduplicated by enemies. Secrecy would be much more difficult if the information is available to the 535 members of Congress, critics of that body argue.

The Constitutional Convention was of course held behind closed doors, a practice that Congress itself has adopted for many of its committee hearings. In recent years more than half of the meetings of the House Committees on Appropriations and Ways and Means, and the Senate Committees on Finance and Armed Services have been held behind closed doors. This is in partial response to the charge that Congress can't keep a secret—that what it knows the world soon learns. But this is fundamentally different from one coordinate branch of the federal government withholding critical information needed by another if the latter is to be able to carry out its legitimate function.

Already cited has been Washington's refusal to turn over to the House the diplomatic instructions used in the negotiation of Jay's treaty with Great Britain. The rejection was solely on the grounds that the House was constitutionally barred from the treaty-making process and not that these documents were classified (the very same papers were delivered to the Senate). It has only been since the Second World War that there has been the massive classification of documents designed to close off from view literally millions of pieces of information. The now familiar triology of CONFIDENTIAL, SECRET, or TOP SECRET began to be stamped on more and more of the files in government possession. Roosevelt's executive order creating the system made it clear that it was designed to prevent public disclosure, not to keep relevant information from the committees of Congress. Truman, like Roosevelt, relied on executive orders to institute his system of secrecy, but unlike Roosevelt, he extended it to cover all agencies of the federal government, rather than just the military. This fear of public disclosure had spread throughout government until at least 1.5 million persons were authorized to classify documents by 1957. The system has been modified by every president since, but the basic outline persists.[51] An example of the extreme to which secrecy has been carried occurred in the spring of 1975. The FBI began an investigation of *Consumer Reports* after the magazine published a comparison of the interest rates on new car loans charged by various banks across the United States. The government document containing that information was classified!

What has changed since the Second World War is the withholding of more and more classified information from Congress itself. The fact that the United States carried out more than thirty-nine hundred separate bombing missions over Cambodia—a country against which Congress had not declared war—came as a complete surprise to the overwhelming majority of senators and representatives. The North Vietnamese knew of these bombings, the Cambodians knew, and undoubtedly the Chinese and Soviets knew as well; only the American people and Congress weren't aware of them. A handful of trusted congressmen were supposedly told by the president what was going on, but Congress as a whole could hardly be expected to stop something of which it had no knowledge.* A historical account of how the United States was drawn into the Vietnam War, the Pentagon Papers, was classified and kept from Congress until Daniel Ellsberg leaked it to several senators. (One of Senator Gravel's aides was prosecuted for his role in accepting these papers.) Nor was Congress told for more than twenty years of special agreements between oil companies and the executive branch that allowed the companies to formulate joint policies in their negotiations with the Arab oil-producing nations without fear of antitrust action from the federal government. The provisions of dozens of secret security agreements between the United States and foreign countries such as Spain, Ethiopia, and the Philippines, agreements pledging our military support, were not made known to the

---

*Congress wasn't the only group to be kept in the dark. High military officers, including the secretary of the air force, learned of the bombing from the newspapers.

Senate. Nor was the fact that Nixon had made secret pledges to reintervene in Vietnam.

Classification has gone so far that even classification designations are now classified and kept from Congress. David Wise tells of how a *New York Times* photograph of McGeorge Bundy, then Johnson's assistant for national security, revealed a spiral notebook in his hand with the legend TOP SECRET DINAR across the cover. The CIA confiscated the negative, but we learned that TOP SECRET no longer constituted the ultimate category of secrecy. A 1964 hearing with Secretary of Defense McNamara before the Senate Foreign Relations Committee included an exchange revealing a portion of what until then had remained unknown to most members of Congress. It begins with the secretary refusing to testify about certain matters because not all of the committee's staff members had the high clearance necessary:

> Secretary McNamara: Clearance is above Top Secret for the particular information involved in this situation.
>
> Senator Gore: . . . would you please clear up the exact identity of this clearance status that is something superior to Top Secret . . . ? I would like to be informed. I never heard of this kind. I thought Top Secret was Top Secret.
>
> Secretary McNamara: . . . Mr. Chairman, may I try to answer it. . . . There are a host of different clearances. I would guess I have perhaps twenty-five. There are certain clearances to which only a handful of people in the government are exposed. There are others with broader coverage, and overlapping coverage, and it is not really a question of degree of clearance. It is a question of need to know, and need to know clearances apply to certain forms of data. . . . There is another clearance, Q clearance, that relates to certain categories of information.
>
> There is another clearance which is the Special Intelligence clearance we are talking about, that relates to intercept information, and it is this latter clearance in particular that is at issue here, and the staff members of this committee have not been cleared for that kind of information. . . . I do not want to get into a further discussion until the room is cleared of those not authorized to handle it. [52]

These special categories of secret information are called SPE-CATS, and besides DINAR, at various times have included classifications with names such as TRINE, UMBRA, SECRET SPOKE, and HARUM. In any case, from McNamara's testimony we know there are more than twenty additional secrecy classifications above TOP SECRET, the names of which are themselves classified.[53] The next level of clearance above TOP SECRET is called COMINT CLEARANCE, and the latter is accessible to only about 120,000 people. This is the clearance that McNamara was describing and the one that Senator Gore and many other members of Congress had never heard of. The information so classified is available to cabinet secretaries, generals, warrant officers, and even many sergeants but by and large not to members of Congress.[54]

Not all secret information is kept from the committees of Congress. And some members (like Senator Stennis) who are considered especially reliable by the administration may be the recipients of a considerable amount of this classified material. But "reliable" here means they can be trusted not to pass on information which Congress as a whole needs if it is to participate effectively in the important decisions concerning the direction of governmental policy. In many cases Congress does not even know what United States policy is, much less have an opportunity to help shape it. George Reedy, former press secretary to President Johnson, has written that the atmosphere of sycophancy surrounding any new president leads to the belief that the chief executive and a few of his closest aides are possessed of special knowledge and abilities; that they alone are capable of deciding the great questions that confront society; and that their information must be kept closely guarded within the White House lest plans be discovered and frustrated by our "enemies." The result is that on the most important issues only a tiny handful of faithful advisers can be entrusted with the right to participate in determining the policies of the United States. "This means that the number of minds which can be brought to bear on any given problem is often in inverse proportion to the importance of the problem."[55]

One of the things learned from the Watergate hearings was the existence of a covert organization operating out of the White House that felt free to violate the Constitution and the laws of the

United States in its attempt to stop "leaks" of information considered of a sensitive nature. The "plumbers" came into existence in the summer of 1971 after Daniel Ellsberg had released the Pentagon Papers to the Senate and various newspapers around the country. Their initial charge from President Nixon was to find out who had been leaking secret information—so they could be dismissed—and the extent to which Ellsberg was involved with other security matters. Whether Nixon himself personally authorized burglary as one of the acceptable methods to carry out this assignment is still open to question, although he has denied it publicly. What is not open to question is what the plumbers actually did in their attempts to "get" Ellsberg.

On June 30, 1971, the Supreme Court ruled that newspapers could not be enjoined from publishing the account of our involvement in Vietnam. It was evidently then decided in the administration that every step would have to be taken to discredit Ellsberg in the public mind to make sure that he did not become a hero, and at the same time to prejudice his chances for a fair trial on the charges of theft and unlawful possession of the Pentagon Papers.

Was this a national security operation, as some of the participants have attempted to argue in their defense? Or was the money paid to the Watergate defendants meant to purchase their silence over an illegal and politically embarrassing search for material that could be used in a smear campaign against Ellsberg? Even the White House–edited transcripts of presidential conversations tend to reveal that the national security rationale was thought up *after* the break-in and was to be used only if the "cap came off the bottle" and E. Howard Hunt revealed the "horrors" he had participated in for the White House. All of the following quotations come from the famous March 21 meeting between the president (P), John Dean (D), and H. R. Haldeman (H):

> D: The Cubans that were used in the Watergate were also the same Cubans that Hunt and Liddy used for this California Ellsberg thing, for the break in out there. So they are aware of that. How high their knowledge is, is something else. Hunt and Liddy, of course, are totally aware of it, of the fact that it is right out of the White House.
>
> P: I don't know what the hell we did that for!

D: I don't either.

[Haldeman enters and the three devise the national security cover to use in case Hunt talks.]

P: You see, John is concerned, as you know, about the Ehrlichman situation. It worries him a great deal because, and this is why the Hunt problem is so serious, because it had nothing to do with the campaign. It has to do with the Ellsberg case. I don't know what the hell the— (unintelligible)

H: But what I was going to say—

P: What is the answer on this? How do you keep it out, I don't know. You can't keep it out if Hunt talks. You see the point is irrelevant. It has gotten to this point—

D: You might put it on a national security grounds basis.

H: It absolutely was.

D: And say that this was—

H: (Unintelligible)—CIA—

D: Ah—

H: Seriously,

P: National Security. We had to get information for national security grounds.

D: Then the question is, why didn't the CIA do it or why didn't the FBI do it?

P: Because we had to do it on a confidential basis.

H: Because we were checking them.

P: Neither could be trusted.

H: It has basically never been proven. There was reason to question their position.

P: With the bombing thing coming out and everything coming out, the whole thing was national security.

D: I think we could get by on that.

P: On that one I think we should simply say this was a national security investigation that was conducted.[56]

Once Watergate started unraveling and the prosecutors learned that the CIA had provided Hunt with disguises, hideouts, and fake documents for the break-in at Ellsberg's psychiatrist's office, the president could firmly tell Assistant Attorney General Henry Petersen, "That was perfectly proper. He was conducting an investigation from the national security area for the White House at that point."[57] The Pentagon Papers of course had already leaked out by the time of the break-in, and there was no question of who had done the leaking. Charles Colson later pleaded guilty to a charge of obstruction of justice for "devising and implementing a scheme to defame and destroy the public image and credibility of Daniel Ellsberg and those engaged in the legal defense of Daniel Ellsberg," and Colson said his acts were committed at the president's insistence to influence the Ellsberg trial then in progress. This was to be accomplished through White House leaks of derogatory information on both Ellsberg and his defense attorneys. Judge Gerhard Gesell ruled out the national security defense in the trial of John Ehrlichman and the others charged with the break-in, and one of those in command of the plumbers, Egil Krogh, pleaded guilty because he could no longer "in conscience" assert national security as a defense. All others involved (who weren't given immunity) were found guilty by a jury.

The need to maintain secrecy in the name of national security, however, was defended by some close to the president as an inherent power knowing almost no bounds. The following exchange took place between Senator Herman Talmadge and the former domestic adviser to the President, John Ehrlichman, during the Senate Watergate hearings:

> Senator Talmadge: . . . I believe you testified yesterday that the President has the power to authorize an inherent break-in in matters concerning national security; was that your testimony? . . .
>
> Mr. Ehrlichman: Yes sir.
>
> Senator Talmadge: Now, in matters involving national security, could the President authorize a forgery?
>
> Mr. Ehrlichman: Well, again, you are getting me into an area that obviously is a subject for the experts. . . . The question of degree here can be carried to unreasonable lengths, and I am not prepared to answer where that line is. It is obviously a judicial question.
>
> Senator Talmadge: You do not think he could authorize murder, do you?
>
> Mr. Ehrlichman: I do not—as I say, I do not think I am the one to try to respond to that kind of question, as to where the line is. . . .

Senator Talmadge: Do you remember when we were in law school, we studied a famous principle of law that came from England and also is well known in this country, that no matter how humble a man's cottage is, that even the King of England cannot enter without his consent.

Mr. Ehrlichman: I am afraid that has been considerably eroded over the years, has it not?

Senator Talmadge: Down in my country we still think it is a pretty legitimate principle of law. [58]

One of the president's closest advisers, then, could not say what, if any, limits could be put on Nixon's "inherent" right to protect national security as defined in the White House. The need for secrecy, according to this opinion, certainly justified burglary; and it wouldn't even automatically rule out murder.

To lend a cloak of legitimacy to the administration's efforts to stop leaks, a proposal was introduced in Congress in 1973 to enact for the first time in the United States an Official Secrets Act. This proposed law would make it a crime to publish any national defense information about the military capability of the United States or an allied nation without the authorization of the Defense Department. A further amendment would prohibit publication of any information that could be used to "the prejudice of interests of the United States." A system of such broad scope could of course be used to control what the press wrote and thus what the Congress and people learn about their government and its policies—a practice which some charged is dangerously close to the Soviet system, where only "authorized" news can be printed. It is questionable whether we would have ever known about the Pentagon Papers, the secret bombing of Cambodia, My Lai, or huge cost overruns on such projects as the C-5A had this law been in effect a few years ago. Critics alleged that what was being sought by the administration here was justification for secrecy practices allowing the government to bury its mistakes and conduct policy free from public scrutiny.

Executive Privilege

Without information Congress cannot investigate or oversee the execution of its laws, and if it can't do these things, it is scarcely in a position to legislate at all. [59] Secrecy is one device that has been used to keep information from Congress; the claim of executive privilege is another. Generally privilege to withhold information is based on the notion that the president has the right to withhold certain knowledge in his possession. Most frequently it has been applied to military or diplomatic areas, but more recently it has been extended to interdepartmental communications, departmental records and files, reports of agents and subordinates, and the advice given the president by his staff members. [60] In the first White House tapes case (*Nixon* v. *Sirica and Cox*, F. 2d-Cir., 1973), the lawyers for the president argued that as long as he remained in office executive privilege remained absolute with respect to communications with the president and that no court could compel him to produce any document. Later Nixon claimed that the separation of powers gave him sole discretion over how much and what information he would release to the House of Representatives—even in his own impeachment case.

Recent presidents have cited the actions of several of their predecessors in withholding information from Congress, most notably Adams, Jefferson, Monroe, Jackson, and Buchanan. Most of these early claims were not based on any inherent right to do so, however, but rather on authorizations granted by Congress itself. For instance, in the House request to Jefferson for documents in the Burr affair, the president was allowed to withhold "such [information] as he may deem the public welfare to require not to be disclosed[61] Later, President James Buchanan refused to turn over information requested by Congress on his alleged involvement in the use of money and patronage to influence members of Congress. His position was that only an investigation into the impeachment of the president would justify the release of such information. [62]

The modern claim of executive privilege in all of its broad scope (as well as the name itself) first appeared in the Eisenhower administration. Although Eisenhower's attorney general could not cite a single court case to support his claim, he wrote that "our Presidents have established, by precedent, that they and members of their Cabinet and other heads of executive departments have an undoubted privilege and discretion to keep confidential, in the public interest, papers and information which require secrecy." He went on to assert that this had been upheld uniformly by the courts, but he failed to cite examples.[63] In the five years that followed, Eisenhower withheld more congressionally requested information than all of our first twenty-five presidents combined.[64] What had been a modest, infrequently used doctrine based on congressional consent had now become an absolute privilege for the executive to deny Congress access to virtually anything the president decided he didn't want them to see. By denying information needed by Congress if it is to legislate, the executive would be given the power to exercise a veto even before a bill was introduced.

The claim of executive privilege was played down once again in the Kennedy and Johnson administrations, as the assertion was made only infrequently. Thus it did not become a matter of intense controversy between the two branches in the years 1961 through 1969. At first it appeared that Nixon would continue with the policy of his two immediate predecessors. He directed his agency and department heads to cooperate with Congress and set out guidelines for the invocation of privilege, which only he could formally authorize.

> The policy of this Administration is to comply to the fullest extent possible with Congressional requests for information. While the Executive branch has the responsibility of withholding certain information the disclosure of which could be incompatible with the public interest, this Administration will invoke this authority only in the most compelling circumstances and after a rigorous inquiry into the actual need for its exercise. For these reasons executive privilege will not be used without specific Presidential approval.[65]

Despite these early good intentions, the administration and its departments and agencies began to withhold more and more requested information as relations between the executive and legislative branches worsened. Most frequently executive privilege was not formally invoked; papers were simply not furnished on request. As the comptroller general of the United States testified, evidently the agencies of the federal government interpreted the president's directive to mean that information would not be provided unless higher authorities approved.[66]

By April 1973 the president was claiming absolute discretion over the testimony and papers of the entire executive branch. His attorney general, Richard Kleindienst (later to plead guilty to a charge of "failure to testify fully" before the Senate—a euphemism for perjury) contended that if the president so ordered he could prohibit the Congress from receiving any information whatsoever from the executive branch and that all of the 2.5 million employees in the departments could be barred from appearing before Congress. Even in his own impeachment proceedings, Kleindienst argued, the president could forbid present or *past* employees from testifying. If Congress didn't like it, there were only two remedies available: impeachment (presumably without witnesses or evidence from the executive branch if the president chose) or a cut off of funds. Kleindienst did not cite constitutional or legal justification for this imperial assertion; he merely implied that this power was inherent in the presidency. The effect of this supposed power would be to put the chief executive in total control of what Congress could learn, and thus what it could legislate. Only through impeachment, a device never successfully used against a president before, would Congress retain any power at all.[67] As Kleindienst well knew, Congress would never undertake impeachment proceedings except on allegations of the most serious kind of wrongdoing, and this would leave the president in splendid isolation to conduct the affairs of government by himself.

To a degree unique in our governmental history, President Nixon ran his administration through White House aides. The cabinet secretaries, with few notable exceptions, were reduced to managing their departments without significant voice in shaping the policies they were responsible for. Foreign policy options originated with Henry Kissinger and the National Security Council, not the State Department. Domestic policy was the province of John Ehrlichman and the Domestic Council staff. However, while Secretary of State William Rogers and the other cabinet secretaries were being called to testify before Congress, the president issued a total prohibition against any of his aides appearing. The people who really knew, those with the power and influence, those who determined the course of the executive branch, were not subject to the scrutiny of those responsible for making the laws. Thus neither John Dean, Charles Colson, H. R. Haldeman, John Ehrlichman, Henry Kissinger, nor any of the other really important people in the administration ever testified before Congress during Nixon's first four years in power.

Perhaps Kleindienst's testimony was prescient of things to come. When impeachment hearings were begun in the spring of 1974, the president refused to turn over evidence demanded by the House of Representatives. The House then issued its first subpoena against an incumbent president, but Nixon failed to comply, basing his refusal on the grounds of separation of powers and executive privilege. Although the Fifth Amendment to the Constitution protects a person from having to testify against himself, it certainly does not allow him to refuse subpoenas for papers and documents relevant to his guilt or innocence. Here, however, was a president claiming that only *he* would be the judge of what those constitutionally charged with the power to impeach would be able to see.

The issue of executive privilege finally reached the Supreme Court in the summer of 1974 (*United States* v. *Nixon*, 94 S. Ct. 3090). The case, however, did not deal with the president's right to withhold information from Congress, but rather his right to withhold from the courts in a criminal proceeding. Although a unanimous Court decided that in this instance the needs of the judicial process for the full evidence outweighed a claim of privilege, Chief Justice Burger's decision gave constitutional sanction to the doctrine for the first time: "Certain powers and privileges flow from the nature of enumerated powers; the protection of the confidentiality of presidential communications has similar constitutional underpinnings." He went on to specify why the claim of privilege had not been upheld in this case: "When the privilege depends solely on the broad, undifferentiated claim of public interest in the confidentiality of such conversations, a confrontation with other values arises. *Absent a claim of need to protect military, diplomatic or sensitive national security secrets*, we find it difficult to accept the argument." [Emphasis added.]

Although absolute privilege was denied, Burger implied that, had Nixon's invocation of the doctrine been based on the need to protect national security, the result may have been somewhat different. He returned to these themes several times: "A President and those who assist him must be free to explore alternatives in the process of shaping policies and making decisions and to do so in a way many would be unwilling to express except privately. These are the considerations justifying a presumptive privilege for presidential communications." And referring specifically to Nixon: "He does not place his claim of privilege on the ground they are military or diplomatic secrets. As to these areas of Art. II duties the courts have traditionally shown the utmost deference to presidential responsibilities." It seems likely that presidents will be careful to include military, diplomatic, or national security claims whenever they seek to invoke the doctrine of privilege in the future.

In the case of his use of executive privilege, as in so many other areas, President Nixon was not inventing wholly new doctrines to spring on Congress and the American people. He simply developed the powers others had asserted tentatively, and with due respect to the sensibilities of the other coordinate branches of the government, into instruments for more complete domination. Perhaps if he had been smoother, if he had not so flagrantly demonstrated his contempt for the traditions of the American political system and the egos of other politicians, what some observers have charged was an attempted coup d'état would have been successful. In that sense he performed a valuable service by illustrating what could be done with all of those powers so joyously heaped on presidents when it seemed they alone could solve all of our problems. It could be argued that for too long Americans had assumed that only people of the highest vision and rectitude would be elevated to the presidency; that if they weren't paragons of virtue and talent when they first came to occupy the White House, then the office itself would ennoble them (Harry Truman is the most frequently cited example).

Emergency Powers

It has long been recognized that democracies, as well as other kinds of political systems, sometimes have to give extraordinary powers to government to preserve the society as a whole. As we have seen, Lincoln, in seizing control of all of the resources at his disposal, violated the Constitution and the laws in his efforts to preserve the Union. The founding fathers themselves, being astute students of Locke, recognized that emergencies sometimes create situations that do not permit the debate or delay inherent in the legislative process. Locke had written:

> The good of the society requires that several things should be left to the discretion of him that has the executive power; for the legislators not being able to foresee and provide by laws for all that may be useful to the community, the executor of the laws, having the power in his hands, has by the common law of nature a right to make use of it for the good of society, in many cases where the municipal law has given no direction, till the legislature can conveniently be assembled to provide for it. Many things there are which the law can by no means provide for; and those must necessarily be left to the discretion of him that has the executive power in his hands . . . nay, it is fit that the laws themselves should in some cases give way to the executive power.[68]

Woodrow Wilson's actions during the First World War have also been discussed. It is important to remember here that almost all of the powers Wilson exercised were delegations from Congress. Once the war was over, all but two of the many emergency laws were repealed. (The two that remained were a food control measure and the Trading with the Enemy Act.) The second Roosevelt is of course also known for his expansive views of the executive power, as illustrated in his inaugural call for the wide latitude necessary to meet the emergency of depression. His suspension of banking was based on one of the emergency statutes left over from Wilson's day—the Trading with the Enemy Act. Here, however, the emergency was purely domestic, whereas the law was intended for use only during wartime. But few who suffered through the depression quibbled with the semantics involved. In any case, the emergency he declared in 1933 to invoke the act is still in effect more than forty years later.[69]

Federal law now embodied in more than 470 statutes grants at least 580 special powers to the president so that in emergency situations he may act to meet the crises in ways which would not be permissible in "normal" times. The Second World War was of course an emergency of immense proportions, one in which we were willing to entrust vast power and resources to the president so he could mobilize the nation to meet the threat of Nazi aggression. Only five years after the end of that war, we found ourselves in a new conflict in Korea. President Truman, too, felt it necessary to declare a state of emergency in order to put into effect the various delegations of power to himself which come with such a declaration. Cold war followed the hot one, and Americans felt endangered both at home and abroad by ubiquitous and monolithic communism. Truman's state of emergency, like FDR's, has not been ended.

Crisis now seems to be a permanent fixture in our lives. (At least every problem we face is pictured in crisis terms.) Whether it is the oil crisis, the crisis of the cities, the Vietnam crisis, inflation, the energy crisis, the gold crisis, the environmental crisis, the Middle East crisis, the population crisis, unemployment, or the balance of payments crisis, new powers have been given to the president to meet the perceived emergency. It is not implied that the difficulties associated with these dilemmas have ready solutions, or that government doesn't have to devise new ways to deal with them. But at the same time it must be realized what the cumulative effect of all this is: the delegation of ever more power to the president. In "doing what needs doing for the people," our chief executives have come to operate a crisis presidency as almost a routine way of doing business. Even relatively minor issues are now cast in terms of emergency—witness President Nixon's declaration of a state of national emergency to treat with a postal strike in 1970, and another one in 1971 to deal with the international monetary situation. These two states of "national emergency," along with Roosevelt's and Truman's, remain in effect. Regardless of the fact that we are not at war anywhere in the world and despite our improving relations with the Soviet Union and the People's Republic of China, the four states of national emergency in existence confer upon the president vast powers that may be used at any time to go outside the normal framework of law to accomplish presidential goals. Utilizing the 470 laws mentioned above, once a state of emergency is declared the president may "seize property; organize and control the means of production; seize commodities; assign military forces abroad; institute martial law; seize and control all transportation and communication; regulate the operation of private enterprise; restrict travel; and, in a plethora of particular ways, control the lives of all American citizens."[70] An example of what is possible under those statutes was Franklin Roosevelt's order during World War II removing American citizens of Japanese ancestry from their homes and imprisoning them in concentration camps. The statute, still on the books, allows the president to establish a military zone of any size anywhere in the United States and exclude potentially dangerous persons from the area. According to Senator Frank Church, cochairman of the Special Committee on the Termination of the National Emergency, the secretary of defense testified during the Cambodian bombing that the president could continue bombing even if Congress were to cut off all funds. This claim was based on authority granted under the Food and Forage Act, which was originally passed in the nineteenth century to allow the United States cavalry to procure food for soldiers and forage for their mounts during periods of congressional recess.[71] As an emergency statute, it had merely been updated by the administration and applied to a situation of its own choosing.

The courts, like the legislature, have been very reluctant to interfere with the president when he exercises emergency powers. As has been seen, no effective roadblocks were put before Lincoln during the Civil War, nor were the courts inclined to limit Wilson or Roosevelt during the two world wars. Even the Japanese-American removal was endorsed. Generally judges have assumed that they should stay out of political questions evoked by national emergencies. (The Supreme Court did, of course, act to strike down much of Franklin Roosevelt's New Deal legislation designed to cope with the emergency of the depression. After the Court-packing threat and the "switch in time that saved nine," however, the Court no longer interfered in any significant way with FDR's domestic program, much less his actions during World War II.) In only one major case has the Supreme Court reversed a president's action when he claimed to be dealing with a national emergency—that of Truman's seizure of the steel industry during the Korean War.

In a concurring opinion in that case, Mr. Justice Jackson wrote:

> That seems to be the logic of an argument tendered at our bar—that the President having, on his own responsibility, sent American troops abroad derives from that act "affirmative power" to seize the means of producing a supply of steel for them.

. . . Nothing in our Constitution is plainer than that declaration of war is entrusted only to Congress. Of course, a state of war may in fact exist without a formal declaration. But no doctrine that the Court could promulgate would seem to me more sinister and alarming than that a President whose conduct of foreign affairs is so largely uncontrolled, and often even is unknown, can vastly enlarge his mastery over the internal affairs of the country by his own commitment of the Nation's armed forces to some foreign venture.

The appeal, however, that we declare the existence of inherent powers ex necessitate to meet an emergency asks us to do what many think would be wise, although it is something the forefathers omitted. They knew what emergencies were, knew the pressures they engendered for authoritative action, knew, too, how they afford a ready pretext for usurpation. We may also suspect that they suspected that emergency powers would tend to kindle emergencies.[72]

Although a minority of three justices felt Truman's seizure justified under his duty "to take care that the laws be faithfully executed," the president obeyed the Court and ordered the steel mills returned to their former owners. With this one rare exception, then, neither the courts nor Congress have proven effective in checking the president during proclaimed periods of "emergency."

Vast new emergency powers were granted the chief executive to deal with the "energy crisis" created by the Arab oil embargo in 1973, despite warnings from some senators that the bill would delegate "extraordinary, unprecedented, dangerous, even dictatorial powers to the executive branch." Said Senator Mark Hatfield, "I cannot think of a single sector of our economic life that will not be under the direct control of President or his agents. Drastic alterations of people's personal and business lives will be implemented at the stroke of a pen."[73] President Nixon vetoed the bill, however, and asked for eighteen separate energy measures without certain objectionable provisions that he found in the first act. Among the offensive features of the original measure were requirements that Congress approve any rationing or conservation plans imposed by the President, a six-month limitation on the life of any conservation measure, and powers given directly to the Federal Energy Administration rather than to the president to delegate as he saw fit. What he did not object to was power to allocate scarce materials, set maximum rates for oil producers, grant exemptions from antitrust laws, restrict the business use of electricity, and provide for the control of transportation to save energy. (These latter provisions would come into effect only after he declared that a state of national emergency existed and Congress had an opportunity to approve or disapprove such plans.) The reason the bill was vetoed, then, was that the president did not believe it went far enough in granting independent emergency powers to him to act as he thought necessary during the crisis.

President Ford, like his immediate predecessors, has given in to the urge to take unilateral action in dealing with emergencies. Citing America's increasing dependence on foreign oil supplies, he decreed a $3 tax on each barrel imported. Although he seemed willing to compromise on his action, he did not consult Congress before making his decision. Federal District Judge Pratt, in upholding Ford's power to act alone, said that we must accept the president's determination of a national security emergency.

The growing concern with unilateral presidental efforts to meet emergencies has led Senator Church to introduce a modest bill which would give Congress at least the opportunity to monitor what the president does in periods of crisis. His proposal would require the publication in the *Federal Register* of any emergency proclamation with a designation of the provisions of the specific laws the President intended to invoke. The emergency would automatically be ended after ninety days unless Congress acted affirmatively to extend it, which it would have to do on a year-to-year basis. In 1974 the Senate finally voted to terminate the four states of emergency still in existence. Whether this will impose any substantial bar to the stampede of demands for presidential action when next we are faced by an "emergency" remains to be seen. Congress and the courts, as much as the public, have largely come to expect the president to act in such situations and to see the responsibility as his.

War Making

The powers just discussed by no means constitute the entire range of weapons in the presidential armory. It has been seen how talented chief executives such as Jefferson, Wilson, and Franklin Roosevelt had been able to use their positions as leaders of their political parties to dominate congressional policy making. Some very persuasive people have been elected to the presidency, people who knew how to use personal contacts with individual members of Congress to convince them that they should go along with the president and his program. Even members of the opposition party sometimes find it difficult to resist when called into the Oval Office for a personal visit with the man shouldering the vast burdens of his office. When this is coupled with pleas for "responsibility," "bipartisanship," or "support for your president," it takes a strong person indeed not to give in. This is especially true when, as Wilson said, the president has the admiration and confidence of the country behind him.

It is foreign and military affairs, however, that have provided the chief executive with his greatest leeway. Some writers have contended that modern presidents exercise more independent control over their nation's power than perhaps any other single leader in the world with the possible exception of Mao Tse-tung. Most Vietnam decisions, as well as the intervention and bombing in Cambodia, for instance, were unilaterally made by Presidents Kennedy, Johnson, and Nixon. On the other hand, the Soviet leadership reportedly had to secure the approval of the politburo before ordering the invasion of Czechoslovakia in 1968. The question that must be faced is whether a democratic society needs more power concentrated in the hands of one man than is the case in most dictatorships. There is little doubt that a large measure of autonomy is essential for the smooth functioning of foreign relations and that most chief executives have behaved responsibly in their execution of our policy toward other nations. Experience with the Vietnam War, however, has convinced many people that some checks must be placed on what kinds of situations presidents will be allowed to get the United States into in the future.

Space does not allow a recounting of the history of American foreign policy and the concomitant growth of presidential control over the war-making power. Suffice it to say the dispute over Congress's power to declare war and the president's to wage it is almost as old as the Republic itself. President Monroe's famous doctrine of 1823, which warned European powers against further colonization in the Americas, certainly could have involved the

United States in wars with one or more of those countries. It was a policy decided upon solely by Monroe and his cabinet. James K. Polk in sending troops to Mexico demonstrated how the president's command of the armed forces could confront the Congress with the *fait accompli* of armed conflict, leaving little alternative but to formalize a state that already existed. Similarly, William McKinley's decision to send American fighting men to China to help put down the Boxer Rebellion illustrated what a determined president could accomplish without reference to the legislature. It has only been since the Second World War, however, that the United States has had the permanent capacity as well as the will to intervene almost anywhere in the world at the president's command.

Fear of Soviet expansion, the "fall" of China, the arms race involving nuclear weapons, and the McCarthy spector of domestic subversion all contributed to an atmosphere that seemed to call for concentrating absolute power in the hands of the commander in chief to deal with unparalleled menace. Truman's decision to commit troops to Korea without awaiting congressional authorization has since been defended by his secretary of state, Dean Acheson, as an action that, like many others in an age which demands instant response, could not be stayed until debate and inquiries had run their course. "I felt that we were in this fight—and it was a desperate fight—and we had better concentrate all our energies in fighting it and not in trying to get people to formally approve what was going on," said Acheson.[74] By 1950, then, congressional authorization of the use of American armed forces abroad in combat was viewed by one of the most experienced foreign policy executives as a mere formality. Subsequent experiences seem to confirm that this notion has been accepted by Truman's successors. President Ford continued in this tradition by ordering American forces to recapture the *Mayaguez* and its crew from the Cambodians. Only after his decision was made and the orders issued to forces in the field did he "consult" with leaders of Congress.

Vietnam soured many intellectuals on the idea of the president being able to act alone in committing troops abroad—and then fighting a war largely without reference to a congressional mandate. Lyndon Johnson referred to the Gulf of Tonkin Resolution as all the mandate he needed to carry out his policies, and one of his undersecretaries of state, Nicholas Katzenbach, frequently cited it as a "functional" declaration of war. When Congress finally got around to repealing that resolution in 1971 during Nixon's administration, the war went on as before. The commander in chief had all the power he needed, said the president, to protect the lives of American boys, and it did not depend upon congressional authorization. The same rationale was used to justify forays into Cambodia and Laos and for the mining of harbors and bombing in North Vietnam. The war powers first enunciated by Lincoln, then, are conceived by some people to be inherent in the presidency and to apply to almost any situation where he and he alone determines that American national security is at stake.

As dissatisfaction with the war spread across the campuses and living rooms of the United States, Congress itself finally became convinced that it had to reassert its constitutional role in the issues of war and peace. As has been seen, the founding fathers feared executive war making and thus had specified that only Congress could declare war. A law enacted in late 1973 seeks, as it says in its first section, "to fulfill the intent of the framers of the Constitution of the United States and insure that the collective judgment of both the Congress and the President will apply to the introduction of United States armed forces into hositilities." This War Powers Resolution constituted the first major slap at what had become almost universally accepted since the Second World War—that is, the power of the president to "go it alone" in deciding when and where the United States would become involved in combat. Paradoxically, it was also the first legislative sanction of his temporary power to do so.

What the new law says is this: The constitutional power of the president as commander in chief to introduce armies into combat situations or areas where fighting is likely is limited to cases where Congress has declared war; or pursuant to specific statutory authorization; or during a national emergency created by attack upon the United States, its territories or possessions, or its armed forces. The president must "consult" with Congress if time permits before sending troops into such situations. Once forces are engaged in combat, he must report such action to the

Congress within forty-eight hours. Unless Congress affirmatively acts within sixty days to declare war or specifically authorizes the use of our armed forces, the president must withdraw the troops. The only exception is that, if the president certifies that the safety of the United States forces in withdrawal requires more time, he may extend by thirty days the removal of those forces. At any time within that sixty-to-ninety-day period Congress could force an immediate pullback by passing a concurrent resolution, which would not be subject to presidential veto.

President Nixon vetoed this measure when it reached his desk, the ninth time he had exercised his veto in 1973. His stated reasons were that, although he agreed with the desire of Congress to assert its "proper role" in foreign affairs, "the restrictions which this resolution would impose upon the authority of the President are both unconstitutional and dangerous to the best interests of our Nation." He went on to declare that the joint resolution would attempt to take away by a mere legislative act authority that presidents had properly exercised under the Constitution for nearly two hundred years. Not only was the measure unconstitutional, but it would seriously erode America's ability to act decisively in times of international crisis. The effect of this would be to undermine the confidence of our allies and strengthen our enemies in their resolve to expand at our expense. "If this resolution had been in operation, America's effective response to a variety of challenges in recent years would have been vastly complicated or even made impossible," wrote the president. It would undercut the ability of the United States to achieve peace. It sought to limit the consitutional powers of the president as commander in chief at the expiration of sixty days. He went on to chastise the Congress for trying to get the power to halt a war merely by sitting still: "In my view, one cannot become a responsible partner unless one is prepared to take responsible action." Finally he suggested the whole matter be submitted to a nonpartisan commission for further study.[75] Despite these vigorous objections the Senate voted to override the veto with a 75 to 18 vote, and the House followed by a margin of 284 to 135, four more than the necessary two-thirds majority. This was the only time in 1973 that Congress was able to overcome one of Nixon's vetoes. A Gallup poll conducted shortly thereafter indicated that 80 percent of the American people approved of the new law.[76]

Despite the jubilation in some quarters that Congress had finally been able to limit the president in this area, others were not nearly so sanguine. It could be pointed out, for instance, that Nixon had asserted the unconstitutionality of the measure, and, if past experience was any guide, some future president would simply ignore the new law and await a congressionally instituted court test. It should also be recalled in this connection that the Supreme Court repeatedly refused to rule on the constitutionality of the Vietnam War despite the efforts of several members of Congress to get it to do so. Even some of the most ardent foes of presidential war found themselves voting against the final version of this new law, contending that it gave congressional sanction to ninety days of combat unilaterally initiated by the chief executive. Senator Thomas Eagleton, an original sponsor of the legislation, maintains that the compromise version finally passed was so watered down that its effect may be the opposite from what Congress intended. He points out, for instance, that the part of the resolution which attempts to limit the president's power to introduce troops into a foreign country is contained in the "Purpose and Policy" section, and this does not have the binding effect of law. It is merely a statement of intention. In addition, Eagleton claims, it gives to the president the inherent right to initiate war whereas the Constitution reserves this right to Congress. The legislative branch is limited to an after-the-fact review. "The Constitution says 'Congress shall declare war,' not 'Congress shall stop war.'"[77] As Congresswoman Elizabeth Holtzman points out, in the nuclear age ninety day limitations don't mean much when the president can launch enough missiles in a few seconds to destroy the world.[78]

Perhaps the most serious criticism of the War Powers Resolution is that Congress would find it exceedingly difficult to invoke. Once the United States is engaged in combat defending the flag or American interests abroad, the president is usually able to generate more than enough support for whatever action he deems necessary. The Gulf of Tonkin Resolution is a clear example of this. It was passed overwhelmingly in both houses of Congress, and the two senators who dared vote against it were defeated when they sought reelection. Both Congress and the people tend to rally around the president when American lives are threatened, even if the president ordered troops into situations where they were likely to be shot at in the first place. American honor becomes involved when our boys are killed, our airplanes shot down, or our men taken prisoner. It took nearly seven years to repeal the Tonkin Resolution. Public opinion polls to the last showed a majority of the American people approved of the president's handling of the Vietnam War, even though they thought it a mistake for us to have gotten involved in it in the first place. Congress could not bring itself to cut off funds for the bombing of Indochina until after the prisoners had been returned and the last American soldier withdrawn from Vietnam. Even then they compromised with the president and allowed him to continue bombing for forty-five days. Both the public and members of Congress applauded President Ford's unilateral decisions in the *Mayaguez* affair, despite his ignoring of the War Powers Act. It thus seems unlikely that Congress will be willing to force the retreat of American power once it has been committed in an area.

There are other drawbacks to the law as well. One has to do with the authorization for the president to get us involved in a fighting situation "created by an attack upon . . . [our] armed forces." We now have approximately 430,000 men stationed around the globe, with army, navy or air force contingents in Europe, Japan, South Korea, Okinawa, Taiwan, the Philippines, Australia, Greenland, Saudi Arabia, Antarctica, Iceland, and Bahrain, among others. Hypothetically, at least, a determined president could manufacture in any one of those countries an incident in which our forces would be "attacked." In addition, the new law permits the president to send troops to defend nations with which the United States has ratified treaty arrangements—almost fifty in number. The SEATO agreement may not seem to have much binding effect any more, but under it the president may determine that one of the signatory countries has been the victim of external attack and thus rush to its aid.

All of these possible loopholes have led some to question whether this law isn't worse than no law at all, whether Congress hasn't given the president authority to initiate war where before he had no legal or constitutional right to do so. Furthermore, it might result in congressional obstruction in those very cases where American interests dictate we should become involved. As

Arthur Schlesinger, Jr. has pointed out, "Had it been on the statute books in past years, it would surely have prevented Roosevelt from responding to Hitler in the North Atlantic in 1941 and would surely not have prevented Johnson from escalating the war in Vietnam."[79]

The powers the Constitution delegated to the Congress are vast, but over the years many of the most important ones have slipped to the executive branch. Whether the attempted reassertion of legislative authority that came in the wake of Vietnam and Watergate will prove permanent or only transitory could determine for all time whether the separation of powers and checks and balances devised by the authors of the Constitution have any meaning in the twentieth century.

NOTES

1. The classic statement on the growth of presidential control over legislative initiative remains Richard E. Neustadt, "Presidency and Legislation: The Growth of Central Clearance," *American Political Science Review*, 48 (September 1954), 641–671, and much of the history here relies on that source.

2. Aaron Wildavsky, *The Politics of the Budgetary Process* (Boston: Little, Brown, 1964), p. 4.

3. Neustadt, "The Growth of Central Clearance," p. 661.

4. Richard E. Neustadt, "Presidency and Legislation: Planning the President's Program," *American Political Science Review*, 49 (December 1955), 981.

5. Robert S. Gilmour, "Central Legislative Clearance: A Revised Perspective," *Public Administration Review*, (March/April 1971), 154–155.

6. Allen Schick, "The Budget Bureau That Was: Thoughts on the Rise, Decline, and Future of a Presidential Agency," *Law and Contemporary Problems*, 35 (Summer 1970), 519–539.

7. Samuel P. Huntington, "Congressional Responses to the Twentieth Century," in *The Congress and America's Future*, ed. David B. Truman, 2nd ed. (Englewood Cliffs, N.J.: Prentice-Hall, 1973), p. 22.

8. Neustadt, "Planning the President's Program," p. 1015.

9. Neustadt, "The Growth of Central Clearance," p. 670.

10. "Controversy Over the Presidential Impoundment of Appropriatiated Funds," *Congressional Digest*, 52, no. 4 (April 1973), 100.

11. Arthur M. Schlesinger, Jr., *The Imperial Presidency* (Boston: Houghton Mifflin, 1973), pp. 235–236.

12. J. D. Williams, "The Impounding of Funds by the Bureau of the Budget," no. 28, *The Inter-University Case Program* (University: University of Alabama Press, 1955), p. 6.

13. Harry S. Truman, letter to Louis A. Johnson, secretary of defense, 8 November 1949, in *Executive Impoundment of Appropriated Funds, Hearings before the Subcommittee of Powers of the Committee on the Judiciary*, Senate, 92nd Cong., 1st Sess., 1971, p. 525. Hereafter referred to as "*Hearings on Impoundment.*"

14. *Congressional Quarterly*, 31 no. 5 (February 3, 1973), p. 213.

15. Louis Fisher, *President and Congress* (New York: Free Press, 1972), pp. 123–124.

16. See Mark Green, James Fallows and David Zwick, *Who Runs Congress?* (New York: Bantam, 1972), pp. 114–117 for a partial list of impoundments in the Nixon administration.

17. Memorandum, "Re Presidential Authority to Impound Funds Appropriated for Assistance to Federally Impacted Schools," reprinted in *Hearings on Impoundment*, pp. 279–284. Quote on p. 283.

18. *New York Times*, 11 January 1974, pp. 1, 38.

19. Sneed's testimony is cited in Larry L. Adams, "The Constitution and Presidential Accountability," paper presented at the Western Political Science Association Meeting, Denver, Colo., April 1974, pp. 24–25.

20. Weinberger's testimony cited in prepared statement by Joseph Cooper in *Hearings on Impoundment*, p. 188

21. Warren J. Archer, "Presidential Impounding of Funds: The Judicial Response," *The University of Chicago Law Review*, 40, no. 2 (Winter 1973), 332.

22. Lewis Carroll, *Through the Looking Glass* (London: Oxford, 1971), p. 190.

23. *Train* v. *City of New York* (95 S.Ct. 839), 1975.

24. For a discussion of these devices, see "Presidential Spending: The Other Side of the Coin," *National Journal*, Center for Political Research, 3, no. 19 (8 May 1971), 1035.

25. Timothy H. Ingram, "The Billions in the White House Basement," *Washington Monthly*, 3, no. 11 (January 1972), 42–44.

26. "Presidential Spending," p. 1035.

27. *Ibid.*

28. Ingram, p. 38. Also see Fisher, chap. 4, for these and other budgetary weapons.

29. "Presidential Spending," p. 1035.

30. Ingram, pp. 41–42.

31. *New York Times*, 12 January 1975.

32. See, for example, Lawrence H. Chamberlain, *The President,*

Congress and Legislation (New York: Columbia University Press, 1946); Ralph K. Huitt, "Congress, the Durable Partner," in *Lawmakers in a Changing World*, ed. Elke Frank (Englewood Cliffs, N.J.: Prentice-Hall, 1966); David Price, *Who Makes the Laws?* (Cambridge, Mass.: Schenkman, 1972); Hugh G. Gallagher, "Presidents, Congress, and the Legislative Functions," in *The Presidency Reappraised*, ed. Rexford G. Tugwell and Thomas E. Cronin (New York: Praeger, 1974); Ronald C. Moe and Steven C. Teel, "Congress as Policy-Maker: A Necessary Reappraisal," *Political Science Quarterly*, 85 (1970), 443–470; Eric Redman, *The Dance of Legislation* (New York: Simon and Schuster, 1973); Richard Fenno, Jr., *Congressmen in Committees* (Boston: Little, Brown, 1973).

33. Thomas E. Cronin and Sanford D. Greenberg, eds., *The Presidential Advisory System* (New York: Harper & Row, 1969), p. xvii.

34. Stanley Kelly, Jr., "Patronage and Presidential Legislative Leadership," in *The Presidency*, ed. Aaron Wildavsky (Boston: Little, Brown, 1969), p. 269.

35. Warren Miller and Donald Stokes, "Constituency Influence in Congress," *American Political Science Review*, 57 (March 1963), 53–54.

36. "National Assessment of Educational Progress," *Report 2: Citizenship: National Results—Partial*, July 1970, p. 37, cited by Fred I. Greenstein, "What the President Means to Americans," in *Choosing the President*, ed. James D. Barber (Englewood Cliffs, N.J.: Prentice-Hall, 1974), p. 125.

37. Kelly, pp. 271–272.

38. See Estes Kefauver, "Executive-Congressional Liaison," *Annals of the American Academy of Political and Social Science*, 289 (September 1953), 108–118 for an early discussion of liaison.

39. Kelly, pp. 268–269.

40. Rowland Evans, Jr., and Robert Novak, *Nixon in the White House* (New York: Vintage, 1971), p. 109.

41. Abraham Holtzman, *Legislative Liaison* (Chicago: Rand McNally, 1970), p. 44.

42. *Ibid.*, p. 174.

43. Cited in Green, Fallows, and Zwick, p. 102.

44. "Legislators and the Lobbyists," 2nd ed. *Congressional Quarterly* (May 1968), pp. 54–55.

45. Holtzman, p. 174.

46. Green, Fallows, and Zwick, p. 126.

47. Quoted in *Time*, 15 January 1973, p. 16.

48. *Ibid.*

49. *Ibid.*

50. Much of this list is taken from Cronin and Greenberg, pp. xvii–xviii.

51. Schlesinger, p. 341.

52. David Wise, *The Politics of Lying* (New York: Random House, 1973), pp. 59–60.

53. *Ibid.*

54. Testimony of Dr. Daniel Ellsberg, *Hearings before the Subcommittee on Intergovernmental Relations, et. al: Executive Privilege, Secrecy in Government, Freedom of Information,* 93rd Cong., 1st Sess., 1973, 1, 431. Hereafter referred to as *Hearings on Executive Privilege.*

55. George E. Reedy, *The Twilight of the Presidency* (New York: New American Library, 1970), p. 23.

56. *Submission of Recorded Presiential Conversations to the Committee on the Judiciary of the House of Representatives by President Richard Nixon, April 30, 1974* (Washington: D.C.: GPO, 1974), pp. 190–222.

57. *Ibid.*, p. 883.

58. *Hearings before the Select Committee on Presidential Campaign Activities of the United States Senate: Watergate and Related Activities,* 93rd Cong., 1st Sess., 1973, Book 6, pp. 2599–2601.

59. Remarks of Senator Fulbright, *Hearings on Executive Privilege,* p. 471.

60. "Executive Privilege," *The Record of the Association of the Bar of the City of New York,* 29, no. 2 (February 1974), 177; see also Raul Berger, "Executive Privilege v. Congressional Inquiry," *UCLA Law Review,* 12 (1965), pp. 1044, 1287.

61. "Executive Privilege," p. 190.

62. *Ibid.*, p. 191.

63. Schlesinger, p. 157.

64. *Ibid.*, p. 158.

65. Memorandum, "Establishing a Procedure to Govern Compliance with Congressional Demands for Information," *"Hearings on Executive Privilege,* p. 116.

66. *Hearings on Executive Privilege,* pp. 115–116.

67. Testimony of Attorney General Richard G. Kleindienst, *Hearings on Executive Privilege,* pp. 18–52. See esp. pp. 18, 45.

68. John Locke, *Of Prerogative: The Second Treatise of Government,* ed. Thomas P. Peardon (Indianapolis: Bobbs-Merrill, 1952), p. 91.

69. "Emergency Powers Statutes: Provision of Federal Law Now in Effect Delegating to the Executive Extraordinary Authority in Time of National Emergency," *Report of the Special Committee on the Termination of the National Emergency,* Senate, 93rd Cong., 1st Sess., September 1973, pp. 1–5.

70. "Summary of Emergency Power Statutes," a working paper prepared by the staff of the *Special Committee on the Termination of the National Emergency,* Senate, 93rd Cong., 1st Sess., October 1973, p. 111.

71. "Sen. Church Cites Curb of Emergency Power," *Spokesman Review*, Spokane, Washington, 26 June 1974.

72. *Youngstown Sheet & Tube Company* v. *Sawyer* (343 U.S. 579), 1952.

73. *Daily Idahonian*, 13 December 1973.

74. Merle Miller, *Plain Speaking: An Oral Biography of Harry S. Truman* (New York: Berkeley, 1973), p. 284.

75. "Veto of War Powers Resolution," *Weekly Compilation of Presidential Documents*, 9, no. 43 (29 October 1973), 1285-1287.

76. Reported in the *New York Times*, 18 November 1973.

77. Thomas F. Eagleton, in *The New York Times*, 3 December 1973.

78. Elizabeth Holtzman, in the *New York Times*, 3 August 1973.

79. Arthur Schlesinger, Jr., "Congress and the Making of American Foreign Policy," *Foreign Affairs*, 51, no. 1 (October 1972), 103.

3

The People and Presidential Power

Power is not simply a quality that a person possesses like blue eyes or intelligence; rather, it is largely a relational phenomenon. That is, someone exercises power in part because others empower him or her to act; leadership implies followers. At the worst, a leader exercises power because the citizens (and officials in the system) do not revolt against him. At best, the citizens actively support their leader because they afford him or her the legitimate right to exercise power. The president is powerful in part because the people as a whole expect him to be; in fact in most cases they now demand it.

The struggle for control between Congress and the president is not carried out in a vacuum. At least partially the battle is fought out in the public arena before the attentive citizenry, and in the long run it influences the diffuse expectations all the people have about the proper role for each branch of government. It thus becomes important to understand how and why the people themselves empower the chief executive, why most people have favored him rather than other governmental institutions with their loyalty and support. To do this we must begin with a discussion of how political attitudes and values are inculcated in the citizens of the country, beginning with childhood experiences.

If a political system is to endure, it must generate support for itself, whether through coercion and force, satisfaction of the expectations of its members, regulation of communications, indifference, or a combination of all of these things.[1] Although

110

each of these is important, what is of interest here is the political socialization process through which political orientations are transmitted across generational lines. Here is the key to public expectations about what presidents should be like, how much power they have (and should exercise), what they should be able to accomplish, and their proper relationship to others (including citizens) in the political system.

Political Socialization

In the late 1950s and early 1960s, David Easton and Robert Hess conducted a survey of more than twelve thousand elementary school children designed to learn when and how political orientations are inculcated in the nation's youth. The authors found significant learning taking place even prior to enrollment in the first grade. To be sure, such knowledge is undeveloped, and it contains little detail with regard to the operation of the political system. What is learned is a general conception of political life in the society in which the child is growing. This occurs gradually, as the child sees its parents operate in a setting wider than the family and observes that even mother and father in some cases have to obey rules set down by others. This could happen in a number of ways, of course. A policeman may stop the parent's automobile, the child may hear mother grumbling about having to pay taxes, or father may reminisce about the time he had to serve in the army. The child learns about outside authorities that partially control what even parents are allowed to do. This serves as a general background for the more specific learning which will take place as the child develops.

Once in school, wherever that may be in the United States, children will probably find a portrait of George Washington, Abraham Lincoln, or both on their classroom walls. Next to the flag, these are probably the most common objects that a young person faces from kindergarten through high school. Virtually the first thing one has to memorize is the pledge of allegiance, a ritual conducted with such reverence and solemnity that Easton and Hess found that up until ages nine or ten many children have difficulty separating God and country. The largest single minority among them thought the pledge *was* to God. They also begin to learn other things from American political lore: about George Washington and the American Revolution, Thomas Jefferson and the Declaration of Independence, James Madison and the Constitution, Abraham Lincoln and the Emancipation Proclamation, and so on. Holidays from school are largely religious, like Christmas and Easter, or patriotic, like Washington's and Lincoln's birthdays. The manipulation of symbols to instill patriotism, then, begins at a very early age. It is through such training that every political system imprints itself on the minds of its citizens. The symbols of course are different; in the Soviet Union it may be the red flag, the hammer and sickle, the October Revolution, and Lenin's tomb, but the process is similar. Thus the Soviet system turns out loyal Russians; the Canadian system, Canadians; and the American system, Americans.

In the United States, early feelings about the political system are extremely positive and warm, especially toward the president, the policeman, the flag, and freedom.[2] The two authority figures mentioned, the president and the policeman, are the only ones children are able to cognize at first. It is through them that they view the entire external political process until they reach the upper grades. Even quite late in their development, the attachment to presidential authority overshadows any notion of the relative importance of Congress or the courts. In their questions to children about who makes the laws, runs the country, helps the country most, or best represents the government, Easton and Hess found the president consistently favored.

> For most children at this stage the President *is* the political structure. Even when the child knows about the Vice-President, he is frequently seen as an aid to the President; and the Senate and House of Representatives as well are considered to be subordinate and subject to the orders of the President.[3]

Thus the attitudes children form toward America, the flag, freedom, and all of the other positive elements in the political system are first viewed through a belief in the transcendent virtue of the presidency.

The children also thought highly of the personal characteristics of the president; he liked other people, was honest, friendly, a

good man, and very knowledgeable. Even when he was compared to their own fathers, the president came out as well or
better in almost all cases. "They uniformly see the President
possessed of all the virtues: benign, wise, helpful, concerned for
the welfare of others, protective, powerful, good, and honest."[4]
The authors hypothesize that this view of the president is so
positive because children generalize their attitudes toward authority figures with whom they are familiar (their parents and
teachers) to cover authority figures beyond their immediate
experience. In fact, they found that all significant authorities tend
to be seen by children as idealized parental figures. Through their
experience with adults, children learn a general frame of reference within which they place those persons they see as most
important in society—namely, high political leaders and especially the president. Their images of these figures are almost
always ones of benevolence and protectiveness. Although positive attitudes decline with age, Fred Greenstein found that at least
through the eighth grade negative comments on the president
were exceedingly rare. In response to the question, "What does
the President do?" he received the following answers: He "is in
charge of the United States and has many wise men to tell him
what is best" (sixth grade boy); "The President worries about all
the problems of all the forty-eight states. Takes care of threaten-
ing wars by holding peace conferences" (seventh grade boy);
"The President deals with foreign countries and takes care of the
U.S." (eighth grade boy); "The President gives us freedom"
(eighth grade girl); "The President makes peace with every
country but bad" (fifth grade boy); "I think that he has the right to
stop bad things before they start" (fifth grade girl).[5]

Idealizing the president and imagining him to make almost all
of the important decisions decrease with age. Children learn
about the law-making function of government and the role of
Congress in that process. Through social studies and civics
classes, they begin to understand the representative nature of
governmental institutions and are instructed in the civics book
norms such as voting. When grade school students were asked to
"pick the two pictures that show best what our government is"
from a set of ten illustrations, younger children most frequently
selected pictures of George Washington and President Kennedy.
By the eighth grade, voting and Congress led the list (with John

Kennedy third).[6] The beliefs that the president is personally responsive to children's needs; that he would care very much if they wrote to him; that he is their favorite person; and that he knows more than anyone, is always a leader, and never makes mistakes also decrease as children grow older. The ideas that he works harder than anyone else and makes important decisions all the time remain constant or actually increase with grade level.[7] Even as children grow older, they maintain an extremely positive opinion of the president. In the second grade 84 percent believed he always or almost always keeps his promises, and this had only fallen off to 70 percent by the eighth grade.[8] Children's basic commitment to the notion of the benevolent leader has already been made by then.

To be sure, the development of political party identification colors somewhat the evaluation that children make of individual Democratic and Republican chief executives. But what is seen as most important is the presidential *role*, and it is this that is evaluated so highly by children regardless of the party affiliation or idiosyncratic personality traits of a particular incumbent.[9] The earliest images that children have of the president tend to be largely personal ones, such as images of his kindness, warmth, helpfulness, goodness, or protectiveness. By the later grades, however, children develop a positive conception of the presidency as an institution apart from the characteristics of any individual president.[10] This has profound impact later on as young persons progress into adulthood.

What is the relevance of all of this for the political system? We know that many enduring political orientations are acquired even before adolescence. Psychologists tell us that early learning has a profound effect on later attitudes. When assessments learned late in life conflict with a child's early attitudes, "the longest held of these would be most likely to influence his response."[11] Even though adults are much more realistic about the governmental system than young children (and more cynical as well), they continue to respect the presidency above other institutions. Most also accept the legitimacy of electoral outcomes despite the fact that they may have voted for another candidate, and this in turn has enormous consequences for the stability of the political system. Such is not the case in many other countries, of course.

The office of the presidency has become a symbol of the nation, and regardless of who occupies it most people believe he should be afforded great respect and deference, plus a substantial degree of leeway in the conduct of his office. This does not mean that citizens view uncritically each possessor of the office, but merely that early idealization of the role continues to influence how much power they believe any president should be allowed to exercise. It also means the president has a "leg up" on the other political institutions in the eyes of the citizenry.

We do not imply that change does not take place through contact with reality and further learning: people change political parties, become apathetic and drop out, get attached to particular candidates and issues, and view negatively the performance of certain presidents. But most studies indicate there is a large residue of affect that colors the way we see things, even though it may largely be subconscious.

Fred Greenstein has pulled together several findings with regard to the way the American people view the president and the psychological uses they make of him.[12] The following discussion draws heavily on what he has written. First, people use the president as a *cognitive aid*. That is, it is much easier to view the buzzing complexity of politics through a single, well-known person than to try to sort through parties, interest groups, institutions, politicians, policies, bureaucrats, and all of the other elements in the political environment. Thus we think of Johnson's war, or of Ford doing poorly with the economy, or of Roosevelt getting us out of the depression, and so on. The existence of the president as a focal point serves to simplify and clarify, to reduce to a manageable level what otherwise would overwhelm our abilities to absorb.

The president is also an *outlet for affect*. He is our equivalent of England's monarch; his family is our royal family. Everything he and his family do is news, whether he is playing touch football or watching the super bowl, or his daughters are dating movie stars. Almost every day the television networks tell about what the president did and how he spent his time. No other figure, political or otherwise, receives this kind of coverage.

Furthermore, Greenstein finds the president to be a *means of vicarious participation*. Citizens who identify with him and his policies, although they aren't able to participate directly in government, may enhance their own senses of power when the president acts in their behalf. When he speaks for the silent majority or attacks the rotton apples, the long hairs, or the news media, those who share these sentiments feel a blow has been struck in their name. It is like watching young boys swagger out of a John Wayne movie: the hero has just smitten the villains and they themselves feel ready to take on bad guys anywhere.

But it is not just partisan identifiers who make use of the president. In a larger sense he serves *as a symbol of national unity.* He represents the United States as a nation, as a people. He not only speaks for America in its dealings with foreign countries and receives kings and prime ministers but buys the first Easter Seal, throws out the first baseball of the season, proclaims Thanksgiving, lights the national Christmas tree, welcomes returning astronauts from the moon, and lays wreaths on the tombs of America's war dead. Even if one doesn't agree with him on all of the issues, he is still "our president" and thus (say millions of people) deserving of support.

Finally, the president serves as *a symbol of stability and predictability.* If we ourselves don't understand the complexities of politics, the intricate nature of dealing with the economy or foreign countries, we at least want to feel that someone is taking care of them for us. We can personify government in the chief executive, and as long as he is there to look after things, we often believe that we need not be concerned. This is perhaps why a substantial number of citizens continued to oppose impeachment despite shock after shock coming out of the White House. What would happen if the president were removed? Would the Soviets take advantage? Would the processes of government collapse, the economy fail? This uncertainty probably led many to prefer what they considered to be a known evil to the unknown consequences of forced removal. By the same token, the sudden death of an incumbent president leads to fears of chaos and turmoil, accompanied by rumors of plots and conspiracies.

The literature on the reaction to John Kennedy's assassination reveals the depth of emotion that attaches people to their president and the degree to which personalization continues in adulthood. Drawing on a national survey conducted by the National

Opinion Research Center within days of Kennedy's death, Paul Sheatsley and Jacob Feldman found people across the country profoundly disturbed by what had happened.[13] The most universal reactions were sorrow, personal shame, and anger. The immediate reactions to the news of the assassination were reported as follows: "Felt sorry that a strong young man had been killed at the height of his powers" (88 percent); "Felt ashamed that this could happen in our country" (83 percent); "Felt the loss of someone very close and dear" (79 percent); and "Felt angry that anyone should do such a terrible deed" (73 percent). The most frequently mentioned emotions, then, were personal ones, the kind felt when a relative or close friend dies. These were followed by shame and anger. Next came a series of three reactions that are political in nature, expressing fear and uncertainty for the country: "Worried about how his death would affect the political situation in his country" (47 percent); "Worried about how his death would affect our relations with other countries" (44 percent); and "Felt worried about how the United States would carry on without its leader" (31 percent). There seems to be some carryover into the later life of adults, then, from early attachments to the president as a person. After that, people begin to worry about how the death of the chief executive will affect the governmental processes.

It should be recalled that less than 50 percent of the electorate had voted for John Kennedy only three years earlier. But in the days following the assassination, half of the people questioned called him one of the two or three best presidents in our history, and nearly 30 percent more described him as better than average. It is obvious that it wasn't only the supporters of the late president who were affected by his death—poll results from shortly before the assassination indicated that only 59 percent approved of the way he was handling his job. In addition, the emotions of grief and sorrow were felt among anti-Kennedy southerners as well as among pro-Kennedy supporters in the North (although not quite as strongly). The authors report that 62 percent of the white southerners who had voted against Kennedy "felt the loss of someone very close and dear."

From the historical evidence presented by Sheatsley and Feldman, the reactions to the death of an incumbent were much the same for Roosevelt, Harding, McKinley, Garfield, and Lincoln. Thus it was not just Kennedy's youth or the fact that he was the victim of an assassin's bullet that accounts for the emotional outpouring at his death. Nor does the death of a past president, no matter how deeply revered, trigger the sense of personal loss and sorrow that occurs when an incumbent president dies. In recent times Eisenhower remained the most popular chief executive while in office and a highly esteemed and loved elder statesman after stepping down. Yet when he died, business went on much as usual; people who remembered him may have been saddened, but there is no indication that the nation suffered from the emotional trauma associated with the death of an incumbent president. When Presidents Truman and Johnson passed away a few years ago, their pictures did not even make the covers of *Time* or *Newsweek*. (The death of a justice of the Supreme Court or of a leader in Congress similarly fails to evoke significant national remorse among the population at large.) Compare this with the physical and emotional symptoms reported by a cross section of the American public at Kennedy's death: 68 percent said they felt nervous and tense, 57 percent felt dazed and numb, 53 percent cried, 48 percent had trouble sleeping, 43 percent didn't feel like eating, and 42 percent said they felt more tired than usual. Only 11 percent of the population reported they felt none of the sixteen emotions listed, and this was almost as equally true for those who opposed Kennedy as it was for his supporters. Obviously, then, the presidency has a hold on the adult imagination and emotion that, although remaining dormant or subconscious much of the time, is aroused to extraordinary levels when the incumbent president dies.

Direct evidence about how much power the people want the president to exert is found in other studies. Roberta Sigel asked a sample of Detroit residents questions designed to elicit their preferences for popular and congressional, as opposed to presidential, leadership.[14] One of the questions read:

> Now, suppose that fighting is breaking out somewhere abroad, and the President thinks it's important to send American troops there. He knows, however, that most Americans are *opposed* to sending our troops there. Now what do you think: Should he *send* these troops, which he may legally do as President, or should he *follow* public opinion and keep them home?[15]

As she hypothesized, a majority said the president should send the troops despite popular disapproval. Seventy-five percent of her respondents answered this question in the affirmative, giving such reasons as "That is his job," "That is what we elected him for," and most frequently, "He knows more than the people." Sigel concludes that, not only does the American electorate feel unqualified to make these complicated decisions in foreign affairs, but also that it trusts the president not to abuse his power.

A second question dealt with domestic affairs and read as follows:

> Now, which of the two statements comes closest to your own ideas: "The President is an inspired leader; he has ideas of his own how to help the country. He should be able to make the people and Congress work along with him," or "It is up to the people through their Congressmen to find solutions to the problems of the day. The President should stick to carrying out what the people and Congress have decided."[16]

Even in matters close to home, a majority (51.5 percent) preferred presidential leadership to that of the people and Congress. The results indicate clearly that the people believe in allowing the president extremely wide latitude in carrying out his office as he sees fit, even when conflict arises between him and others in the political system. The only apparent limit they want to set to his power is in terms of a fixed tenure, believing that one person should not hold this powerful office for more than two terms.

There is also evidence from public opinion polling sources about the extent to which the people are willing to follow the president—that is to empower him to carry out his policies, especially in foreign affairs. For instance, during the 1960s favorable responses on national polls concerning the admission of "Red" China to the U.N. could be substantially increased if the question were prefaced with the notation "if the president suggested it." Results from President Nixon's trips to China and the Soviet Union indicate that these were two of his most popular moves with the people; despite his earlier speeches against "being soft on communism," people were able to change their perceptions and support "détente" rather than confrontation. By the same token public opinion followed Presidents Johnson and Nixon as they escalated or de-escalated the conflict in Vietnam.

Before Johnson called off the bombing of North Vietnam, only 40 percent approved of such a policy; after he announced that that was what he was going to do, 64 percent said they approved. Only 7 percent of the people approved an invasion of Cambodia before Nixon ordered troops there; after his speech explaining his action, 50 percent said that the president was right to do so.[17]

John Mueller has described a "rally round the flag" phenomenon in presidential popularity that takes place when an event "(1) is international and (2) involves the United States and particularly the President directly; and ... (3) [is] specific, dramatic, and sharply focused."[18] Almost any event of this kind leads to a surge of support for the president, some with relatively lasting effects (like the Cuban missile crisis), and others that are transitory and leave the president in the long run with less support than when he started (the U-2 crisis and the Bay of Pigs). It is of little relevance whether the action directed by the president is a flop or a success; people tend to rally to their leader when occurrences of this sort take place. Truman increased his opinion poll showing by 9 percentage points when he sent troops to Korea in 1950, Eisenhower gained 8 during the Suez crisis, Kennedy's popularity went up 13 points after the Cuban missile crisis, and Ford gained 10 points with the *Mayaguez*.[19] Mueller has identified thirty-four such "rally points" in the administrations of presidents from Truman through Johnson, and there is evidence that this continued in the Nixon and Ford administrations. Prior to the announcement that he intended to travel to China, Nixon had been holding steady for several months at around 49 percent approval. With that trip, his popularity increased to 57 percent, and his visit to Russia increased his positive image to 61 percent. Even the first manned moon landing led to a slight increase in the rating of the president.[20] In early 1973 the end of American fighting in Vietnam and the return of American prisoners were responsible for Nixon's highest approval ever, 68 percent.

There are many persons, then, who tend to follow the president in whatever direction he chooses to lead. They take their opinion cues almost exclusively from him in foreign affairs, and it matters little what leaders in Congress or others are saying. According to Mueller:

Chief of State

The President's strength in this area seems to derive from the majesty of the office and from his singular position as head of state. Followers seem to identify with the country and with its leadership and tend to be susceptible to the social and political influences in this direction. . . . For them, the President *is* the country for many purposes and, therefore, there is a certain popular loyalty to the man that comes with the office which tends to place him above politics.[21]

If this is the case, it may be misleading for opinion pollsters to try to gauge public sentiment toward specific policies in this area; what is important to know is where the *president* stands. If we know that, we can be fairly certain that a substantial portion of citizens will go along. Watergate has illustrated that a large number of people will continue to support an incumbent president in spite of almost any evidence of wrongdoing, as this quote from a full page ad in the *Los Angeles Times* makes clear: "Every President's right to our loyalty is non-forfeitable. Whether we voted for him or not, he is entitled to it for as long as he discharges the awesome responsibility of that office, regardless of the charges against him."[22]

Notice loyalty according to the quotation is not determined by the performance of an incumbent president but is owed solely because he occupies the office. The use of the term "loyalty" itself indicates some sort of familial bond that ties the president to his people in much the same way children are bound to father; they are expected to support him even though he may be a drunk. ("He's the only father we've got.") It is inconceivable to imagine loyalty being owed to one's member of Congress or a Supreme Court justice accused of wrongdoing; in addition to having other judges and representatives, few people think in terms of the duty of loyalty to such public officials. If anything, it is believed that they owe the people an honest and conscientious performance of their jobs; the loyalty involved is to the Constitution and the laws of the land. The danger is that investing unquestioning loyalty in the head of state may run the risk of putting him above the standards used to judge ordinary mortals.

Presidential popularity goes down in the polls as well as up, of course. Although we have few measurements of public opinion prior to the 1940s, we know from historical accounts and contemporary newspaper stories that many past presidents were vilified by large segments of the population as well as by the press itself. Even the most revered presidents, such as Washington, Jefferson, Jackson, and Lincoln, did not escape calumny heaped upon them by their fellow citizens. It is likely that their popularity fluctuated considerably during their terms of office, as Table 1 shows.

TABLE 1   JOB RATINGS FOR LAST SIX PRESIDENTS
(PERCENT APPROVING)

	High	Low
Nixon	68%	25%
Johnson	80	35
Kennedy	83	57
Eisenhower	79	49
Truman	87	23
Roosevelt	84	54

SOURCE: *The Gallup Opinion Index*, Report No. 106 (April 1974), p. 2. Reprinted by permission.

Mueller has pointed out with regard to modern incumbents that generally the approval ratings of presidents tend to decline with length of service. He has identified four factors that partially account for this decrease.[23] First, presidents are elected because they are able to forge coalitions of various political, ethnic, economic, occupational, and geographical groups. Many times the interests of these groups come into conflict, and the longer a person is in office, the more likely he is to have made decisions which please some factions but alienate others. In some cases, of course, unpopular actions may have the effect of making him less popular with both sides in a dispute. This "coalition of minorities" effect accounts for some of the decrease in popularity as the years go by.

We have already mentioned the "rally round the flag" phenomenon that occurs during dramatic international events; the longer it has been since the last rally point, however, the more likely a president is to decline in popularity (about 5 or 6 percentage points for every year since the last rally). Another variable acting to depress the ratings of the chief executive is the existence of an economic slump. Mueller's findings indicate that for every percentage point increase in the unemployment rate there is a drop in presidential popularity of 3 percent. Unfortunately from the president's standpoint, the reverse is not true: a decrease in unemployment does not lead to increased presidential approval. Finally, the existence of a long war may depress evaluations of an incumbent. In the case of Harry Truman, the Korean War alone accounted for a loss of 18 percentage points. However, the Vietnam conflict did not seem to have an independent effect on Lyndon Johnson's popularity. This may be attributable to Johnson's efforts to keep the war bipartisan, as well as to the existence of racial turmoil in the cities that was enough in and of itself for many of the unfavorable assessments he received.

Of course other events, personality variables, and issues affect the popularity of incumbent presidents. (Dwight Eisenhower's ratings, for instance, remained high for his entire eight years in office.) There is evidence that inflation seriously erodes support for a president, as does the existence of scandal that can be laid at the chief executive's door. Watergate is an excellent example of the loss of confidence that can occur when many of the American people conclude the president is guilty of illegal or unethical behavior. Perhaps it is because the office is so idealized in the imagined presidencies of historical myth that some people are so quickly disillusioned. In any case, just as the corruption in government under Nixon was unparalleled in previous administrations, so too no president suffered a more precipitous drop in popularity than Nixon did in 1973. From a high point of 68 percent in January shortly after the end of our formal participation in the Vietnam War, his rating plummeted 39 points to a low of only 29 percent approval in December. In 1974 the indications were that Nixon had fallen to a bedrock support of between 25 and 30 percent of the people. No new "horrors" that were revealed seemed able to shake the confidence of that hard-core following, but at the same time not even trips to the Middle East or the Soviet Union served to increase his appeal significantly. The rallying potential of these trips seemed to have disappeared. No president since Truman (when he fired MacArthur) had been so unpopular with such a large percentage of the American people.

Overall, who were the people who supported and who were those who opposed removal of President Nixon? The latest detailed poll results available before Nixon's resignation are presented in Table 2. Even a casual inspection reveals that the greatest difference in opinion is associated with partisan identification: Democrats strongly favored removal, Republicans more strongly opposed it, and independents were somewhere in between (although closer to Democratic opinion).

In the same poll, only 25 percent of the national sample said they approved of the way President Nixon was handling his job. Confirming evidence presented in Chapter 2, Congress did not fare much better in the eyes of the electorate. Overall, 30 percent gave Congress a favorable rating, with Republicans the most negative in their views and Democrats split evenly between approval and disapproval. Thus only 5 percentage points separated the president from Congress in popular support, despite the massive belief in the guilt of Nixon and no comparable belief in the criminality of the legislative branch. Clearly there exists a predisposition to favor the chief executive over Congress except in the most unusual of circumstances.

Perhaps the most fundamental question to ask is why approximately one-fourth to one-third of the population continued to believe the president was doing a good job despite inflation and unemployment (both at the same time), Watergate, and all of the other problems besetting the administration. Part of the answer is attributable to the achievements of President Nixon and his chief foreign policy adviser, Henry Kissinger, in seeming to end the war in Vietnam and in arranging for a separation of the warring parties in the Middle East. When this is coupled with improved relations with China and the Soviet Union, it is possible to see how many people became convinced that the president had been remarkably successful in his dealings with foreign countries. Domestically as well, those who agreed with Nixon's policies on such matters as his opposition to busing to achieve racial balance in the schools, his promotion of revenue sharing, or the reduction or elimination of many Great Society programs continued to support the President. Ideological or policy agreement, then, probably accounted for some of the continued favorable ratings of President Nixon.

TABLE 2   PERCENTAGE OF POPULATION FAVORING
NIXON'S REMOVAL°

	Yes	No	No Opinion
National	46%	42%	12%
Sex			
Male	49	42	9
Female	43	42	15
Race			
White	43	45	12
Nonwhite	67	17	16
Education			
College	47	45	8
High School	46	42	12
Grade School	42	39	19
Region			
East	47	40	13
Midwest	46	42	12
South	41	45	14
West	50	39	11
Age			
Under 30	59	31	10
30–49	45	44	11
50 and older	38	47	15
Politics			
Republican	18	74	8
Democrat	60	28	12
So. Democrat	56	30	14
No. Democrat	62	26	12
Independent	47	38	15
Religion			
Protestant	40	48	12
Catholic	53	35	12
Occupation			
Prof. and Bus.	39	50	11
Clerical and Sales	37	55	8
Manual Workers	53	35	12
Nonlabor Force	41	43	16

SOURCE: *The Gallup Opinion Index*, Report No. 107 (May 1974), p. 6. Reprinted
by permission.

° Question: "Just from the way you feel now, do you think his actions are serious
enough to warrant his being removed from the Presidency, or not?"

How much support for any president results from lingering effects of early idealization of the office is impossible to determine. We know from the studies cited earlier, however, that the impact of childhood socialization contributes to the attitudes that adults display later on in life. We can speculate, at least, that some people (most likely those who do not pay a great deal of attention to current political happenings) say they approve of the way a president is handling his job merely because he is the president. Despite the antipolitical folklore in the United States, they have learned that presidents are good; that they are responsible for the conduct of government; and that it is the responsibility of citizens to support whoever occupies the office at a given time. Future studies should be able to reveal the size and composition of such a group of citizens; they are important because they contribute to the stability and generally pacific tenor of the political system. On the other hand, some critics have viewed it as unhealthy that a large body of people in a democracy are willing to accept passively almost any course of action determined by a single person.

The President and the News Media

As has been pointed out, not all attitudes and values are permanently fixed in childhood. The adult continues to learn, to test former beliefs against reality as he or she experiences it, and to change and modify opinions as further information is acquired. In the United States, once a person leaves school, the great bulk of his or her new knowledge about government comes from the mass media, but the plural nature of Congress and the judiciary deprives journalists of a handy focus for their stories about those institutions. There is no one authority who can speak with definitiveness for the legislative branch, but rather a confusing multiplicity of "leaders," each with a measure of independence from the others. What Senator Hruska says may be interesting to Nebraska residents, but by and large those who live in other states are uninterested. Thus the national media only infrequently carry stories or statements by the vast bulk of the members of Congress. Moreover, journalists, like most of the rest of the people, have grown up believing that what the president does is comparatively more important than what the legislature does, except possibly in reaction to presidential initiatives. In addition, much of the real work of Congress goes on behind closed doors in committee sessions, and this too poses a problem for reporters. As for the Supreme Court, its deliberations are always barred to the public and journalists. Almost never do stories leak from behind the purple curtain, and the justices rarely make public statements on important issues that may someday be brought before them as cases. When the Court speaks it is in the form of legal opinions, and these are written in a style that most laymen find difficult to penetrate. Thus only the gist of Court orders is generally reported to the public.

The vast majority of news about the national political system that reaches the eyes and ears of the average citizen tends to be about the president. Once again his ability to act while most others merely react is important here. When he or his spokesmen issue statements, it is relatively certain that he is in a position to commit the executive branch to a particular course of action. The existence of a single individual in such a position makes it possible to personalize all of the activity carried out under his direction. He of course does have vast authority, both under the Constitution and in the form of powers delegated to him by laws of Congress. What he attempts to do about inflation and the economy, or what his position is with regard to antitrust policy, or civil rights enforcement, or arms limitation, or détente, or social programs affects the lives of almost all of the American people. Thus it becomes important for citizens to know where their president stands on these issues.

Not only is the press interested in the president, but the president is interested in the press as well. The relationship between the two is a symbiotic one. The media use the chief executive as a source of news and interesting stories, and the president uses the press to reach the people in an attempt to shape opinion into a source of support for his administration. It was Teddy Roosevelt who originated the modern presidential press conference and provided space in the White House itself for reporters. Only relatively small numbers of people had been able to see the chief executive in personal appearances, but with the aid of newspapers Roosevelt could have his image and views transmitted to the farthest corners of the United States. Although newspaper readership was probably more widespread at that time than it is today, the president was still dependent upon reporters and editors, party leaders, and locally influential citizens for what the people learned of him. This is no longer entirely the case, since modern presidents have the capability to go over the heads of political parties, local opinion elites, and newspaper editors and reporters directly into the homes of almost every American citizen.

With the advent of radio, and later television, it has become possible for the president to speak simultaneously to people in Maine and California, Minnesota and Mississippi. He can, and does, preempt every available channel on the broadcast band, leaving the listener the choice between hearing what the president has to say or turning off the set. The timing, frequency, subject matter, and format are almost totally up to him; no other political figure has this opportunity. Franklin Roosevelt was the first to make extensive use of the potential of radio. As governor of New York he had spoken directly to the people of his state and found the radio talk to be an extremely popular enterprise with his listeners. Once elected president, he initiated the practice on a national scale, even shaping his messages to Congress as much for their impact on the people as on the legislators. If he could generate popular enthusiasm, he could bring additional pressure to bear on senators and representatives to pass his programs.

Roosevelt's most successful and memorable such efforts were probably his famous "fireside chats," which calmed fears generated by the depression and inspired confidence in his leadership. After he asked in one of his broadcasts for listeners to write telling him of their troubles, he was deluged with more than half a million letters. Seldom had a political leader been more effective in communicating a warm, confident, soothing, and friendly personality to the American people. Seldom, too, had people been more willing to entrust power to the president. In the first "Hundred Days," he made four such broadcasts, but anticipating that they would lose their dramatic impact if overused, he cut back to an average of one every six months for the remainder of his twelve years in office.

Most surveys now indicate that it is the broadcast media that the public considers to be its prime source of political information. At the outbreak of the Korean War in 1950, Truman could go on nationwide TV to announce his decision to send troops to that country. Viewers not only heard the solemn voice of the president but also saw his expression and demeanor as he explained the hardships that lay ahead for the American people. As never before in our history, they were made an immediate part of a presidential decision. But it was really Eisenhower who became the first "television president," with the addition to his staff of a TV advisor in the person of Robert Montgomery, the actor and producer. The main thing for television, said Montgomery, was to project a picture of a relaxed, informal, and spontaneous leader. Since most people saw Eisenhower as a warm and sincere man, strategies would have to be devised to convey that image in visual form. All sorts of formats were experimented with to get away from the stilted, straight-reading-from-the-written-page early TV efforts of the administration, and ultimately some success was obtained. To the end of his term, Eisenhower was able to maintain his image as a nonpartisan, "above politics," benevolent leader. It didn't seem to matter so much what he said, as long as he was there.

The four televised debates between candidates Nixon and Kennedy in the 1960 election were viewed by between forty-eight and seventy-five million people. Many observers credit Kennedy's narrow victory over Nixon to his performance on the first broadcast. Television was indeed the dynamic, young president's medium, and in this sense he was to presidential television what Roosevelt had been to presidential radio. He averaged about three televised speeches to the nation each year, and mixed in press conferences and informal interview shows on top of that. In addition, documentaries on the president at work seemed to bring viewers into the very decision-making process of the nation's chief executive and gave them an intimate look at their president on the job. Even his wife was pressed into service to give the cameras a guided tour of the White House (now a staple of each administration). The public reactions to these TV efforts were overwhelmingly favorable. [24]

One of Lyndon Johnson's first tasks as president was to convey to the people a sense of the continuity of leadership in the United States, to reassure them he would carry on where John Kennedy had left off. Within five days of the assassination, Johnson addressed a nationally televised joint session of Congress, promising the legislators and the American people that the slain leader's initiatives in space, equal rights, education, jobs, and care for the elderly would be pushed with renewed vigor. In this period of national trauma, he sought to heal the divisions and fears plaguing society: "These are the United States—a united people with a united purpose. . . . The time has come for Americans of all races and creeds and political beliefs to understand and to respect one another." [25] All indications from the press and public opinion polls were that the overwhelming majority rallied to the support of their new president, even those who had been suspicious of this Texas politician with a reputation for arm twisting and "wheeling and dealing."

Television of course played a significant role in familiarizing the people with their new president. Within hours of Kennedy's death, the major networks were broadcasting film biographies of Lyndon Johnson, stressing his vast governmental experience. The people saw the parade of world leaders who had come to the funeral of Kennedy stay to meet the new chief executive. In the days that followed, extensive coverage of the administration, as well as continued stories on Johnson the man, his family, and his interests, made him almost as familiar to America as his predecessor had been. The people could sit in their living rooms and be reassured that their government was unimpaired, that Lyndon Johnson had firmly taken over the helm of state, and that they could trust their new president to handle the difficult job to which he had been suddenly elevated. Much the same kind of soothing reassurance was communicated by President Ford eleven years later when he took over from Richard Nixon.

The wave of unity generated for Johnson in late 1963 carried through the 1964 election. It can be argued that the Republican choice for an opponent in that election, Barry Goldwater, contributed significantly to the continuation of support for the incumbent president. Johnson, however, had difficulty relating effectively to the people over television, especially when his style and manner were compared with that of his urbane predecessor. Perhaps it is true, as Eric Goldman suggests, that the contrast in the minds of the intellectuals and opinion shapers in the media would not really let them judge Johnson neutrally. They had become accustomed to having in the White House a leader whom they considered to be one of their own—now they found the office occupied by a rough Texan who seemed to them to ooze insincerity and pious platitudes.[26] Johnson himself believed that it was his southern accent and the hostility of the "Eastern establishment" that was responsible for his widespread lack of acclaim.

> I did not believe . . . that the nation would unite indefinitely behind any Southerner. One reason the country could not rally behind a Southern President, I was convinced, was that the metropolitan press of the Eastern Seaboard would never permit it. My experience in office had confirmed this reaction.[27]

Marshall McLuhan contends that television is a "cool" medium, one that demands equally cool personalities if they are to be projected favorably. That is, a politician should come across with low intensity and with a certain undefined generality in order to allow the viewer to fill in the details of "image" for himself. Lyndon Johnson, on the other hand, projected an intense, "hot" personality unsuited for the television cameras. What is acceptable in person or in print is simply not suitable for the living room via television. Johnny Carson in this sense is the competitor for our affections and support, and what an individual politician says and stands for is less important. If a president can't come across on television today, some infer a fatal flaw in his leadership ability. Joe McGinniss posits that Hubert Humphrey would probably have been elected President in 1968 had he been able to project better through television: "The performer must talk to one person at a time. He is brought into the living room. He is a guest. It is improper for him to shout. Humphrey vomited on the rug."[28] By the same token, we were willing to accept almost anything from Kennedy, but from Johnson almost nothing:

> We forgave, followed, and accepted Kennedy because we liked the way he looked. And he had a pretty wife. Camelot was fun, even for the peasants, as long as it was televised to their huts.
>
> Then came Lyndon Johnson, heavy and gross, and he was forgiven nothing. He might have survived the sniping of the displaced intellectuals had he only been able to charm. But no one taught him how. Johnson was syrupy. He stuck to the lens. There was no place for him in our culture.[29]

Despite this lack of effectiveness, Johnson never gave up trying to use television to reach the people directly. He insisted on having almost instant access to the television cameras any time he had a message worthy of sharing with the public. To this end, a studio was set up in the White House itself, with three color cameras constantly kept in readiness should the president request free time. Within his first twelve months in office, Johnson appeared on television more than Kennedy had in three years; by the end of his second year, his appearances outnumbered those of Eisenhower in eight years in office.[30] He requested, and received, live coverage for bill signings and for announcements of strike settlements. As with his predecessor, news conferences, speeches, informal chats with news anchormen and extensive coverage of his trips were also broadcast. Sometimes he would break into regular programs almost without any warning at all. On one such occasion, the technicians requested that he delay for a moment so they could put up the presidential seal. The reported response was, "Son, I'm the leader of the free world, and I'll go on the air when I want to."[31] Yet for all of his efforts, he never truly succeeded in mastering the projection of the kind of image that television requires, "never communicated the personal qualities Americans demand of their presidents."[32] Perhaps therein lies part of the explanation for the vehemence with which his critics denounced him.

Richard Nixon, like Lyndon Johnson before him, distinguished between two kinds of presidential television. In one category are news reports and news conferences, in which reporters can at least partially interject what they consider to be relevant for the American people to hear. This is the kind of television that the administration attacked through Spiro Agnew, citing what it considered to be biased reports (including the raised eyebrows of newsmen as they read certain stories) as evidence of a medium hostile to the incumbent administration. The president himself joined the attack in October 1973, criticizing the Watergate coverage he was receiving:

I have never heard or seen such outrageous, vicious, distorted reporting in 27 years of public life. I am not blaming anybody for that. Perhaps what happened is that what we did brought it about, and therefore, the media decided that they would have to take that particular line.

But when people are pounded night after night with that kind of frantic, hysterical reporting, it naturally shakes their confidence.[33]

Some observers have seen in this an effort to focus public attention and hostility on the bearer, rather than on the subject, of the message. If the people could be made to believe that the media treated the president unfairly, that reporters were prejudiced against a conservative administration, perhaps the people would put less credence in the message itself. Even the comments of reporters after Nixon's broadcast were attacked as "instant analysis," and were, at least for a time, discontinued by CBS.

The other kind of presidential television, the kind that was approved, is "pure" television. That is, direct access to the viewer without the intervening influence or participation of reporters. Here the incumbent president is in almost total control of the format and content of the message he wishes the people to hear. What is desired is a direct link between the people and their president. Television viewed simply as a mechanism for transmission of the chief executive's image and views is "good" television; allowing others to share partially in this process is "bad" television. Acting on this belief, President Nixon held fewer press conferences than any other modern chief executive, sometimes going four or five months without subjecting himself to the questioning of reporters. The president was said to believe that the "grandstanding" of newsmen detracted from the effectiveness of the media in getting across the information and policies he wanted to communicate to the people.[34] In his first term in office, Nixon held 16 televised press conferences and 15 untelevised ones, for a total of 31. In all he had 37 conferences in five and a half years. Kennedy had held 64 in three years, Johnson 126 in five years, Eisenhower 193 in eight years, Truman 322 in eight years, and Roosevelt 998 in twelve years. The averages for these presidents are 7 press conferences a year for Nixon, 21 for Kennedy, 24 for Johnson and Eisenhower, 42 for Truman, and 83 for Roosevelt.[35] Gerald Ford held 18 news conferences in his first year in office.

Nixon's "pure" use of the media, on the other hand, far

exceeded that of any of his predecessors. During his first eighteen months in office, he appeared in prime time (between the hours of 7 and 11 P.M.) more than had Johnson, Kennedy, and Eisenhower *combined* during their respective first eighteen months in office.[36] By the end of thirty-six months, Nixon had preempted all three TV networks simultaneously for seventeen reports, announcements, or briefings. If one had to purchase this amount of time, it would have cost between $2 and $3 million.[37] In his first four years, President Nixon made fifty-seven televised addresses or special appearances on television, and this excluded the coverage he received on his trips to China and the USSR and his news conferences. In the period from October 1973 through March 1974, he appeared in eight evening performances (six of them in the choicest slots at 7 or 7:30 P.M.).[38] Jeb Stuart Magruder tells us that in an early conversation with H. R. Haldeman he was informed that

> the President understood he lacked the charisma or personal appeal of a Kennedy or an Eisenhower. He assumed, too, that he would never win over the liberal opinion makers in the media and elsewhere who had always loathed him. So the challenge was to develop a public relations program that could circumvent the liberal opinion makers and take the President's message directly to the people.[39]

Part of this effort to devise means of controlling the image projected by the White House was to divide the public relations (PR) function between Ron Ziegler, press secretary for the president, and Herb Klein, who functioned as communications director in the newly created Office of Communications. Theoretically at least, the latter organization was to coordinate all news from the executive branch and facilitate access to the departments for reporters. In practice, however, it did not work out that way. In addition to the staffs accumulated in these two offices, Charles Colson during his tenure in the White House also took on PR functions, specializing in news leaks designed either to help the president or harm his enemies. Finally, another new agency, the Office of Telecommunications Policy under Clay Whitehead, concerned itself with developing strategies to influence the media in directions favorable to the president. It was Whitehead who

issued the following veiled threat to television and radio executives: "Station managers and network officials who fail to act to
correct imbalance or consistent bias in the networks—or who
acquiesce by silence—can only be considered willing participants
to be held fully accountable . . . at license renewal time."[40] Of
course no station can operate without a license from the federal
government. Whitehead's broadside was aimed at putting
double-barreled pressure on the networks: first, by indicating
administration displeasure with CBS, ABC, and NBC directly;
and second, by hinting that the locally owned affiliates would be
in trouble unless they took steps to "balance" the programs they
carried from the networks with programs more favorable to the
administration (on penalty of being forced out of business).

The transcripts released by the president, as well as testimony
by former administration aides and internal memos that were
introduced into evidence in the impeachment proceedings, show
that much of the time of those in the White House was taken up
with trying to devise public relations strategies. "How will it play
in Peoria?" became a consuming preoccupation of much of the
top leadership. The wording of releases, how they were to be put
out, through whom, and their timing and content were the subject
of prolonged brainstorming sessions between Nixon, Haldeman,
Ehrlichman, and Ziegler. Farther down the line, in response to
memos from these men, Klein, Higby, Magruder, Colson, and
their staffs worked on lists of suggested PR actions. A major part
of this effort was to put pressure on the networks to cease
criticism of the Administration and to deny Democrats free air
time to respond to presidential speeches. Charles Colson met
with broadcast officials and reported in a memo afterwards that
they were "very much afraid of us and are trying to prove they
are 'good guys.'" He let them know that "we are not going to
permit them to get away with anything that interferes with the
President's ability to communicate. . . . The harder I pressed
them [CBS and NBC], the more accommodating, cordial and
almost apologetic they became."[41]

As Chet Huntley, one of the NBC television anchormen, was
about to retire in 1970, he gave an interview to *Life* magazine in
which he was quoted as saying of Nixon: "The shallowness of the
man overwhelms me; the fact that he is President frightens me."

(Huntley later claimed he had been misquoted.) This criticism proved to those in the White House what they believed all along—that television reporters were prejudiced against the president. Huntley's statement also offered them an opportunity to attack the media. Suggestions and memos outlining diverse plans and courses of action flew back and forth between various staffers. Among them was this suggestion from Larry Higby:

> We need to get some creative thinking going on an attack on Huntley for his statements in *Life*. One thought that comes to mind is getting all the people to sign a petition calling for the immediate removal of Huntley right now. The point behind the whole thing is that we don't care about Huntley—he is going to leave anyway. *What we are trying to do here is to tear down the institution. . . . Let's put a full plan on this and get the thing moving.* [Emphasis added.] [42]

Magruder responded with a four-page memo of his own, listing eighteen possible actions. He insists that not much came of these two "game plans," but, as he points out, Haldeman (and presumably the president) liked memos that suggested solutions to problems.

One of Magruder's first efforts in this area came shortly after he arrived at the White House in the fall of 1969. He proposed that the administration set up a monitoring system on the networks through the Federal Communications Commission to document unfair coverage, that the Antitrust Division of the Justice Department be used to investigate news organizations, and that the Internal Revenue Service be loosed upon the newspapers and networks considered most hostile to the president. [43] (Misuse of federal agencies comprised the second article of impeachment voted by the House Judiciary Committee.)

In public Clay Whitehead attacked reporters for engaging in what he called "elitist gossip" and "ideological plugola" and suggested that local stations "jump on the networks" over their supposed bias. [44] Klein's operation was put to work stimulating letters supporting the president's position to Congress and newspapers. One Washington woman alone wrote fifty to sixty letters a week, which were then sent out to Republican loyalists across the country to sign with their own names and forward to the target papers and representatives. A staff of sixteen speechwriters was available when the administration decided that one of its officials should blast its critics. A computerized mailing list of more than 150,000 names was developed so the White House could flood supporters with information useful to any "grass roots" campaign they wished to undertake. This list was individualized, so that by pushing the right buttons the administration could "mail to middle-aged black dentists or the presidents of small Midwestern colleges or whatever."[45]

It is difficult to obtain exact figures on the size of the staff in the White House charged with promoting the image of the administration. As David Wise points out, no official has the words "public relations" in his or her title. Jeb Stuart Magruder tells us that he was able to expand Herb Klein's (later Ken W. Clawson's) Office of Communications staff from four to twelve assistants. Ron Ziegler had his own aides, Charles Colson built his own mini-empire, Patrick Buchanan not only prepared the president's daily news briefing but also helped write speeches, and there was a television adviser as well as a staff of official photographers. The estimates for the totals of all persons engaged in one or another of these public relations areas in the Nixon administration range from sixty to one hundred.[46] When the cabinet secretaries who from time to time spoke for the administration and all of the "information officers" and "executive assistants" in the departments with publicity functions are added to this number, the total becomes truly awesome. It is clear that no other branch of government can come close to matching the scope of PR activities carried out on behalf of the executive. This is important, not only for individual disputes between the branches where public relations can sway the outcome, but also in creating a public climate of expectations focused on the presidency. The more they "sell" and convince the people that only the chief executive is in a position to solve the nation's problems, the more power ultimately flows to the president and his assistants.

Gerald Ford began his administration promising openness and frankness. Reporters have seen this as a welcome change from the Nixon administration policies. David Kennerly, the President's official photographer, has a staff of seven assistants helping get photos of the first family out to the media, and Ron Nessen, the press spokesman, has forty-five aides. On his first day in office,

Ford personally went to the White House newsroom to introduce his first press secretary, Jerald F. terHorst, to those covering the White House. This indicated the importance that the new president attached to friendly relations with the media and his realization of what can happen to an administration when the press comes to view with suspicion the statements issued in its name. Ford had witnessed at first hand the lack of credibility of Nixon's spokesman, Ron Ziegler, who had to admit that he had "misspoken" himself and that past declarations were "inoperative."

The new president did not abjure attempts to use the media, however. His PR staff is even larger than Nixon's. Just three weeks before the fall 1974 Congressional elections, Mr. Ford announced that he would be making an important economic address to the Future Farmers of America in Kansas City and that all of the people could benefit from hearing his suggestions for controlling inflation and saving energy. After examining his proposed remarks, all three networks decided against broadcasting the speech. The administration then formally requested, and received, live coverage of the address. (No formal presidential request has ever been refused by the networks). The beginning of the third game of the World Series had to be delayed for fifteen minutes to allow the president to complete his remarks. In the speech, the president's listeners were urged to plant vegetable gardens, drive slowly, shop wisely, and clean up their plates. The next day the president also let it be known that he would be available for exclusive interviews with television reporters for the first time in his administration. Critics charged that this was an attempt to dominate the television screen prior to the election.

As Johnson and Nixon complained, reporters do to a degree define situations for the public. The Tet offensive by the North Vietnamese was seen as a failure by LBJ because their forces could not hold any of the gains they had made. Newsmen and television reporters, however, saw the offensive as a success, as proof that the back of the Viet Cong had not been broken. Evidently the majority of the American people viewed it this way as well, despite the president's attempts to persuade them otherwise. In their pursuit of truth as they see it, the press (and especially television) may have a real impact on how the public interprets events, what conclusions it draws, and what it thinks about and sees in a particular situation.

Every recent administration has begun with a pledge of openness. Despite these good intentions, it usually does not work out this way. Part of the reason lies in what the press considers news stories—usually conflicts, controversies, scandals, disputes, or complaints. Thus instead of insuring a good press, openness may sometimes bring to public view matters which reflect badly on an administration. Rather than reporting on how well most policies are succeeding (a difficult chore and usually not very exciting), the press frequently concentrates on what has gone wrong. This is of course necessary to keep the public informed and hold government responsible for its mistakes, but from the politician's standpoint it often seems unfair.

Harry Truman was open to his aides, members of Congress, the press, and the people. Yet no President, including Richard Nixon in the midst of Watergate, fell lower in the opinion polls. Candor and frankness seem very attractive in retrospect, but they did not do much for Truman during his incumbency. (It is illustrative of the reverence for the institution of the presidency that this most unpopular of chief executives is now remembered fondly by the American people and rated as one of the "near-greats" by historians.) George McGovern also discovered that, although the press may clamor for openness, the provision of it may result in disaster for a campaign. Every complaint by third-level officials in the McGovern organization was picked up by the press and spread across the United States. The result was the image of an internally divided, bickering, disorganized campaign structure and a candidate who couldn't even keep his own house in order. This of course resulted from the almost total access which the press had to the McGovern organization. (He has said since that if he were ever to run again he would keep the press more at arm's length.) On the other hand, Nixon's inpenetrable campaign received an excellent press, with few damaging stories on the Committee to Re-elect the President emerging until after the election was over. Despite the enormity of the crimes that went on, there were few reporters engaged in the investigative reporting. that might have exposed the situation earlier. Instead

Washington-based reporters and the White House press corps dutifully covered the campaign as Nixon wanted it covered. Future candidates may well learn the lessons to be drawn from this experience by running "closed" as opposed to "open" election campaigns.

Unauthorized leaks of opinions or information from within their administrations have frustrated most recent presidents. Such leaks spoil the image of a united front, convey impressions the president doesn't want broadcast, indicate that some "high officials" disagree with the policy of the chief executive, foreclose the desired element of surprise, or narrow the "options" of the president. Lyndon Johnson is said to have been so infuriated with such disclosures that he would change plans if his original intentions leaked out before he was ready to announce them. If it became known that he intended to appoint John Jones to the Federal Communications Commission, a story to that effect in the newspapers could result in another person being appointed in his stead. (The story floated around Washington that some rumors were deliberately started with the very purpose of insuring that John Jones *not* be appointed.) Even the news of when he intended to leave for the LBJ ranch is said to have resulted in altered travel plans by the president. He would then deny that decisions had been firmly made and maintain that the leaked hour and date for departure had merely been among one of the "options" under consideration.

More serious evidence of the frustration experienced over unauthorized leaks came with the wiretaps on White House aides and newsmen that began in the first year of the Nixon administration. Later the plumbers were organized to plug leaks. What seems to have set off the first wave of this spying was a news story in the *New York Times* on May 9, 1969, dealing with the secret (from the American people) bombing of Cambodia. The president asserted that this information could only have come from within the National Security Council and thus the defense of the nation would be compromised unless the leaks were shut off. The taps began in that month and lasted until February 1971 but never did turn up the persons guilty of leaking. As Nixon told John Dean on February 28, 1973, "They never helped us. Just gobs and gobs and gobs of material: gossip and bull shitting."* Nor were the taps authorized by court order as is required in ordinary criminal cases. Rather they were approved by the president acting under a claim of "inherent power" to protect the security of the United States. At least one of the original seventeen taps (there were thirteen on White House staffers and four on reporters) was continued for nineteen months after the FBI had concluded that it had discovered nothing concerning national security. This tap remained on the private telephone of Morton Halperin for months after he had left the White House and had gone to work for the then leading Democratic challenger to the president, Edmund Muskie. Political information thus gathered was passed on to H. R. Haldeman, the president's chief of staff.

One of these "national security" taps was placed on the phone of William Safire, a presidential speechwriter; another on Jamie McLane, an expert on problems of the aging; and yet another on a White House lawyer, John Sears. None of these people had access to the security information that supposedly prompted the investigation in the first place. They were, however, known to consort with members of the press, and this in itself was reason for suspicion by some White House officials.[47] By 1974 all White House staff members were ordered to report their contacts with the press to presidential assistant Ronald Ziegler. Administration spokesman Gerald Warren told reporters that it was not the purpose of the new policy to intimidate officials from talking to the media, nor was it a form of censorship, but rather merely a policy designed to keep the White House press office informed

---

* This is the same man who as a candidate for the presidency against John Kennedy criticized former President Truman in the televised debate of Oct. 13, 1960 with these words: "I can only say that I'm very proud that President Eisenhower restored dignity and decency and, frankly, good language to the conduct of the Presidency of the United States, and I only hope that, should I win this election, that I could approach President Eisenhower in maintaining the dignity of the office; in seeing to it that whenever any mother or father talks to his child, he can look at the man in the White House and . . . say: 'Well, there is a man who maintains the kind of standards personally that I would want my child to follow.'" The texts of these debates are printed in Sidney Kraus, ed., *The Great Debates* (Bloomington: Indiana University Press, 1962). The quote is from p. 397.

about the concerns of reporters and the kinds of questions they were asking.[48] The policy has been dropped under Ford.

One other instance of presidential concern with leaks will suffice to demonstratrate the point. This had to do with yet another story in the *New York Times*, published in July 1971 and dealing with the administration's fall-back position in the SALT negotiations with the Soviet Union. This leak, the president informed Egil Krogh and John Ehrlichman on July 24 of that year, "does affect the national security—this particular one. This isn't like the Pentagon papers." The president then discussed subjecting everybody in the administration with TOP SECRET clearance to lie detector tests to discover the person or persons guilty of the leak. "I don't care whether he's a hawk or a dove or a ————. If the son-of-a-bitch leaked, he's not for the government. . . . I've studied these cases long enough, and it's always a son of a bitch that leaks," Nixon told his listeners. He went on to say that it didn't matter if one million people had to take lie detectors: "Listen, I don't know anything about polygraphs and I don't know how accurate they are but I know they'll scare the hell out of people."[49] With such measures, it was evidently hoped, only "official" stories (and favorable leaks) would ever come out of the White House. The administration could speak with one voice, and that voice would convey a scenario worked out for its maximum public relations impact.

There is no doubt that presidential access to the media and the successes of recent chief executives in utilizing it in furthering their goals has added immensely to their ability to lead the people and shape opinion. Frederick Wilhelmsen and Jane Bret argue that "the governed are not so preoccupied at [sic] *what* is done by its elected representatives, as *how* they do it."[50] This has led to a preoccupation with "image" not only during campaigns but between elections as well. Speeches and policies (or the semblance of policies) may be crafted as much for their intended impact on the viewer as for their revelation of governmental intentions. Those best adapted to the TV medium by their "physical appearance . . . poise, assertiveness, determination, reaction to pressure, and all the various complex attributes that go into making up [their] particular 'style'"[51] hold a tremendous advantage over those less suited for the TV cameras. When a president has such a style (or at least learns to project it), he can, because of his unmatched access to national TV, dominate the political arena.

An example of the impact of presidential television in helping shape the outcome of events in the United States occurred in the election year of 1972. In the spring of that year, Democratic candidates for their party's nomination, including George McGovern, Hubert Humphrey, Edmund Muskie, and George Wallace, were busily cutting each other up in the primaries. Richard Nixon, on the other hand, could concentrate on playing the greatly respected presidential role before millions of viewers. As we have seen earlier, his popularity at the beginning of 1972 was only around 49 percent. But he then did something that only a president could do, and he did it on nationwide television. He went to China to improve relations with that country, and later to the Soviet Union. More than seventy tons of broadcast equipment had been flown to China for this television event. Forty-one hours of live coverage were provided during the next seven days to an estimated 100 million viewers in the United States. The American people saw the president walk along the Great Wall of China and watched him being toasted by Premier Chou En-lai at a lavish banquet. The president's arrivals both in China and back in the United States were staged during prime time.[52] The next public opinion poll showed that the president's approval rating had gone up to 57 percent, and with the equally well covered Russian trip this increased to 61 percent. No Democratic challenger stood a chance after that, whether he had been McGovern, Muskie, or another candidate. As Fred Friendly, former president of CBS news has said:

> The drafters of the American Constitution strove diligently to prevent the power of the president from becoming a monopoly, but our inability to manage television has allowed the medium to be converted into an electronic throne.
>
> No mighty king, no ambitious emperor, no pope, or prophet ever dreamt of such an awesome pulpit, so potent a magic wand. In the American experiment with its delicate checks and balances, this device permits the First Amendment and the very heart of the Constitution to be breached, as it bestows on one politician a weapon denied to all others.[53]

The president can effectively set the agenda, as well as the parameters of acceptable solutions, for the problems he chooses to bring to the forefront of public attention. Ben Bagdikian tells us of how Kennedy was able in the first five minutes of a televised news conference in 1962 to demolish the opposition to his attempts to get the steel industry to roll back their new price increases. Before the editorial writers or the steel executives themselves could even formulate a defense against the president, "the general public, or that part of it that saw television and heard radio that same day, had an opinion, based on the words and image of the president himself in their living rooms."[54] By the same token, Kennedy's speech to the nation during the Cuban missile crisis effectively foreclosed as serious possibilities either the direct invasion of Cuba or a milder reaction than the one he announced.

When the president schedules an address to the nation, the people assume that his message must be of great importance. When he takes to the air waves, it is now expected that he will serve as the nation's single national spokesman. Radio and television have played a major role in perpetuating a circular pattern of these expectations: the president is the focus of attention because he is powerful; the more attention that is focused on him, the more it is expected that he should solve the nation's problems; and the more powerful he ultimately becomes. He now can go directly to the citizens with appeals for support against Congress or any other institution and count on a sizable favorable response. The result has been yet another major accretion to his ability to ignore the separation of powers and the checks and balances thought so necessary by the authors of the American Constitution.

The Effects of Vietnam and Watergate

If the above assertions and findings about socialization and the media are correct, how do we account for the fates of Presidents Johnson and Nixon? The first was forced to retire from office in 1968 when he was constitutionally eligible to run for reelection, and the second became one of the most unpopular presidents in our history (or at least since pollsters have been able to measure these things). Rarely have the American people suspected their presidents of criminal behavior, and before Nixon never had one been forced from office in midterm. Even Andrew Johnson, who faced the fury of the Radical Reconstructionists after the trauma of the Civil War, was able to avoid conviction in the Senate and to serve out the remainder of his term. Lyndon Johnson and Richard Nixon were presidents in an era when they could dominate national attention as their early predecessors could not. They had the advantage of huge public relations staffs; they could command free and immediate access to almost every American home via television; they were the inheritors of the relatively new but widely shared academic and popular belief in the permanently dominant presidency; and they were the beneficiaries of the socialization process of the last forty years that has placed the chief executive above all others in the political system.

The question of their failures admits of no ready answer, but several possible explanations offer themselves for consideration. It has already been seen that television is a mixed blessing for those without the personality, style, or training for its use. Neither Johnson nor Nixon had natural talent for the cameras, and the former was never able to master the technique of successfully projecting the kind of image he wanted to convey to the American people. After his poor showing in the first televised debate with John Kennedy, Nixon spent considerable time and effort in learning how better to utilize the medium. One of the television advisers he hired in 1968, Roger Ailes, discussed why Nixon needed a "new" image:

> Let's face it, a lot of people think Nixon is dull. Think he's a bore, a pain in the ass. They look at him as the kind of kid who always carried a bookbag. Who was forty-two years old the day he was born. They figure other kids got footballs for Christmas, Nixon got a briefcase and loved it. He'd always have his homework done and he'd never let you copy.
>
> Now you put him on television, you've got a problem right away. He's a funny looking guy. He looks like somebody hung him in a closet over night and he jumps out in the morning with his suit all bunched up and starts running around saying "I want to be President." I mean this is how he strikes some people. That's why these shows are important. To make them forget all that.[55]

Nixon was an apt pupil, learning his television lessons well. But despite his early intentions, perhaps he, like Johnson, overused the medium as president. The dramatic impact of an occasional interruption of regularly scheduled programs for some momentous presidential announcement is debased when it becomes almost routine to see the president supplanting the shows people are accustomed to watching. The frequency of his appearances suggests that perhaps this did occur.

Nixon became so committed to television coverage that in some cases his judgment seemed to be lacking. Spiro Agnew had just been forced to plead no contest to a criminal charge when the President staged a gala TV extravaganza for his "man who" speech nominating Gerald Ford to be Agnew's successor. The speech seemed to many to be more fitting for a political convention in happy times than for a period in which the second-in-command in the administration had been publicly disgraced. Even at the end, Nixon allowed live coverage of his farewell address to his cabinet and staff, a moment that seemingly called for privacy for the emotions expressed.

Paradoxically, it may have been President Nixon's success in routinizing summit meetings and in improving relations with Russia and China that drained his trips to foreign countries of their rallying potential in the final months of his administration. With tensions and fears reduced, many felt less compulsion to watch their peripatetic chief executive. At the same time, allegations of corruption and abuse of power gradually began to take on meaning for increasing numbers of citizens. Daily stories about new confessions or indictments of some of the president's closest aides may have bored many, but their cumulative impact quite obviously eroded confidence in his leadership. Television also worked against Johnson and Nixon in another way. "Johnson's war," with all of its frustrations, was brought nightly in living color to almost every American home. For Nixon, the televised Senate Watergate hearings exposed the viewers not only to new folk heroes in the legislative branch like Senators Ervin and Baker but also to John Dean, John Ehrlichman, Bob Haldeman, John Mitchell, and others with whom Nixon had surrounded himself. Individual judgments about these aides were formed by the viewers, but many did not like what they saw and heard. It may be because the American people expect so much of the president, and have come to believe so wholeheartedly in the myths of office, that revelations of possible wrongdoing or the inability to get us out of a protracted war shatter their illusions and make the incumbent seem that much more unworthy of wearing the mantle handed down from Washington and Lincoln.

In fact it is nearly impossible for any president to live up to the images that are implanted in childhood (or for that matter even the TV version of the presidency). If that indeed is the case, many are sure to be disappointed with the current possessor of the office, whoever he may be. Besides the president's necessarily making enemies by choosing among alternatives, this reasoning goes, the more the people learn of the "real" man (as opposed to the "ideal" they thought they were electing), the more unfavorable they are apt to become toward him. The textbook versions of our heroes came without warts; once the new president's honeymoon period with the press is over, citizens may be inundated with stories to the effect that the man they selected is a veritable toad. (Reporters, despite their supposed cynicism, are as much believers in the myth as are ordinary citizens. They too become disillusioned when a president fails to live up to the exaggerated model against which politicians in the highest office are judged).

What of the attitudes of children? Have the Vietnam War and Watergate massively altered the kind of idealization of the presidency discovered by earlier studies? It should be remembered that Easton and Dennis posited: "Early idealization may create latent feelings that are hard to undo or shake off. This is the major significance of the first bond to the system through the Presidency. The positive feelings for political authority generated there can be expected to have lasting consequences."[56] Can it be implied that a generation of children learning political values during the Johnson and Nixon administrations have come to distrust political authority, with profound implications for future political stability? Has the ultimate legitimacy of the system itself been damaged? It is of course too early to offer definitive answers to these questions. There has not been sufficient passage of time to study the long-range implications of the events of the last two administrations. However some preliminary studies have been conducted, and they may provide insights into the continuing process of socialization after Watergate.

Even before the events of recent years, some groups of children in the society did not share the broad cultural belief in the benevolence of authority. For instance, white children in the relatively poor rural area of Appalachia were much less favorably disposed toward political objects than were the children studied in much of the rest of the country.[57] Differences also exist to a degree for black children.[58] The latest findings present something of a changed picture for young people growing up today in white, middle-class America as well. Howard Tolley found, for instance, children much more willing to criticize a president for involving America in war.[59] In a 1969–1970 survey Fred Greenstein, however, discovered young people still to be *"extraordinarily positive in their spontaneous descriptions of the President."*[60] The "benevolent leader imagery" of earlier socialization studies still persisted in those he surveyed. These were some of the responses he received. "If a person is going to be the head of a country like the United States for four years, he just has to be about perfect." "He tries to help his country. Like if there's a war on he tries to stop it or he tries to win it, and he tries to do the best for his people in things that will . . . that will do good." "[He] tries to make America a better place to live." "[He] tries to make things equal and fair."[61] Thus Vietnam, for all of its unpopularity, did not seem to effect seriously the idealization of the presidency in the abstract, at least among the children in this survey. It was not that these students couldn't imagine the chief executive breaking the law when an imaginary case of lawbreaking was presented to them. Rather, many of them saw the president as being above the law.

In a follow-up survey in early June 1973, Greenstein sought to explore the effects of Watergate on the attitudes of children toward the president. This, it should be recalled, was during the televised Watergate hearings (but before the testimony of John Dean). At the time, the president's approval rate among the general population stood at 44 percent, while his disapproval rate was 45 percent. Many of the seventh-grade students surveyed mentioned Watergate spontaneously, as the interviewers had been instructed not to bring the subject up and not to probe if the children should do so. But at the same time, many of the idealized stereotypes so prevalent in earlier studies were repeated by these students. "He makes sure that the laws are fair and that people are governed fairly." "He tries to help people, he tries to stop crime and everything." "He tries to stop pollution and he finished the war in Vietnam, and he does lots of stuff that's good." "Well he makes some good laws and some not-so-good laws. *But you should obey him anyhow.*" [62] Overall levels of affect and idealization had decreased from 56 percent positive (with 1 percent negative) before Watergate to 45 percent positive (and 7 percent negative) after Watergate.

The most striking change noted in these findings was an increase both in the percentage of children enunciating the norm that all people are equal before the law and at the same time in the feeling that the president is above the law. The post-Watergate survey found 58 percent stating this belief. Sometimes the same child mentioned both assumptions. Greenstein's interpretation is that rather than merely having a disillusioning effect on young people, Watergate has led to a view of the president as being unresponsive: "The climate of political communication during a period when an unresponsive President is widely viewed as having been implicated in an unraveling scandal may be to encourage fatalism and quiescence toward presidential authority." [63] Thus preliminary studies indicate that idealization of the presidential role continues despite all that has happened in recent years, but that this is now coupled with an image of a chief executive unencumbered by legal restraints binding on others in the political system. What the consequences of such attitudes will be on the political life of America in the years to come remains to be seen.

While Greenstein still found many children with positive attitudes toward the president, Christopher Arterton in a December 1973 survey of third, fourth, and fifth graders discovered many more with negative ones. "The once benevolent leader has been transformed into the malevolent leader by the impact of current events," [64] he wrote. Utilizing many of the questions from the Easton and Dennis survey of the early sixties (cited earlier), the change in responses was dramatic in the December 1973 survey. For instance, in 1962, 21 percent of the fifth graders said the president "is my favorite of all." This had decreased to 2 percent in the Arterton study. Conversely, whereas only 8 percent rated the president as "not one of my favorites" in the Easton and Dennis study, this figure had increased to 64 percent in 1973. Almost all of the positive affective components of their attitudes toward the chief executive had been drained away, but not their beliefs in his power. Cynicism and rejection of the president were the key elements observed in these children.[65]

The impact of Watergate on children's attitudes toward the president was seen in other responses in this survey as well. Whereas only 22 percent of the fifth graders in 1962 said the "government has too much power" this belief had increased to 42 percent by 1973. The conviction that "the government meddles too much in our private lives" more than doubled, from 17 to 35 percent. What were once considered to be distrusting, conservative attitudes toward government were now widely shared by these children. The conclusion to be drawn is that individual presidents and political events (and not just the presidential role) are important factors in the socialization process. If, as Easton and Dennis maintain, the chief executive is the early mechanism through which children are socialized to diffuse support for the entire political system, then a generation growing up believing their president is "truly malevolent, undependable, untrustworthy, yet powerful and dangerous" could be expected to behave politically far differently from its predecessors.[66]

Arterton points us toward a different explanation for both the 1962 and 1973 findings, however. Citing Lawrence Kohlberg's work on the moral development of children, he speculates that these students may be in a stage of "pre-conventional thinking." That is, they tend to see things in terms of absolutes—a president is thus all "good" (like Eisenhower and Kennedy in the early studies) or all "bad" (like Nixon). This could account for the positive evaluations across the board in the studies of Easton, Hess, Dennis, et al. some time ago, as well as the negative feelings in recent years. If this is the case, the resignation of Richard Nixon in the summer of 1974 could mean a return to near the former levels of youthful idealization of the presidency (or at least for as long as Gerald Ford maintains public confidence). Since children now react more negatively not only to the president but to other political figures and institutions as well, however, it may be that Watergate has had a permanent effect on attachment to the political system generally.[67]

We can only speculate as to the reasons for the more positive reactions found in the Greenstein study than in the Arterton one. While the former conducted his interviews in June 1973, the latter carried his out in December of that year. In that time period, the president's popularity had slipped to 29 percent among the general population, and this could have had an impact on the children's views. The questions and methodology of the surveys also differed, and thus their findings are not strictly comparable. Selection of the samples of children to be interviewed may also have contributed to somewhat different results. At the same time, it is important to remember that both studies did find widespread belief in a president essentially outside the control of the law—a powerful and nearly unrestrained leader not responsive to the wishes of the people. Since democratic governments must be based on trust between the people and their leaders, any permanent adherence to this kind of belief could result in the instability of government itself. Perhaps the forced resignation of Nixon will lead to altered images of just how independent of popular control a president can be.

Have some of the myths of the presidency been destroyed by the administrations of Lyndon Johnson and Richard Nixon? Or do the people adhere as strongly as ever to these beliefs and simply view the incumbents of the last ten years as betrayers of the dream? It may well be the case (although little empirical evidence exists on this point) that the public has become so imbued with the image of the heroic presidency that many believe their problems could be solved and America set straight again if only the right person could be found to fill the office—the "right" person being in this instance one in the gallant mold of the past presidential greats. This search for the ideal is almost sure to be disillusioning. Although campaigns are able to convince millions that their candidates are indeed the possessors of all the attributes of greatness, the realities of insoluble problems and inadequate responses once in office nearly assure frustrations for the electorate. The people have learned to expect too much from their president, to believe that he can accomplish almost anything. This may be one of the greatest dangers in the presidency of the hyperbolic imagination—centering all hopes and expectations on the institution guarantees that no one will be able to measure up. In the real world there are few magical solutions, and the only people who can match the legendary feats of past presidents are themselves chimerical creations of the myth makers.

In the future, some president well suited for television by personality, training, or style may be able to project the image of the exaggerated heroes of the past. If this ability is united with the knowledge of how to charm rather than bludgeon Congress and how to use the institutional pride and sensibilities of the legislature rather than flaunt his own hubris, there is no telling how much power such a person could accumulate and what he would be able to do with it. Although Gerald Ford himself may not pose a serious threat to democracy, recent experience has demonstrated that the country may not always be so fortunate. The elevation of the presidency to a position approaching divine right power, coupled with the monarchical reverence afforded the institution by the people, provides the matrix for the ultimate peril to a free society.

NOTES

1. David Easton and Robert D. Hess, "The Child's Political World," *Midwest Journal of Political Science*, no. 3 (August 1962), 231.

2. *Ibid.*, p. 237.

3. *Ibid.*, p. 241.

4. *Ibid.*, pp. 241–242.

5. Fred I. Greenstein, "The Benevolent Leader: Children's Images of Political Authority," *The American Political Science Review*, no. 4 (December 1960), 939.

6. See David Easton and Jack Dennis, "The Child's Image of Government," *The Annals of the American Academy of Political and Social Science*, 361 (September 1965), 40–57. The other pictures from which the children could choose were a policeman, Uncle Sam, the Supreme Court, the Capitol, the flag, and the Statue of Liberty.

7. Robert D. Hess and Judith V. Torney, *The Development of Political Attitudes in Children* (Chicago: Aldine, 1967), pp. 37–50.

8. David Easton and Jack Dennis, *Children in the Political System* (New York: McGraw-Hill, 1969), pp. 185–186.

9. *Ibid.*, pp. 193–200.

10. Hess and Torney, p. 214.

11. Greenstein, p. 942. The linkage between early learning and later behavior has been the subject of debate among political scientists in recent years. See, for instance, Donald D. Searing, Joel J. Schwartz, and Allen E. Lind, "The Structuring Principle: Political Socialization and Belief Systems," *American Political Science Review*, no. 2 (June 1973), and the letters that followed that article in subsequent issues.

12. Fred I Greenstein, "Popular Images of the President," *American Journal of Psychiatry*, 122, no. 5 (November 1965), 523–529.

13. Paul B. Sheatsley and Jacob J. Feldman, "The Assassination of President Kennedy: A Preliminary Report on Public Reactions and Behavior," *Public Opinion Quarterly*, 28 (Summer 1964), 189–215.

14. Roberta S. Sigel, "Image of the American Presidency: Part II of an Exploration into Popular Views of Presidential Power," *Midwest Journal of Political Science*, 10, no. 1 (February 1966), 123–137.

15. *Ibid.*

16. *Ibid.*

17. See Robert S. Erikson and Norman R. Luttbeg, *American Public Opinion: Its Origins, Content, and Impact* (New York: Wiley, 1973), pp. 155–156, and the studies cited therein.

18. John E. Mueller, "Presidential Popularity from Truman to Johnson," *The American Political Science Review*, no. 1 (March 1970), 21.

19. Eriksen and Luttbeg, p. 155, and *Seattle Post-Intelligencer*, 26 May 1975.

20. Gallup surveys reported in *Newsweek*, 28 August 1972, p. 16. Daniel Yankelovich's polls indicate that it was the two summit meetings, and not McGovern's candidacy, that had convinced a majority of people to vote for the president, and this was long before the Democrats even had a candidate. See Daniel Yankelovich, "Why Nixon Won," *New York Review of Books*, 30 November 1972, p. 7.

21. John E. Mueller, *War Presidents and Public Opinion* (New York: Wiley, 1973), pp. 69–70.

22. *Los Angeles Times*, 28 October 1973.

23. Mueller, "Presidential Popularity from Truman to Johnson," p. 21.

24. Elmer E. Cornwell, Jr., *Presidential Leadership of Public Opinion* (Bloomington: Indiana University Press, 1965), pp. 272–274.

25. Cited in Bernard Rubin, *Political Television* (Belmont, Calif.: Wadsworth, 1967), p. 115.

26. Eric F. Goldman, *The Tragedy of Lyndon Johnson* (New York: Dell, 1968), ch. 16.

27. Lyndon B. Johnson, *The Vantage Point* (New York: Popular, 1971), p. 95.

28. Joe McGinniss, *The Selling of the President 1968*, (New York: Trident Press, 1969), pp. 30–31.

29. *Ibid.*, p. 30.

30. Newton N. Minow, John B. Martin, and Lee M. Mitchell, *Presidential Television* (New York: Basic Books, 1973), pp. 44–45.

31. David Wise, *The Politics of Lying* (New York: Random House, 1973), p. 256.

32. Dan Nimmo, *The Political Persuaders* (Englewood Cliffs, N.J.: Prentice-Hall, 1970), p. 145. See also the interview with Lady Bird Johnson rpt. in Harold Mendelsohn and Irving Crespi, *Polls, Television, and the New Politics* (Scranton, Pa.: Chandler, 1970), p. 267.

33. Presidential news conference, *Weekly Compilation of Presidential Documents*, 9, no. 43 (29 October, 1973), 1291.

34. James Keogh, *President Nixon and the Press*, (New York: Funk & Wagnalls, 1972), p. 45.

35. For these figures see Wise, pp. 246, 312.

36. Minnow *et al.*, p. 56.

37. *Ibid.*, pp. 63–64.

38. *New York Times*, 30 April 1974.

39. Jeb Stuart Magruder, *An American Life* (New York: Atheneum, 1974), p. 5.

40. Speech to Sigma Delta Chi, 18 December 1972, quoted in Wise, p. 276.

41. Memo from Charles Colson to Herb Klein, reprinted as Exhibit No. 13 in *The Final Report of the Select Committee on Presidential Campaign Activities*, Senate, 93rd Cong., 2nd Sess., June 1974, pp. 281–283. Hereafter referred to as *Final Report*.

42. Memo reprinted in Magruder, p. 106.

43. *Ibid.*, p. 85. See also *Final Report*, Exhibit No. 10, pp. 267–268.

44. *New York Times*, 17 December 1973.

45. Magruder, p. 95.

46. The figure of sixty PR aides is from Wise, p. 198, and the estimate of one hundred is made by Thomas E. Cronin in "The Swelling of the Presidency," *Saturday Review of the Society*, 1, no. 1 (February 1973), 36.

47. Material developed by the House Judiciary Committee while investigating possible impeachment charges against the president, reported in the *New York Times*, 23 March 1974 and 7 June 1974.

48. *New York Times*, 22 January 1974.

49. "Transcript Prepared by the Impeachment Inquiry Staff for the House Judiciary Committee of a Recording of a Meeting . . . July 24,

THE PEOPLE AND PRESIDENTIAL POWER

1971 . . . ," *Hearings Before the Committee on the Judiciary, Statement of Information,* House of Representatives, 93rd Cong. 2nd Sess., Document 52. 2, VII-XX (May/June 1974), 867–885.

50. Frederick D. Wilhelmsen and Jane Bret, *Telepolitics* (Plattsburg, N.Y.: Tundra, 1972), p. 214.

51. Mendelsohn and Crespi, p. 268.

52. Minow et al., pp. 66–68.

53. Fred W. Friendly in his forward to Minnow et al., pp. vii-viii.

54. Ben H. Bagdikian, *The Effete Conspiracy* (New York: Harper & Row, 1972), p. 100.

55. McGinniss, p. 103.

56. Easton and Dennis, *Children in the Political System,* p. 207.

57. See Dean Jaros, Herbert Hirsch, and Frederic J. Fleron, Jr., "The Malevolent Leader: Political Socialization in an American Sub-Culture," *American Political Science Review,* LXII, No. 2 (June 1968), 564–575.

58. See, for instance, Charles E. Billings, "Black Student Activism and Political Socialization," paper presented at the 1971 American Political Science Association meeting; Edward S. Greenberg, "Political Socialization to Support of the System," unpublished Ph.D. dissertation, University of Wisconsin, 1969; Charles S. Bullock III and Harrell R. Rodgers, Jr., eds., *Black Political Attitudes* (Chicago: Markham, 1972); James W. Clarke, "Family Structure and Political Socializaton among Urban Black Children," *American Journal of Political Science,* 17, no. 2 (May 1973), 302–315.

59. Howard Tolley, *Children and War: Socialization to International Conflict* (New York: Teachers College, 1973).

60. Fred I. Greenstein, "The Benevolent Leader Revisited: Children's Images of Political Leaders in Three Democracies," *American Political Science Review,* forthcoming, p. 36.

61. *Ibid.,* pp. 37–38.

62. *Ibid.,* pp. 60–61.

63. *Ibid.,* pp. 63–65.

64. F. Christopher Arterton, "The Impact of Watergate on Children's Attitudes toward Political Authority," *Political Science Quarterly,* 89, no. 2 (June 1974), 272.

65. *Ibid.,* pp. 276–277.

66. *Ibid.,* pp. 281–286.

67. *Ibid.,* p. 287.

4

Elevation and Isolation
in the White House

It is tempting to write off Watergate as the product of an overzealous staff functioning under a president with a unique penchant for selecting the wrong people. If this is the assumption, then the whole episode can be dismissed as an aberration in the otherwise long and successful history of the American presidency. The problem is that there remains the task of explaining how such a man could come to hold the office in the first place, and why he was reelected by one of the largest majorities in American history. Surely no politician was more familiar to the electorate than Richard Nixon. It had seen him over a period of twenty-five years as he moved through his "six crises," many of them on television. The people had also witnessed successive incarnations of "new" Nixons, and "new, new" Nixons, often before they had had an opportunity to forget the "old" Nixon. Even for those without interest in politics, it was impossible to escape the daily coverage of Nixon as president both in print and in the broadcast media. Could it be, then, that the defect lay in the electorate, who had voted for a candidate with such disqualifying characteristics? This too could be rationalized, for in the words of one of the greatest presidents: "You can fool all of the people some of the time, and some of the people all of the time. . . ."

But perhaps the flaw lay in the political parties that offered the people the kind of candidates who in retrospect seem so unsuited for the office. Such an explanation neatly disposes not only of

Richard Nixon but of Lyndon Johnson as well (another unpopular incumbent prone to mistakes in office). For both of these politicians first served their parties as vice-presidential candidates selected to "balance" the tickets on which they ran. Thus, in 1952 there was little contention that the hard-line, aggressive young senator from California was fitted for the presidency, just as in 1960 few believed that the former Senate majority leader would do anything but finish out his political career in the relative obscurity of the vice-presidency. But if nothing else, these two men were judged by their contemporaries to be shrewd political men, capable of maximizing their advantages with the resources at hand.

Once in the presidency, however, with unmatched opportunities to use the leverage of the office, each stumbled badly into mistakes even ordinary politicians should have been able to avoid. Lyndon Johnson stubbornly pursued his course in Vietnam long after it became clear to most observers that his policies were doomed to failure and only served to divide the American people. He followed those policies to unpopularity and into political oblivion. Even before Watergate, Nixon had lost several of his battles needlessly, thus damaging his professional reputation among fellow politicians. The Haynsworth and Carswell nominations offer examples, as does his futile struggle to win approval for an American supersonic transport plane (SST).

There are seemingly inexplicable lapses in the political acumen of other recent chief executives as well. Franklin Roosevelt attempted to pack the Supreme Court and suffered greatly for his lack of sensitivity to how far any president could go. Harry Truman seized the steel plants. And John Kennedy approved the disasterous Bay of Pigs invasion.

To be sure, explanations for these political blunders that focus either on the individual character traits of the incumbents or on the weakness of the selection process of the political parties cannot be rejected out of hand. The personality of a president is an important factor in any administration.[1] Delegate selection procedures, primaries, and conventions have resulted in candidates chosen primarily for internal party reasons. In recent years, the Democrats have designated Lyndon Johnson, Hubert Humphrey, Edmund Muskie, George McGovern, and Thomas

Eagleton to carry their party's banners, while the Republicans have offered Barry Goldwater, William Miller, Richard Nixon, and Spiro Agnew (Gerald Ford was never seriously considered either for the top spot or the vice-presidency under the normal selection mechanism). In this chapter, however, the focus is on the institution of the presidency itself and how its operation may predispose those who labor there to serious errors of judgment.

Some recent authors have suggested that systemic conditions may be responsible for many of the questionable decisions emanating from the White House. If "Nixon's Nazis" (the term is William Saxbe's), as well as 'the best and the brightest" (David Halberstam, from the poet Shelley) produce policies resulting in the Bay of Pigs, Vietnam, the Saturday night massacre, and Watergate, then perhaps looking at the presidency as an institution can offer insight into how such conduct originates. George Reedy, himself a former White House staffer, has told us that "it is only an inference but an inescapable one that the White House is an institution which dulls the sensitivity of political men and ultimately reduces them to bungling amateurs in their basic craft—the art of politics."[2] If this kind of analysis is correct, then merely selecting "better" people to serve there would not eliminate the pitfalls awaiting any new administration (assuming for the moment it is known how to select better people). That is, individual aberrations may not be as important as the combination of presidential power with White House isolation, a combination that produces a system that almost assures the loss of touch with political reality for all who serve there. The first part of this chapter will deal with the perquisites of office and some possible consequences of treating the president in a manner once reserved for royalty. The second part discusses the operation of the staff system that functions in this atmosphere.

The Sun King

George Washington felt that the protocol he established for the office of the presidency would serve as precedent for those who were to follow. An aristocrat himself, he seemed convinced that the position of chief magistrate of the new nation should be afforded a measure of deference that would set it apart from all others. Accordingly, he decided not to accept any private invitations once he became president. Rather, he issued invitations to prominent citizens and political leaders to his own elegant dinners, parties, ceremonial receptions, and levees (defined by Webster's as "a morning reception held by a sovereign or person of high rank when rising from bed"), where he would bow to his guests instead of shaking hands as they entered. When he traveled, it was either in a splendid coach drawn by six matched horses or astride his own white horse with leopard-skin saddle blanket. John Adams would have gone even further with regard to protocol, since he evidently felt the office had been slighted when the House of Representatives decided against officially designating the President as "His highness, the President of the United States of America, and Protector of their Liberties."[3]

Thomas Jefferson abandoned the practice of bowing to his guests and instead relied on the simple handshake. This, as well as other of his policies, no doubt was to emphasize the equalitarian nature of his administration. The story is told of how the new president walked back to his rooming house after his inaugural (the White House was not yet completed and there was no official carriage or escort) only to find all of the places taken at the common table. At first no one stopped eating or indicated anyone of special importance was in their midst. Finally, a woman arose to offer Mr. Jefferson her seat, but the gentleman from Virginia declined and waited for a fellow boarder to finish his meal before taking his place at the table.[4] In the decades that ensued, it tended to be Jefferson's examples that were followed rather than Washington's. Even though some of those who came to occupy the White House could be considered aristocrats, and despite the prestige of the office, few believed that the current incumbent had to be singled out for magisterial treatment. Being born in a log cabin of humble origins was seen as an advantage in the popular imagination. In a democracy the president was merely *primus inter pares.* His conduct and decisions were not automatically accepted by unquestioning subjects, but rather evaluated by citizens. Even Washington had seen the necessity of keeping open the channels of communication between the masses of people and himself. Accordingly, he set aside time each week when any citizen desiring to do so could appraise the president of facts or opinions he felt the president should hear.

Early life in the White House was somewhat austere. John Adams spent the last few months of his administration there, but the building was not yet complete. His wife used the unfinished audience hall to dry the washing she had done and complained even that the outdoor privy had not been dug. Early presidents were not provided with servants, staff assistants had to be paid out of the chief executive's own pocket (or found a job in one of the departments), the Secret Service was not yet in existence to provide protection, and entertainment costs (even for state dinners) had to be born by the incumbent himself. The pay was $25,000 a year, a figure that was not increased until Grant became president after the Civil War. Not even transportation was provided by the federal government. The chief executive had to furnish his own horses and carriage. As a result, Thomas Jefferson left office $20,000 in debt. No funds were spent to protect or refurbish the private homes of presidents—security equipment at residences came only in 1968. The first men to serve in the office brought their own furniture to the White House, and some, like Monroe, left it there for future tenants. Finally, in the 1920s, an entertainment allowance was awarded each new incumbent, and under Truman meals for servants came under the federal budget as well.

These rather modest beginnings offer little hint of the life-style to which latter-day chief executives have become accustomed. As the power of the presidency grew, so did the perquisites that went along with attaining the office. The more public and congressional expectations came to be focused on the man occupying the White House, the more it seemed right that he should live in a manner beyond the means of other citizens. It has been claimed that Americans sorely miss having royalty that would enable them vicariously to enjoy the pageantry and privilege of rank. Perhaps modern chief executives and their families have come to serve that function for the people. It also seems clear to many that when a person must deal with the Soviets, assure peace in Cyprus, heal the divisions in society at home, cure inflation, and devise solutions to energy difficulties, every facility must be provided to remove the frustrations of everyday life from his shoulders.

What are some of the advantages of holding the office that Jefferson once referred to as that "splendid misery"?[5] To begin with, there is a $200,000 yearly salary, supplemented by a $50,000 expense allowance. The president lives rent-free in the 132-room White House cared for by seventy-five full-time staff employees. A budget now totalling more than $1.3 million pays the salaries of these carpenters, electricians, painters, plumbers (the kind who deal with pipes), masons, and domestics. On the staff are a housekeeper, five maids, two chefs, two cooks, two kitchen helpers, one pantry assistant, two laundrywomen, one seamstress, two storekeepers, one linen supervisor, four doormen, and five housemen. Anytime of the day or night, the president may order a gourmet meal or cottage cheese with ketchup (Nixon's favorite). A masseur is also in attendance, and a barber makes weekly trips to cut the presidential hair and that of privileged aides. Twenty-one gardeners at a cost of more than $200,000 a year are provided by the National Park Service. A $1.5 million "special projects" fund may be spent at the president's discretion, with the limitation that none of it is to go for additional staff salaries. Since the chief executive does not have to account for this money at all, the uses to which it has been put are not always known.

Within the confines of the White House grounds and the adjoining Executive Office Building, the president may bowl, work out in his gym, play tennis, putt on his green, cut flowers from the greenhouses, view virtually any movie he decides to order, be entertained at "command performances" by Hollywood and Broadway stars, read from the library kept fully stocked by the publishing industry, get a rubdown, take a sauna, pose for his official photographer, or swim in his pool. The latter exercise posed somewhat of a problem for Ford, since President Nixon had the pool covered and converted into a press room. Most recent incumbents have ordered renovations and additions, depending upon their own recreational interests and those of their families. Within a month of his inauguration, plans were being discussed for a $500,000 pool and physical fitness center for Gerald Ford. Given the recession, however, these plans were dropped and a $55,000 pool paid for by private contributions was substituted. All of the White House recreational activities are of course free of charge to the president and his guests.

If the chief executive tires of the White House grounds, he may decide on an excursion down the Potomac on one of the yachts kept in readiness by the navy for that purpose. He may choose between ninety-two and sixty-foot vessels for his dining and cruising pleasure. (Sometimes a president worried at the extravagance of all of this will order one of these boats into dry dock, or even on occasion put one up for sale.) To get even further away from the Executive Mansion, a trip to Camp David is always possible. Established as a rustic mountain retreat by Franklin Roosevelt and furnished with hand-me-down White House furniture, the hideaway was converted by Eisenhower into a comfortable resort. Eisenhower used the place as an alternate White House and changed the name from Shangri-La to Camp David, after his grandson. Nixon went even further, spending more than $1.5 million adding a new heated pool and otherwise converting the residence into a luxurious resort. The navy maintains security for this retreat, with one hundred fifty guards on duty. As it is only thirty minutes by helicopter from Washington and since it offered him a place to "get away," President Nixon averaged spending two or three nights a week there. It also served as a honeymoon cottage for his daughter Tricia and her new husband, Edward Cox. Aides to the president may use Camp David for vacations at presidential invitation. There they may enjoy bowling, archery, tennis, pool, skeet shooting, swimming, nature-trail hiking, or pitch-and-putt golf.

All presidents are expected to entertain foreign heads of state, visiting governmental leaders, and American notables. An allowance is now included in the federal budget to cover these expenses. State banquets, of which there were thirteen in 1973, however, are billed to the State Department. Artists and performers are usually invited to entertain the guests, and the honor is so great that stars will cancel scheduled performances in order to attend. In addition, continuous music is provided by the army, air force, navy, and marine bands. Smaller aggregations, such as the Army Chorus, the Air Force Strolling Strings, and the Navy Sea Chanters also play and sing for the visitors. These costs are born by the Defense Department. President Kennedy ordered the marine band to dress in bright red formal tunics for these special occasions.

President Nixon exceeded even Kennedy in the formality of White House pageantry. Evidently it was on one of his first trips abroad as president that Nixon became inspired by the resplen-

dence of Rumanian formal uniforms and determined that something should be done about the dress of the White House police. A
tailor was ordered to produce a costume befitting guards for a
royal family. The result (at first approved by the president)
reminded many of the Graustarkian grandeur of comic opera.
Peaked caps with leather bills were complemented by white
tunics crossed with a strap attached to the patent leather holster.
Dark pants with a single stripe down each leg and formal shoes
completed the ensemble. The resulting laughter forced cancellation of this dress, but a similar effect was achieved when the army
agreed to outfit a seventy-two-man unit in revolutionary-war–era
uniforms to serve as official escorts at White House functions.
Three marine guards in full dress uniform did nothing but open
limousine doors for arriving guests. "Herald pages" blowing
straight trumpets with banners draped underneath signaled the
arrival of the president and Mrs. Nixon. Processional music
accompanied the pair down the staircase, and "Ruffles and
Flourishes" and "Hail to the Chief" greeted them as they entered
the banquet room.[6] White-gloved waiters (no waitresses allowed)
served the food and wines in the White House. After entertainment there was usually dancing, sometimes until the wee hours of
the morning. President Nixon himself seldom danced but often
indicated as he left that he hoped his guests would stay as long as
they liked. Once again a march by one of the bands accompanied
the exit of the first family as they disappeared up the staircase.
The most expensive function ever held at the White House was a
party for the returned prisoners of war. The Defense Department
paid the bills.

One of the more costly items in maintaining the modern
presidency has to do with travel. The White House air armada
now includes five Boeing 707s (up from three under Johnson),
eleven Lockheed Jetstars, and sixteen soundproofed helicopters.° On order are four more medium-range jets. It is obvious
that the official $75,000-a-year travel budget barely scratches
the surface of what is actually spent. For instance, in 1973 a

---

°On one occasion, Lyndon Johnson, out on an excursion, was about to climb
into the wrong helicopter. When this was pointed out to him by a young marine,
the president fixed him with a steely stare and said, "Son, they're all my helicopters."

new *Spirit of '76* (rechristened *Air Force 1* under President Ford) was ordered for $7.5 million and then "reconfigured" on order of H. R. Haldeman. After that job was completed, Mrs. Nixon decided she did not like the arrangement of the cabins, since the staff had to walk through her quarters to reach the president's office. Another "reconfiguration" at a cost of $285,000 was carried out to eliminate this oversight.[7] At least three big jets make each trip—the president's own plane, a back-up aircraft, and a communications plane. The president's plane has sophisticated communications gear of its own, including eighteen telephones and two teletypewriters linked directly to the White House. Instantaneous contact with any part of the globe is guaranteed. Sometimes a giant cargo plane flies ahead with the bulletproof Lincoln limousine. Wherever the chief executive flies the air force clears the air lanes of other planes and flies sorties to insure safety from attack.

On a routine trip to San Clemente or Key Biscayne, as many as two hundred people would accompany the Nixons. Rather like when the Tsar moved from Moscow to the Winter Palace, this retinue included the president's top staff men plus their wives, Secret Service agents, mess stewards, eight White House telephone operators, members of the press corps, Mr. Nixon's valet and dog handler, and Mrs. Nixon's hairdresser. When they reached one of their estates, the permanent staff was already on hand. Several days before any of this occurred, an advance team would check on airport security, set up emergency medical facilities (including a supply of the president's blood type), and arrange for a fleet of limousines and marine chauffeurs. On duty would be bomb disposal squads, fire-fighting teams, rescue helicopters, and the Coast Guard. Navy frogmen checked surrounding waters for potential trouble, and a shark net was raised.[8] (One of the last perquisites to disappear when Mr. Nixon resigned from office was the Coast Guard cutter patrolling offshore from his villa. The public was also allowed back on the beach in front of his estate.) When a president goes into the ocean, he is surrounded by Secret Service agents swimming in unison on either side of him. In 1973 alone, Nixon made four round trips to San Clemente (staying a total of six weeks), and fifteen to Key Biscayne. Innumerable weekends and overnight stays were also spent at Camp David. Several helicopter flights were made to Grand Cay, an island retreat off the Florida coast belonging to a wealthy friend. Helicopter pads and an office were installed there for these visits.

When a president travels to an unfamiliar city or to a foreign country, his pilot makes trial runs beforehand to test the runway, atmospheric conditions, and special instructions needed for landing. The Army Signal Corps installs banks of telephones, communications gear, and teletype machines. At least one of the two bulletproof Lincolns, built at a cost of $500,000 each, awaits the presidential arrival. The cost of the vehicles is not as bad as it may seem, since the Ford Motor Company pays for their construction and leases them to the government for a modest $15,000 a year. Secret Service personnel confer with local police on security arrangements, buildings along the motorcade route are checked out, and persons who may be considered a threat to the first family put under surveillance. After the assassination of John Kennedy, few chances can be taken. Foreign countries frequently arrest anyone who may be expected to demonstrate or cause an unpleasant scene. On President Nixon's last trip to the Soviet Union, thousands of Jews were rounded up for fear they would embarrass the regime by publicly demanding the right to emigrate to Israel.

Back home in the United States the White House has a fleet of limousines at its disposal. The Secret Service provides drivers for the president, vice-president, and members of their families. Other cars (about thirty in number) are leased from Chrysler Motors for one dollar a year and provide transportation for White House aides. The top dozen or so of these officials are driven to and from work by their military chauffeurs and have unlimited access to the cars for use in carrying out their duties. Abuses are frequently alleged, as when the drivers are employed to take children to school, do the shopping, or run other errands for the family. Lesser aides are restricted to getting cars when their work requires them to travel around Washington. Attending cocktail parties, dinners, and receptions are part of the "duties" of office, so generally there are few complaints when the automobiles are used for this purpose. Especially favored staffers have been known to enjoy the use of presidential helicopters to lift them over the traffic in going to and coming from the airport or to save precious minutes in getting to Camp David. Dan Cordtz tells of an outing in Florida where Ron Ziegler and a journalist friend were transported to the tennis courts in a Continental Mark IV rented by the government, and of another occasion when one of President Nixon's dogs, King Timahoe, was the sole passenger on a trip to Camp David.[9]

It is impossible to determine exactly how much all of this travel costs the taxpayer. Much of the expense is charged to the Pentagon's budget. It is estimated, however, that it takes approximately $1,000 an hour to keep each of the big four-engine jets in the air. Pilot salaries are on top of that, as are the sorties flown by the air force in defense of the presidential planes. The trips to San Clemente and Key Biscayne in 1973 alone probably cost at least $300,000.[10] During the oil crisis caused by the Arab embargo, President Nixon took to television to order the shutdown of service stations on Sundays and urged Americans to reduce the temperature in their homes as a fuel economy measure. That same Thanksgiving weekend he made two helicopter flights to Camp David accompanied by his Secret Service escort. The Associated Press estimated that twelve hundred gallons of fuel were consumed. In addition, the presidential limousine and staff cars made the trip on the ground.[11]

Other travel costs are incurred when a president takes a "working vacation"* as well. Staff aides and cabinet members shuttle back and forth between Washington and the president's retreat, as do courier flights with important documents. Offices have to be provided, and communications gear installed. At the nearby Coast Guard station in San Clemente, the General Services Administration spent at least $1.7 million setting up an operations center for staff working with president Nixon. An office was also installed for the chief executive in this building, as well as one in his private home. A new office (there was an old one in existence) was created at Camp David, another added in Key

---

*Eisenhower was the last chief executive to feel he did not have to give excuses for taking a break from the office. Even under his administration, however, his press secretary felt it necessary to save up announcements to be released while Ike was vacationing in order to prove that the president was never off duty. See the account in George Reedy, *The Twilight of the Presidency,* p. 32.

Biscayne, and one at Robert Abplanalp's estate on Grand Cay in the Bahamas. When the cost of helicopter pads, security equipment, and service personnel are joined to these other costs, the House Government Activities Subcommittee estimated an expenditure of almost $17 million for Nixon's first four years in office to enable the president to work away from the White House.[12]

Providing security for the president is an obvious necessity. Four chief executives—Lincoln, Garfield, McKinley, and Kennedy—were assassinated while in office. Attempts were also made on the lives of Jackson, Theodore Roosevelt, Truman, and Ford. In addition, Lincoln and Franklin Roosevelt were the victims of plots or assassination attempts even before they were inaugurated. The security net has tightened, especially since Kennedy's death. The Secret Service believes that if it has to err, better to err on the side of too much, rather than too little, security. Few would argue with these sentiments. One of the criticisms of the Nixon administration, however, was that security became a rationale for enriching the estates of the president. Congressional testimony in 1973 estimated a cost of $500,000 a year on the part of the Secret Service, General Services Administration, and the military for protecting, maintaining, and operating Key Biscayne and San Clemente.[13] What drew more censure was the almost $100,000 spent on these two estates ostensibly for security but in reality, the Joint Committee on Internal Revenue Taxation decided, to benefit Mr. Nixon personally.

Among the items paid for by the taxpayers at San Clemente or Key Biscayne was $18,494 for a forced-air heating system, $1,600 to install four picture windows facing the ocean, $621.50 for an ice-cube–making machine (the president reportedly disliked the machine he had which produced cubes with holes through them), $2,329 for a flagpole at San Clemente (a cheaper model was found for Key Biscayne—at only $587), and $2,000 for a terrazzo shuffleboard court. This last expense was justified as a replacement for an existing court that had been destroyed when security equipment was installed. However, the concrete court which was taken up could have been duplicated for $400 had a tile model not been insisted upon. Besides these items, $388.78 was spent on an exhaust fan for the fireplace in the president's den at San Clemente after it was discovered the chimney did not draw well enough on its own. Other expenditures which the joint committee ruled should have been considered as taxable income by Nixon included $4,981.50 for a gazebo, $3,800 for sewer construction, $998.50 for handrails, $5,866.66 for paving costs, and $5,472.59 for boundary surveys. By far the largest amount was spent on landscape construction and maintenance at the two residences.[14]

Clearly some of these outlays had only the most tenuous connection to protecting the chief executive. When existing structures had to be modified for the provision of security devices, they were almost always replaced with more expensive or more esthetically pleasing ones. For instance, there is little doubt that a security fence was desirable to ward off intruders at Key Biscayne. The President's family, however, decided that the one installed should be remodeled to resemble the fence at the White House—at an additional cost of $12,679. Expensive Japanese lanterns were provided to light the way for the chief executive, and the cost of pruning trees was born by the government as well (falling limbs could injure the president). Even such items as $71.96 for an electric "Weed Eater" and $86.00 for decorative pillows for the chief executive's den were picked up by the government. (The General Services Administration insisted when the story of these expenditures reached the newspapers that it would reclaim all removable items once the president was out of office.)

It has become commonplace for many Americans to assume that "they all do it," that politicians at whatever level enrich themselves at the public expense. This excuse was also given by defenders of President Nixon for the political crimes subsumed under the name of Watergate. It is difficult to dispel these widely held myths, since there has been just enough corruption, just enough wrongdoing by politicians in American history to contribute a patina of truth to this cynical view. Perhaps a measure of distrust of political leaders is a healthy indication that citizens are not willing to entrust their fortunes completely to any elite, elected or otherwise. At the same time, a total lack of confidence in the probity of its officials would soon cripple a democracy. The scandals that have touched previous administrations never involved the president directly. Some of Grant's and Harding's appointees may have been corrupt, but there was no indication that the chief executives themselves benefited from the misdeeds of their subordinates. None grew rich in the office or believed that the taxpayers were responsible for outfitting their private residences.

Presidential claims on the government purse are a relatively recent phenomenon. The first pensions to former presidents were provided in 1958. In that year Congress voted for annual retirement benefits of $25,000 a year, or $10,000 to the widows of chief executives. An additional $50,000 a year was included for office staff. These benefits have now been increased to $60,000 for a former president, plus $96,000 for staff salaries. When Richard Nixon was forced from office in 1974, his successor requested $850,000 in support for the former chief executive in the first year. (Congress reduced this figure to $200,000.) Among the items asked for was $65,000 for office furnishings, $40,000 for travel, and $100,000 for "miscellaneous" expenses. Former President Johnson had never spent more than $1,760 for travel in a year. A butler, a maid, secretaries, a speechwriter, a military aide, gardeners, and press secretaries were put on other governmental payrolls and were in addition to Ford's request for Nixon. By the same token, not much was done until recently for the residences or property of incumbent presidents, nor were personal expenses paid for. About the only addition to the Truman home in Independence was a fence erected to keep out the curious. Three guard booths were constructed at Eisenhower's Gettysburg farm, and a similar number at Kennedy's presidential compound at Hyannisport. A fence to insure privacy was paid for by the Kennedy family itself.

Truman bought his own postage stamps for use on private letters mailed from the White House. When his wife and daughter returned to Missouri for vacations, they did so on regularly scheduled trains, and paid for their own tickets. Eleanor Roosevelt flew to Europe at her own expense during World War II to visit with American soldiers. Lady Bird Johnson took the commercial shuttle flights to New York, rather than commanding a government plane. When John Kennedy's father commissioned a mural for the swimming pool in the Executive Mansion and an aide ordered special lighting for it at government expense, the president insisted on paying the $56,000 cost himself.[15]

The first major capital outlay on a president occurred in the Johnson administration. The House Government Operations Committee in 1974 estimated that approximately $5.9 million had been spent for the convenience of the former chief executive. This, however, had been spread over a period of ten years, and none of it was spent directly on the president's house at Johnson City. Most of the money went for the Federal Office Building in Austin, the installation of communications equipment at the ranch, security lighting, lengthening of the runway for the presidential jet, and Secret Service facilities.[16] Perhaps the problem for President Nixon and his aides was that they could no longer see Richard Nixon as a person distinct from the president. For instance, Jack Anderson quoted from a June 16, 1969 memo from John Ehrlichman:

> The President holds the view that a public man does very little of a personal nature. Virtually all of his entertainment and activity is related to his "business." He wants to be sure that his business deductions include all allowable items. For instance, wedding gifts to Congressmen's daughters, flowers at funerals, etc.[17]

Dan Cordtz blames "the advance-man mentality" for a multitude of the resulting abuses. Many of the top staffers in the Nixon White House had first served the candidate as advance men, where one of their functions was to insure Nixon that everything would be taken care of. Comfort and ease were deserved by the hard-driving president-to-be. Once in office, they simply had more resources at their disposal.[18]

As a result of the donation of his vice-presidential papers, the various tax write-offs, and the failure to report the improvements on his homes as income, Nixon was able to triple his net worth in his first four years in the White House. The Internal Revenue Service routinely approved his returns. Then, as questions mounted about the large sums being spent on his estates, an employee of the tax-gathering agency leaked the presidential returns to the press. Both Congress and the Internal Revenue Service itself opened investigations into the matter. The result was a finding that the chief executive had underpaid his taxes by nearly $500,000, and a civil penalty for "negligence" was imposed.[19] Three aides were charged with tax fraud. Some saw in this a healthy reminder to future incumbents that election to office does not destroy the separate existence of the private person apart from the presidency. Any person who sits as president merely occupies the role; he does not become the institution. Even the electorate may once again distinguish between the man and the office.

Apart from the question of tax matters and the necessary outlays for security, the perquisites of the presidency and the manner in which any incumbent is treated remain important issues. Few leaders in the world enjoy the kind of advantages showered on American chief executives. Former President Georges Pompidou of France got away from Paris to an old farmhouse overlooking the Lot River. The structure had been bought for $4,000 and then remodeled. Hordes of police, newsmen, and aides did not surround the leader when he took a vacation. Juscelino Kubitschek of Brazil drove his own Volkswagen to work in the morning, even though he was president of the country. Prime Minister Tanaka of Japan arrived at work in his privately owned Dodge sedan and traveled by commercial air lines when he had to fly. The prime minister of England receives only $57,000 a year in salary and gets the same $20 a day travel allowance as any other governmental official.[20] Golda Meir of Israel entertained in the kitchen of her own modest home in Jerusalem. And even Leonid Brezhnev of the Soviet Union is expected to make do with a five-room official apartment in Moscow and a cottage in the suburbs. Of all the worlds' heads of state, no democratic leader, and few absolute rulers, can match the style and expense of the American president. Critics argue that in "the world's greatest democracy," the land of the common people, the elected leader should be treated as if he were *of* the people, rather than above the people.

How much does the modern presidency cost to maintain? No exact figures can be given, for as has been shown, much of the real expense is born by other departments. Even as unpretentious a first lady as Betty Ford has a staff of twenty-eight to help her in her duties. In 1969 there were estimates that a private citizen would need an income of at least $35 million a year to live in the way in which modern chief executives live.[21] Interviews with members of Congress in 1973 resulted in guesses of a cost to the federal government of around $50 million a year to support the presidency. And Dan Cordtz, after discussion with an official in the Office of Management and Budget, puts the figure at $100 million a year. The problem of attributing those portions of the Defense, State, and other federal department and agency budgets which actually go to the White House is so great, however, that many conclude that no one knows for sure.[22]

Richard Nixon was the originator of very few of the perquisites of the office he held. Rather, his administration was but the logical culmination of years of ever increasing benefits heaped upon the president. With so many of the nation's expectations focused on the office, so much deference afforded the incumbent, and with power ever more concentrated in the hands of one man and his aides, it is perhaps not surprising that mere mortals could forget that the United States is a nation of laws, not men. People inside and outside the White House tended to overlook the fact that the person occupying the office was just another man—a politician by trade—who did not become endowed with infallibility the moment he took the oath of office. It is difficult to expect that when a person is treated like a monarch he will not behave like one. When that subject of reverence and awe also possesses great discretionary powers, there is the danger that he will see himself as an absolute monarch, unrestrained by the Constitution or laws. Everything around him, the treatment he receives from his subordinates (and he has no equals), his reception by the people as he travels around the country—all tend to confirm a notion of omnipotence.

Isolation

Obviously it was not simply the opulent living that was responsible for the errors in judgment on the part of recent presidents. In fact, life-style is partially a reflection of other problems. Possibly the greatest hazard to intelligent decision making and responsive leadership is the loss of touch with political reality that has almost become built into the presidency. It begins even before a politician is elected to the office. Most have large egos to begin with. The candidate and his supporters believe that he has something valuable to offer to the nation, even when he begins a political career at a relatively low level. After many years in politics, moving to more prominent positions, with frequent reelection and increasing mention as a presidential possibility, the candidate and his backers may be ready to pursue the highest office of them all.

Once he becomes the nominee of his political party, the accuracy of the candidate's self-estimate is reaffirmed. The press and political leaders will marvel at his acumen in putting together an organization that had the nomination sewed up months or years in advance. (Alternately, if he comes from behind or is a dark horse, his talents in beating the front-runners may seem all the more extraordinary.) As the party drums up support and tries to heal divisions that may have been created in the primaries, the candidate is perceived by increasing numbers of people to be just what they have been looking for. Advertising helps in this process. Thousands of people around the country (aided by advance men) turn out to hear and see the person who may be the next president of the United States. Even candidates who were swamped in the general election, such as Goldwater and McGovern, drew huge crowds of admiring supporters. The most lackluster of nominees is sure to be seen by millions as a new Washington, Lincoln, or Roosevelt once the buildup gets underway. It must be difficult to keep all of this in perspective, to maintain a balanced self-image in light of all of this adulation flowing from the people. The danger is that one will come to accept press notices as reality.

Once the election is over, there is an almost immediate intensification of support and admiration for the victorious candidate. John Kennedy won the 1960 election with less than 50 percent of the popular vote, but by inauguration day 69 percent of the people approved of their new chief executive. The so-called honeymoon with the press, the people, and Congress adds further credence to the belief that the new incumbent has an inherent knack for making the right decisions. All of a sudden Jack, or Lyndon, or Dick becomes "Mr. President," even to those who have been with the candidate for years.°

°"After his 1968 election, Mr. Nixon grew furious that the board of directors of Fisher's Island would pay him only double, not triple, the par value of his holdings, and Hoke T. Maroon, the largest shareholder, tried to reason with him. He got as far as 'But Dick . . .' when Mr. Nixon exploded: 'Don't you dare call me Dick. I am the President of the United States. When you speak to me, you call me Mr. President.'" (*Newsweek*, 20 August 1973, p. 31)

Glowing stories appear in the media, even in the papers that had opposed the new president as a candidate. Presidential platitudes are reported as if they were beatitudes. It is difficult to recall the high hopes and effusive praise that greeted each new administration, since recent ones have ended on such sour notes. Perhaps a reminder from Theodore H. White's popular *The Making of the President 1968* will illustrate this point.

> No more plastic President, none more open to suggestion and ideas, none more willing to admit mistakes or learn from error, has sat in the White House in recent times. . . . The style of the man, as President, had begun to change within days of the election; and calling on the President, two days after the inauguration, it was as if history itself was now taking a hand in finishing the portrait I had watched so long. . . .
>
> Few, in the past century, have come from origins so humble and made their way, solitary, against such odds, to influence so great. None has shown himself, on the way to power, so susceptible to strain, yet apparently learned better how to cope with strain within himself. Richard Nixon has roved across the entire map of the United States. . . . But no passage of this public wandering has been more impressive than the transformation of the impulsive, wrathful man of the 1950's, so eager for combat and lustful for vengeance, to the man in the White House, cautious and thoughtful, intent on conciliation.[23]

Surely White had been no apologist for Nixon in the past. But now he saw the presidency in just two days work its miracle and transform the man in the office. "Plastic" did not mean phony, but rather pliable, pragmatic, adaptable, capable of growing. By the same token, Eisenhower had been greeted with stories in the press about his cosmopolitan experience, calm assurance, sense of humility, command ability reminiscent of FDR, the dignity he "restored" to the office, how tough he was on his staff—making them work the same ten-and twelve-hour days he put in. This last assertion is a common feature of all new administrations, as a whirlwind of activity creates a sense of mission and institutes change in the old order. A wise new incumbent will try to seem as different from his immediate predecessor as possible. Eisenhower listened to others, had an amazing understanding of the legislative process, and treated Congress with respect, while Truman and Roosevelt had used coercion and threats on that body, reported the media.

When Kennedy began his term, journalists were just as enthusiastic. A new tempo, verve, and drive had replaced the somnolence of Eisenhower's administration. The Kennedy people were always on the move, bright young Harvard men who understood how to make the system work. Idealism was combined with self-deprecating humor. They were going to "get the country moving again," and Kennedy himself intuitively knew what had to be done to stay on top of this turbulent but exciting experiment. Gone was the cluttered and hierarchical chain of command system under Eisenhower; in its place was a fluid process allowing the president to cut across organizational lines and get the information and people he needed. He and his people could read rapidly and digest mountains of information; they had a way of cutting through the irrelevant and getting right down to the heart of issues. Kennedy (like every president before and since) was going to revitalize the cabinet, delegate unprecedented authority to these men of such stature whom he had chosen. No White House clique or chief of staff (as under Eisenhower) would dictate to the heads of departments.

In the aftermath of the Kennedy assassination, it was in poor taste to criticize his administration. What this meant in practice was that the new president had to be praised without depreciating his predecessor. If anything, however, he worked even harder than Kennedy, the press informed the people. He labored day and night and would take no less from his staff. Not that this meant he was an impulsive, shoot-from-the-hip decision maker. Rather, he consulted widely both inside and outside his administration to assure himself that he had learned all relevant information and touched all bases. He sought dissenting opinions. Jack Valenti, one of the president's aides, perhaps went too far even for an admiring country when he announced that he could sleep a little better each night "knowing Lyndon Johnson is my President." As a combination FDR New Dealer and Jack Kennedy New Frontiersman, Johnson retained his faith that the people, and not the president alone, would solve American's problems. The old image as an arm twister was false; Johnson relied on persuasion and consensus. He had had more governmental service than any other twentieth-century president and thus was able to secure passage of the legislation which Kennedy could only request. As a southerner he could get civil rights laws enacted where northern presidents had failed. He invited members of Congress to the White House for briefings on important issues and reminded all that if they ever needed to talk to him, he was as close as the telephone. He welcomed questions from any and all sources and met frequently with members of the press in both formal and informal sessions. That these impressions were shared by the people was indicated by his 80 percent approval rating in the polls shortly after he assumed the office. One quote illustrates how immediately the cloak of office transforms opinions about new presidents:

> Getting to Johnson . . . this strikes me again . . . the fact that we immediately began to think of Johnson in slightly better terms than we have before. . . . I at least began to think things like, well, he's the man who put the two civil rights bill [sic] through the Senate, the first time this had been done since the Civil War. He was a Roosevelt New Dealer, and so forth.[24]

Richard Nixon, too, was greeted by a wave of acclaim. Walter Lippmann wrote that, because of his reputation as an anti-Communist, Nixon could improve relations with the Soviet Union without appearing to sell out to them. Others wrote that he did not overdominate meetings as Johnson had done but rather listened to dissenting opinions. His White House operation was far less structured and rigid than Eisenhower's but more efficient and businesslike than Kennedy's or Johnson's. He was happy and relaxed on the job. Seeing too many people, as Roosevelt and Truman had done, would make it impossible to concentrate his energies on the "big questions," the ones only the president could deal with. His relative seclusion was seen as an advantage. Thus it was wise to allow his staff to take the petty burdens off the president's shoulders and bring him only the conflicts that could not be resolved at a lower level. He had a knack for asking the right questions, for separating the wheat from the chaff. He probed aides and advisers without tipping his own position to make sure they were not giving him what they thought he wanted to hear. His cabinet was composed of "men of extra dimensions," and it would be restored to a place of prominence in his administration.

When Gerald Ford came to the presidency, the public, press,

and Congress breathed a sigh of relief. He was as honest as Lincoln, warm as Eisenhower, and as experienced as Johnson (without being an arm-twister). The greatest contrasts were of course with his immediate predecessor, since Ford was as self-effacing as Nixon had been grandiose, was open rather than isolated, and viewed Congress as a partner rather than as an object of contempt. In short, he was an ideal American president. It was difficult to understand how his obvious talents had so long been overlooked. He was the healer, would put to rest suspicions that had divided the country, could ask Americans to pray without seeming hypocritical or corny. He was everything Richard Nixon only pretended to be. He was genuinely of middle America; rather than viewing that group as an object of manipulation, he believed in its values. Here are some of the things *Time* magazine said of him in his first week in office: "Loyalty, honesty, diligence, patience, a fear of the Lord . . . Gerald Ford has all these qualities." "He has demonstrated his skills in one of the most complex parliamentary arenas on earth, winning the respect of adversaries and allies alike." He has a passion for compromise, "a tolerance of differing views, a desire to accommodate, a sense that at the heart of government lies the right to disagree." "Ford has a minor ego that does not get in the way of his politics." "Gerald Ford *is* middle America. His roots reach deeply, tenaciously into the thrifty-hard-toiling community of Grand Rapids." "Ford's colleagues are astounded by his stamina." "It is his plainspokenness that makes him such a welcome contrast to his predecessor; for the moment, he is living proof that nice guys sometimes finish first."[25]

This kind of praise greeting new presidents surely does nothing to detract from their beliefs in their own innate wisdom. (It also perhaps guarantees that the people will be disappointed with the performance of any president. It would be difficult, if not impossible, to live up to the advance billing that each of them receives.) Once the new chief executive has taken the oath of office, he moves into the White House and is the recipient of all of the perquisites discussed earlier. At first it probably is somewhat embarrassing, as it was for Ford, having all of those services at one's fingertips. A person not used to being waited on or catered to may wish to continue his plain and humble ways. The chances are, however, that he will soon learn that as president of the United States he must maintain the respect and dignity of the office. Harry Truman suffered in the popularity polls and in the eyes of Congress because his common style and language did not match the elevated standards expected of a president. Lyndon Johnson, too, transgressed the bounds of acceptable behavior, as when he showed his gall bladder scar to reporters or picked up his beagle by its ears. These are the kinds of actions that may be acceptable or overlooked in friends and acquaintances but not in presidents. In any case, privileges are fairly easy for most people to get used to, and taking advantage of them soon becomes second nature. They come to be expected as nothing more than what is due to the "leader of the free world."

In the White House the chief executive is engulfed in deference. What he wants, or even what others think he wants, is provided as a matter of course. The very history of the building itself must have a psychological impact on those who labor there. The president walks where Jefferson walked, sleeps where Lincoln slept, writes on Wilson's desk, and dines where the Roosevelts dined. Only thirty-six men in the whole history of the world held the office he now occupies, and he is assured, as few other men are, of a place in history. There is the temptation to disregard what mere politicians in the political system may want today and to let history be the judge. He has, as everyone keeps telling him, vast powers and responsibilities. The future of the entire world may depend upon his decisions. There is no doubt that the mental burden of all of this must be great, and at the same time it tends to remove him from the confines of everyday reality within which others are operating. Each of the last four presidents has adopted the imperial "we" when referring to himself, (as in "we, Nicholas, Tsar of all the Russias").[26]

Everywhere he moves he is surrounded by the trappings of power. The officer from the army Signal Corps with the briefcase containing the code to launch a nuclear attack is always at his elbow. Secret Service men are ubiquitous. White House police, marine guards, and Executive Mansion staff personnel open doors for him and ease his way. Few, if any, of his old friends and colleagues are willing to argue with him. They may politely put a case to him, but one does not freely enter a heated debate with the president of the United States. Most are rather willing to try to go along with what he wants if they possibly can, even if they have reason to believe he may be wrong. But even this notion usually can give way to the assumption that the president is in fact right. Do not his election, his surroundings, his superior sources of information prove that the president knows best? Many at least assume so. It is because the chief executive is set apart from—in fact set above—other men that insures that no one can talk to him as an equal or pierce the cocoon of obsequiousness that envelopes his every waking hour.

But is it not true that the president knows more than anyone else, that he is in the best position to decide all important questions? That certainly is what the conventional wisdom outlined in earlier chapters would have us believe. After all, the president can draw information from the State Department, CIA, FBI, National Security Agency, National Security Council, Defense Intelligence Agency, and a host of expert advisers. Reedy contends, however, that on the major policy decisions involving war and peace a president has the same kind of information available to the close reader of the *New York Times*. Thus FDR's decision to commit America to World War II was not based on anything the American people did not know about German or Japanese policies. Truman's sending of troops to Korea in 1950 was grounded primarily on the publicly known incident of the North Korean invasion of the South. And Johnson's dispatch of marines to the Dominican Republic was based on facts possessed by every aware citizen.[27] The president's position may in fact guarantee that he knows less about certain key political realities of some of the problems that are brought to him. His elevation and isolation partially serve to remove him from the hurly-burly of everyday politics within which others are immersed. In addition, he has to deal with such a range and variety of issues that he can hardly be expected to possess expertise on all of them. Thus he has to rely on the information that is brought to him by subordinates and the "options" that they outline for him. There is no guarantee that the "experts" will have his broad political perspective in mind or that their commitments to certain solutions will not prejudice the information they provide.

Charles Frankel, who served in the State Department in the

Johnson administration, asserts that executives do indeed possess information denied to others, but frequently that information is false. "After a while I came to suspect that I might not be dealing with hard facts, but rather with a world created out of hunch, hope and collective illusions," he writes.[28] There are several reasons why this is so. One factor is an institutionalized proclivity toward optimism. The people who gather information in the agencies see as one of their functions the supplying of evidence that the policymaker's decisions are correct. Thus they generate "proof" that enables the executive to defend his policies against attack. The facts are usually ambiguous enough to justify the selection of evidence favorable to the administration. In addition, a report from the field to the effect that the policy is not working is subject to only two interpretations: either the boss's policies are wrong or the man on the spot is incompetent. There is little doubt which interpretation most policymakers will believe is the accurate one. Thus military reports from Vietnam concerning "body counts," the number of hamlets secured, the size of trained South Vietnamese forces, and the number of people served by Revolutionary Development teams conveyed eternal optimism to those who served in the White House. Pacification, Vietnamization, and "strategic hamlets" were succeeding because they were the policies of the people back in Washington.

Another factor leading to distortion in the information executives get is that what is assumed to be true is often what is politically acceptable to those who receive the information. Political judgments as well as facts are combined in judging what is reality. Part of the political reality taken into account is the power of the person or organization supplying the information. Thus a report from J. Edgar Hoover was likely to carry more weight than one from an agent in the field who had firsthand knowledge of the problem. The former had power and "clout," while the latter was an unknown. Under Secretary of State George Ball argued against the president's Vietnam policy within the administration itself, but his view of reality could not overcome that of Secretary of State Dean Rusk, of the Defense Department, or of the president himself. Whom does one believe, an undersecretary of state, or the heads of departments and the collective military wisdom of the generals? This is not to argue that such officials are always or even persistently wrong. It is necessary, however, to recognize that officials have commitments to certain policies, that they have a stake in being proved right in their recommendations. Thus what one sees in the present tends to confirm the sagacity of what was decided in the past. The very act of supplying justification may lead to a stronger belief in the necessity of a policy. Even officials who seek objective information may emanate their own policy biases. What they get back most frequently is proof that they have been right all along.[29]

The White House Staff System and the Decline of the Cabinet

The exalted treatment afforded any president, the public expectations that he can and should solve the nation's problems, along with deference from fellow politicians and policy makers, all help create an atmosphere of unreality in the White House. The chief executive is primarily responsible for setting the tone and ambience of his administration, and when he operates in a world removed from the ordinary existence of most others, his aides are apt to do so as well. In fact they are likely to be among the chief contributors to the isolation which presidents must struggle against. It is with his staff that a president most frequently interacts. If cabinet officials and members of Congress merely defer to chief executives, then White House aides are veritable toadies. Their one function is to do the president's bidding. For most of them, no price is too high to pay to serve their chief, no task too humble to perform. (Lyndon Johnson sometimes used Jack Valenti's lap as a footstool in front of visiting officials.[30]) Few would conceive of the possibility of arguing with the chief executive; their duty is to carry out what he wants, not to give him disagreement.

It is an age-old custom to slay the bearer of bad news. Thus associates of the president are reluctant to burden him with news of the failures of policies or programs that the chief has supported. Although each administration within memory has begun with a pledge of openness, those who find themselves too frequently disagreeing with the president will probably not last long. Richard Nixon promised to bring dissent into the cabinet, saying he did not want a group of "yes men" surrounding him. However, when Walter Hickel, secretary of the interior, found he could not see the president to voice his concerns about Vietnam policy and leaked a letter to the press containing those opinions, he was soon fired. (Lack of mutual confidence was the stated reason.) Even John Connally, once thought being groomed by Nixon as his successor, found himself without access or power after he had advised the president to fire Ron Ziegler—advice the president did not want to hear. It does not take too long for aides to learn that it is better to bring the president proof of success rather than doubts or misgivings about his policies.

After all, are not most people sure that those who agree with them are perceptive, intelligent, and capable, while those who share differing opinions are either uninformed, knaves, or fools? Thus most people tend to associate with like-minded persons who reinforce their opinions. Since it is the president who holds the power, it is important for those who wish to be thought well of by him to know where he stands on issues. Robert Kennedy asserted that "personalities change when the President is present, and frequently even strong men make recommendations on the basis of what they believe the President wishes to hear." The president's brother believed that the recommendations that emerged from the Ex Com's meetings during the Cuban missile crisis were as valuable as they were precisely because Jack Kennedy did not attend most of the sessions:

> His office creates such respect and awe that it has almost a cowering effect on men. Frequently I saw advisers adapt their opinions to what they believed President Kennedy and, later, President Johnson wished to hear.
>
> I once attended a preliminary meeting with a Cabinet officer, where we agreed on a recommendation to be made to the President. It came as a *slight* surprise to me when, a few minutes later, in the meeting with the President himself, the Cabinet officer vigorously and fervently expressed the opposite view, which, from the discussion he quite accurately learned would be more sympathetically received by the President. [Emphasis added.][31]

If even cabinet members, who usually have at least a measure of independence from the president, seek to adapt their thinking to that of the chief executive, then White House staff aides are even more anxious to do so. As Ted Sorensen has pointed out, these people are chosen for "their ability to serve the President's needs and to talk the President's language."[32] Those closest to the chief generally do not have to do a great deal of adapting to his viewpoint. In part they rise to their positions because they think the way he does in the first place. They serve as extra eyes, ears, and hands for him, doing what he would do himself if he had the time. A president needs extra help, of course, since the number of tasks expected of any chief executive today far exceeds what one person can do. It is natural to rely on those who think the same way he does, for in doing so a president can be fairly confident his aides will not alter in the execution the policy they agree on in principle. Thus those in tune with a president's thinking, style, and personality become the most trusted aides, the ones who come to wield the most power in his name. Henry Fairlie has compared this to eunuch rule in the Chinese, Turkish, Roman, and Mogul empires.[33]

John Kennedy brought to the White House a group of men sometimes referred to as the "Irish Mafia," men whom he felt he could communicate with and who shared his particular view of the world. When Lyndon Johnson succeeded to the office, he asked everyone in the administration to stay on, assuring each that he needed his services more then Kennedy had. Several cabinet members, including Dean Rusk, Stewart Udall, Willard Wirtz, and Orville Freeman, remained until the end of his term. The White House staff aides of Kennedy, however, were sooner or later replaced by men more in tune with the new president. Thus the "Texas Mafia" came to fill the place close to the Oval Office once occupied by men with eastern accents. Personal loyalty is desired by each incumbent of the office. Richard Nixon had his Bob Haldeman and John Ehrlichman, men who identified so closely with their chief that they reportedly adopted his luncheon habit of eating cottage cheese with ketchup. And Gerald Ford, despite his desire for continuity, almost immediately added his old friends and associates Philip Buchen, Robert Hartman, John Marsh, and Jerry terHorst to his inner circle. Most of those people either were from Michigan or had served the new president previously. Ron Ziegler, John McLaughlin, J. Fred Buzhardt, and Fred Malek from the old administration lasted less than two weeks into the new one. Almost all of Nixon's White House staff were replaced within four months. One of the risks of being surrounded by like-minded people is that such aides come to reinforce a president's predispositions rather than to serve to enlarge his perspective. Inflexibility and a lack of diversity in a staff is sure to lead to further isolation of the president himself, and in a country as diverse as the United States and with as many different interests depending on the chief executive, this can spell political trouble for the incumbent.

Ford, as Nixon had done before him, entered office with a pledge to reduce the power and influence of the White House staff. Critics had seen in the growth of the institution a danger to representative government. Its members are not elected by the people and, unlike cabinet officers, are not subject to senatorial approval. In addition, whereas the heads of departments can be called to testify before congressional committees, White House aides have often refused to testify on the grounds of separation of powers and executive privilege. Thus means of holding them accountable are notably lacking. Why then has the staff seemed to increase in importance while the cabinet members individually and as a body have lost esteem?

Part of the answer lies in the criteria used in the selection of these two bodies. While a staff member may be virtually unknown to everybody except the new president or a member of his inner circle, a cabinet secretary generally is a person of some prominence. Thus talented but obscure figures may be asked to join the staff of a chief executive but not his cabinet. In addition, personal factors figure saliently in the choice of those who will work directly with the president on a day-to-day basis. Loyalty to the president as a person is seen as an ideal characteristic. Frequently his top aides have worked for the new president in the past and have demonstrated their commitment to him as well as learned the way he prefers to organize his energies and run his office. Bill Moyers, an aide to Lyndon Johnson, was quoted as saying, "Any President has to have around him some people who are so unquestioningly loyal that their very loyalty is a source of strength to him."[34] While it is desirable to have people in the cabinet who pledge their fealty to the chief executive, it is not as necessary to have their personal commitment. In fact, it is nearly impossible to to do so when a president takes into account the other qualifications he seeks in his cabinet secretaries. The staff member must, in Sorensen's words, "speak the President's language," while department heads will speak with varying accents and for different interests.

Balance is a factor (at least for public relations purposes) in selecting a cabinet; it is not of the same importance in a staff. For political reasons as well as by custom, a president seeks to give representation at the top level of his administration to as many relevant interests as possible. Party is one such interest. Each important element of the chief executive's political party will generally be represented. Thus a liberal president will appoint to office some persons who are more conservative than he, lest that wing of the party become further alienated. It is important to try to maintain as much party support as possible if a president is to be successful with Congress and the states and if he is to help his own reelection chances. Jerry Ford's selection of Nelson Rockefeller as vice-president offers an example of a conservative moving to nail down the moderate-to-liberal elements among the Republicans. A unified party is the desired outcome. In the past, presidents have offered cabinet positions to those whom they defeated for the nomination (as when Nixon chose Romney in his first cabinet). Such an appointment to his own personal staff is unlikely.

Geographical balance is another consideration in appointing cabinets. Though Kennedy was from the East, it would have been unthinkable for him to select his secretaries solely from that region. Areas of the nation must be represented as well as wings of the party. At least one southerner is generally appointed, whether the chief executive is a Democrat or a Republican. Similarly, the Middle West, New England, and the West will all have representation in the cabinet. The largest states are almost sure to get at least one appointee. Historically, different regions of the country also have had claims on particular departments. The Middle West has provided most of the secretaries of agriculture in recent years, while the West furnished the secretaries of the interior. Nixon may have altered that pattern when he chose Rogers Morton of Maryland in 1970 to head the Interior Department. White House aides usually are not chosen for their geographical distribution. Thus Kennedy's Boston Irish, Johnson's Texans, Nixon's Californians, and Ford's Michiganders were all out of proportion to their numbers in the general population.

Yet another factor that accounts for balance in a cabinet is the appointment of officials from various occupational and socio-economic groups. Lawyers are usually prominently represented in the selections (especially for attorney general), as are politicians. Nixon's first cabinet contained three governors—Romney, Hickel, and Volpe. Senators, and to a lesser degree, representatives, are also frequently chosen. Part of this is an effort to get party balance in the cabinet. Farmers will want a cabinet secretary with direct experience in Agriculture, business executives seek to place one of their own in Commerce, and organized labor prefers a person with a record of promoting the cause of the worker in the Labor Department. Nixon chose Peter Brennan, himself a labor union leader, to head the latter department. Even when a president seeks to represent an interest in his cabinet, however, he sometimes runs into trouble with other factions of the group. For instance, farmers are split between the family farmers and the corporate farmers, between adherents of the American Farm Bureau, the National Farmers Union, and the National Farmers Organization, among others. There will also generally be a mixture of religious backgrounds in the cabinet.[35]

The executive agencies of the federal government have become huge organizations demanding management capabilities on the part of those who run them. Sometimes this function can be left to undersecretaries and professionals, but the chances are a president will want heads of departments with at least some experience in management. Unless he allows his staff to develop large staffs of their own, this ability is not as crucial in his aides. Every president is faced with the problem of making the bureaucracy bend to his will, of getting a hold on the executive machinery to insure that the entrenched civil servants will be responsive to the program of the administration. There is no guarantee that someone who has run a large organization in the private sector can be successful in this effort, but a president probably will try to minimize trouble on his own door step by selecting appointees he believes can do the job for him.

Another set of reasons why the White House staff has gained at the expense of the cabinet in recent years centers upon the different interests each has come to represent. For the staff people, the president is the only client. His welfare, his program, his reputation, his power, and his popularity occupy their working hours. (This is not to deny them individual ambitions of their own.) Cabinet members, on the other hand, as Richard Neustadt has written, serve five masters.[36] They do owe their loyalty to the president. He nominates and removes them from their positions, and under the Constitution he is ultimately responsible for "taking care" that the laws be faithfully executed. In this sense the president as chief executive is at the top of the chain of command for the departments.

But cabinet secretaries also serve other interests. Each department of the executive branch was created by Congress under a separate statute. Each has different laws to administer, laws that may change from year to year. Thus the relationship between the departments and Congress is a special one not shared by members of the White House staff. Every year the representatives of the agencies and departments must go to Congress for funding. Cabinet members themselves testify before committees of the legislature to justify their budget requests. Each agency deals with different subcommittees of Congress, and over the years close ties are built up. The important members of Congress (the committee and subcommittee chairmen) develop expertise in the program areas of the agencies they oversee. Many times they come to take a proprietary interest in the internal affairs of the departments for which they are responsible. To be effective, a cabinet secretary must take care that these ties between his department and specific members of Congress are nurtured and not allowed to go sour. Thus department heads serve not only the president but Congress as well.

Another set of "masters" that the cabinet members must be responsive to if they are to fulfill the missions of their agencies is composed of the "clients" served by their departments. Those in business want a Commerce secretary who will articulate their needs, who will do everything in his or her power to further their interests within the administration, who will push for programs designed to foster the growth of profits in the private sector of the economy. Commerce is "their" department, and its head should be as closely identified with their goals as possible. Secretary of Agriculture Butz has spoken consistently in favor of higher prices for farmers for the crops they produce. Even during wage and price controls, he let it be known that he believed a freeze on farm commodities would have disastrous effects in the long run on costs to consumers. This was a challenge to the policies of the president who appointed him, but he was serving the interests of the Agriculture Department's clients, which he believed to be ultimately in the best interests of the administration as well. On several occasions he said that farm prices should go higher to encourage production, and that expensive beef guaranteed that when he went to the supermarket all the steaks would not have already been purchased by poorer people. These statements proved so popular among some farmers that one of the slogans during the 1972 campaign was "vote for Nixon or you'll lose your Butz." A president and his staff have to concern themselves with more than just one set of clients in the population. They are expected to look out for the interests of the president and, thus, of all the people.

A cabinet secretary must also spend considerable time and energy promoting the interests of the permanent civil servants within his or her own department. Many of these people have devoted years of service to developing expertise in carrying out their agency's mission. Presidents and administrations come and go, but the careerists linger on. They are the ones who are most familiar with the legislative mandate of their departments and who have the oldest and closest ties to the clients served by the departments. In many cases they believe that their experience and professionalism puts them in a better position than the president to determine which policies best further agriculture, the defense of the United States, business, or urban housing. (They of course may be right.) Careerists also develop institutional loyalties to the agencies that employ them. Thus pride in their achievements and their integrity, concern for maintaining their reputations among fellow professionals, and an interest in fostering morale all mean that the cabinet secretary has to be aware that his or her department has interests as an institution that set it apart from others in government. Civil servants, too, have families to support and are concerned with receiving promotion and recognition for their accomplishments.

Those who watched Assistant Attorney General Henry Petersen during the Watergate hearings received an instructive lesson in the pride careerists develop in their agencies. In emotional testimony he told the senators that he "resented" the appointment of a special prosecutor, that the Justice Department lawyers had completed 90 percent of the case against those involved, and that "we would have convicted those people." He said that his twenty-six-year period of professional service was "too long to jeopardize my reputation for anyone." Turning over the work of his staff to an outsider was an insult to the integrity of the men and women who had devoted their lives to the cause of justice. No White House aide and not even the president could subvert their dedication to the highest professional standards. Petersen was obviously concerned with the Justice Department as an institution and took deep satisfaction in its work. If cabinet secretaries are to assure full working cooperation with the permanent members of the bureaucracy, they must come to identify with the goals and standards of those professionals and seek to protect their interests.

The problem that arises when they do so, however, is that they are then perceived as "going native" by those in the White House. They are viewed as being controlled by the department, rather than controlling it for the president. The more they speak for the agency and its clients, the less they speak for the chief executive. In the president's and his staffers' eyes, such a secretary has been captured by the bureaucracy and can no longer serve effectively as the agent of the administration. Since it may not be feasible to replace him or her (as the new one may be captured as well), White House aides have been used more and more to give orders to the departments. They are not identified with either the clients or the interests of the agency. A president could try to get around these diverse loyalties by appointing close friends who have proved their devotion to him in the past to important cabinet positions. Many recent presidents have done just that in some departments. John Kennedy chose his own brother to serve as attorney general, and Richard Nixon appointed his close associates Robert Finch to HEW and John Mitchell to the Justice Department. But this creates other problems. The closer cabinet members stick to the president, the more trouble they may have within their departments. Finch faced a near rebellion of the professional staffers in HEW over proposed administration programs that they felt the secretary was not doing enough to try to change. They demanded mass meetings with him, and, after a near breakdown, he had to be withdrawn from the department and offered a position in the White House. John Mitchell saw careerists angrily resign their positions with public blasts at the administration, and sixty-five lawyers in the Civil Rights Division signed a protest petition to the attorney general and otherwise embarrassed him and the president.

One other master that cabinet members serve should be mentioned. Besides the president, Congress, their clients, and their departments' interests, they also have their own individual concerns to think about. One consideration may be a further political career. That is, they may view their service in the cabinet as a stepping-stone to another office or into the presidency itself, and thus the decisions they make in the present may be colored by considerations of how their futures will be affected. Cabinet secretaries also have their own pride and integrity, and sometimes this clashes with a president's desires. A good example of this was Elliot Richardson's refusal to fire Special Prosecutor Cox. Even though Alexander Haig, President Nixon's chief of staff, told the attorney general "this is an order from your commander in chief," Richardson felt his commitment to the independence of Cox left him no alternative but to resign from government himself rather than carry out the President's wishes.* It is hard to think of a White House aide who would refuse to implement a presidential directive. Although staffers have their own careers and ambitions to think about, most frequently these are bound up in close identification with the chief executive. Usually they have no independent base of power to fall back upon, as many cabinet secretaries do. Recent cabinet members have not been very successful in picking up their political careers, but most White House aides have fared even more poorly. Despite the great popularity of Kennedy, the electorate has repeatedly turned down the bids of aides such as Kenneth O'Donnell, Ted Sorensen, and Pierre Sallinger to seek office on their own.

Because cabinet secretaries have so many masters to serve, the president cannot always count on them, and he soon learns to

---

* The use of the military term "commander in chief" is itself an interesting revelation of how the Nixon White House viewed the relationship between itself and members of the cabinet.

count on his aides instead. "The members of the Cabinet are a President's natural enemies," remarked Charles G. Dawes, who served Harding, Coolidge, and Hoover.[37] Even Roosevelt, the president who has been cited as the most successful of all in bending the departments to his will, complained:

> The Treasury is so large and far-flung and ingrained in its practices that I find it almost impossible to get the action and results I want even with Henry (Morgenthau) there. But the Treasury is not to be compared with the State Department. You should go through the experience of trying to get any changes in the thinking, policy, and action of the career diplomats and then you'd know what a real problem was. But the Treasury and the State Department put together are nothing compared with the Na-a-vy. The admirals are really something to cope with—and I should know. To change anything in the Na-a-vy is like punching a feather bed. You punch it with your right and you punch it with your left until you are finally exhausted, and then you find the damn bed just as it was before you started punching.[38]

The government is now twice the size it was in Roosevelt's day, and it is probably at least twice as difficult for a president to work his will within its confines. President Nixon prided himself on his mastery of foreign affairs and spent much of his time in this area. Yet when Pakistan and India went to war over Bangladesh, he grew furious when he and Henry Kissinger were unable to get the machinery of government to "tilt" toward Pakistan. The war was over before he could accomplish his purpose. The only result was poorer relations with India.

One solution Nixon attempted for this dilemma was to place his own trusted aides and friends in second-level positions within the departments. There they could serve both to shape the policy of the agencies and as listening posts for the White House. Thus a Nixon "presence" would guarantee a measure of control in what was considered a hostile environment. Fred Malek had been chief of the White House Personnel Office. He was offered a cabinet position but turned it down for a job as deputy director of the Office of Management and Budget (which says something about the relative importance of the OMB and the departments). Jeb Stuart Magruder went to the Commerce Department. Robert Mardian was already an assistant attorney general. Gordon

Strachan was made general counsel of the U.S. Information Agency. John Caulfield was found a position in the Treasury Department. Egil Krogh became an undersecretary in Transportation. Edward Morgan, a former deputy to Ehrlichman, became assistant secretary of the Treasury. Frank Carlucci was made undersecretary of HEW. And John Whitaker went to the Interior Department as undersecretary. Some saw in this a White House spy network designed to ferret out of the departments anyone who might oppose the president's programs. Others felt these people would be the real powers in the agencies, while cabinet members themselves only served as fronts. Thus a president could select secretaries for their administrative ability, or their lack of outside power sources, or for their willingness to obey. If Nixon did not have to rely on them for policy advice, then reward for former political support or their "representativeness" would not lessen his control of the departments. It did not matter so much if the cabinet did "go native"; the real power would be behind the throne. Nixon announced at the beginning of his second term that his staff would be cut in half—that the remainder would be sent to work in the departments.

Growth of the Staff

It is time to take a step back and look at the historical growth of the staff that has seemed to replace so many of the functions once performed by members of the cabinet. In its present size and scope, the formalized structure of the White House staff is a relatively recent phenomenon. Presidents have always had their private aides, going all the way back to Washington, who hired his nephew Howell Lewis as "a writer in my office . . . at a rate of three hundred dollars a year." He also added a former aide-de-camp, Major William Jackson, as a personal secretary. That was the extent of his office help, and both were paid out of his own pocket. Edward Corwin wrote that it was not until 1857 that Congress appropriated the first money for a presidential clerk. He went on to say:

> Others, like Jackson, set up "kitchen cabinets," advisers who "kept backstage," but aided the President in various capacities. Grant presided over "the great barbecue," comprising six White House

Assistants whose salaries totaled $13,900. McKinley lavished $44,340 on a staff of 27; Coolidge was given 46 employees, costing the public exchequer $93,520; FDR ran the show before the Second World War with 37 employees.[39]

President Benjamin Harrison, who served in the early 1890's, was able to give his entire staff office space on the second floor of the White House, which it shared with the living quarters of the first family. It was not until William McKinley that Congress provided funds for the entire staff, and even then most presidents found they had to continue the practice of putting an aide on the payroll of one of the departments and then "borrowing" his services. (This practice continues today, and thus it is impossible to give an exact figure for the number of people who actually work for the president.)

With some notable exceptions, being a "presidential secretary" was not a very prestigious occupation before the administration of Franklin Roosevelt. (The job was what today would be considered a presidential aide.) Hoover had drawn criticism for doubling the number of these top assistants from two to four. In addition, he was served by two military aides and a staff of approximately forty messengers, clerks, and typists.[40] With the New Deal and World War II, however, the rapid expansion of the White House establishment got under way, and the power and desirability of these posts increased apace. It became clear that the departments as constituted were incapable of dealing with the crisis brought on by the depression. Government involvement in matters such as unemployment, falling farm prices, foreclosure of mortgages, taxation, welfare, labor policies, stimulation of business, and resource development on an integrated basis required new mechanisms, Roosevelt believed. The existing cabinet structure, which divided problems into neat categories, would no longer suffice. By creating entirely new structures, he could bypass entrenched bureaucracies with their established ties to interest groups and their inherent conservatism.

To modernize his own staff operation, Roosevelt sought the advice of a committee made up of some of the preeminent scholars of the day. This Committee on Administrative Management reported back with conclusions pleasing to the presidential ear. In a message transmitting the report to Congress he wrote:

They say . . . that the President cannot adequately handle his responsibilities; that he is overworked; that it is humanly impossible, under the system which we have, for him fully to carry out his constitutional duty as Chief Executive, because he is overwhelmed with minor details and needless contacts arising from the bad organization and equipment of the government. . . .[41]

The recommendations which Roosevelt wanted most to impress upon Congress and the people were the ones dealing with the necessity of increasing the number of the aides to the president. The committee said:

The President needs help. His immediate staff assistance is entirely inadequate. He should be given a small number of executive assistants who would be his direct aides in dealing with the managerial agencies and administrative departments of government. . . . *They would remain in the background, issue no orders, make no decisions, emit no public statements. . . . They should be men in whom the President has personal confidence and whose character and attitude is such that they would not attempt to exercise power on their own account.* They should be possessed of high competence, great physical vigor and a passion for anonymity. [Emphasis added.][42]

Acting on these recommendations, Roosevelt issued an executive order in 1939 creating the Executive Office of the President. Two agencies were among the first to be included within this new structure—the White House Office and the Bureau of the Budget (now the OMB). Congress gave the president power to create and abolish divisions within the Executive Office, a power every president has utilized fully to meet his own particular operating needs. Mostly, however, agencies have been added, and only a relative few abolished. There are now approximately twenty of them. Roosevelt was granted authority to hire six top aides to run the office. By the end of 1939, there were eight hundred employees working in the Bureau of the Budget, the National Resources Planning Board, the Liaison Office for Personnel Management, the Office of Government Reports, and the White House Office itself.[43] This is what some writers refer to in part as the "invisible" presidency. This new structure was intended, in the analysis of Leonard D. White:

1. to insure that the chief executive is adequately and currently informed
2. to assist him in foreseeing problems and planning future programs
3. to insure that matters for his decision reach his desk promptly, in condition to be settled intelligently and without delay; and to protect him against hasty and ill-considered judgments
4. to exclude every matter that can be settled elsewhere in the system
5. to protect his time
6. to secure means of insuring compliance by subordinates with established policy and executive direction[44]

These admirable purposes were accompanied by the assumption that the people who occupied staff roles would not be interposed between the president and the cabinet secretaries or agency heads. They were not to have authority over the regular operating departments or officials in them. The reality as this new structure developed, however, was that power and influence steadily moved to those closest to the chief, and a new layer of government was created. For 1975, President Nixon had requested a $11.2 million salary authorization for White House staff members, but this figure did not include $22 million for the OMB or other agencies within the Executive Office. In addition, many people who actually work for the White House are carried on the payroll of the regular departments and agencies. At the top of the pyramid were fourteen aides with salaries of $42,500 a year, the same amount that members of Congress received. These fourteen, along with others in the elite corps of aides, now go by a variety of titles including assistant to the president, special assistant, counsel to the president, special counselor, special consultant, director, and staff director. They number more than fifty. It is this figure which Gerald Ford has pledged to reduce, along with the staffs that serve them (so far without much success).

Roosevelt is noted for his disdain for organizational charts and "channels." He insisted that creative ideas and the information he needed for his decisions could not flow to the top if he did not go beyond the formal structures of government or even outside his own staff. Thus he divided his day into fifteen-minute segments, seeing a wide variety of people who felt they had something that the president should hear. Around one hundred people could call him directly on the phone without having to explain their business to a secretary. He read at least six newspapers a day, in addition to the mountain of official papers and documents that came across his desk. He preferred, however, to learn through conversation with those whom he met. At least in the years before the war, he would dig down into the lower levels of the agencies to invite promising young people to the White House for their opinions and suggestions. He talked with everyone about what interested him at the moment rather than just the subject of their appointment. Thus he was sure of a wide range of opinions and protected himself from being confined to the views of those officially responsible for a problem. Although this infuriated aides and cabinet secretaries alike, they were often astounded by the amount of information he had secured beyond what they had sent to him. These conversations gave him an opportunity not only to hear diverse opinions but also to refine his own ideas by bouncing them off his listeners. At least in the early years, he encouraged a free-wheeling airing of candid and critical evaluations of his administration and its policies.[45]

Nor did Roosevelt limit his information gathering to Washington, D.C. Realizing how isolated that city was from the currents of thought that flow across the country, he traveled so that he could listen to them. Mainly, however, he had to rely on his wife and aides for this kind of looking and listening. Eleanor went everywhere for him, even into the poorest and most miserable sections of the land. The president had great confidence in her observations, frequently citing them in cabinet meetings. When she was in the capital, she traveled about the city by streetcars or on foot, getting away from "official" Washington and hearing what the ordinary people had to say. She became a finely trained observer of the human condition. To seek even further afield, Roosevelt read a random selection of the letters that average citizens wrote to him.

Part of this insatiable curiosity came from a genuinely inquiring mind. But even more of his thirst for information resulted from his insistence that the president had to be possessed of all the facts if he were to keep control of decision making in the executive branch. To quote Schlesinger again:

> Given this conception of the Presidency, he deliberately organized—or disorganized—his system of command to insure that important decisions were passed to the top. His favorite technique was to keep grants of authority incomplete, jurisdictions uncertain, charters overlapping. The result of this competitive theory of administration was often confusion and exasperation on the operating level; but no other method could so reliably insure that in a large bureaucracy filled with ambitious men eager for power, the decisions, and the power to make them, would remain with the President.[46]

Conflict among aides, cabinet members, bureaucrats, members of Congress, or others guaranteed that he would receive many different views of an issue, and that he would retain control over the final decision himself. Like the hub of a wheel, with his aides and officials arrayed around him, no important movement could take place without disturbing the center. Communication through the hub might sometimes prove a bottleneck, but there was no doubt that the conflict thus encouraged would bubble up to Roosevelt himself.

No president since has been able to sit astride government as FDR did. In part this has been due to the enormous growth and proliferation of agencies and programs since his death, but even in his day few people would have had either the capacity or the style to operate in the Roosevelt manner. The total lack of hierarchy among aides and his habit of giving two or more of them the same assignment to insure competition takes a special kind of president to keep the system from falling apart. Even Roosevelt's system had to become more formalized with the advent of war and as specialities were developed by individual staffers.

As every president does, Truman brought his own manner of doing things to the White House. The staff was one of the first things reorganized, becoming more structured and specialized. Though he still relied on trusted aides for general advice on the whole range of governmental problems, some among them were given specific responsibility for problem areas. While Roosevelt often played off one aide against another, Truman almost never did so. But in a sense this staff was not as important as his predecessor's had been, for Truman believed in government through the cabinet rather than through his aides. The assistant to the president, John Steelman, was expected to make sure that unwanted problems from the agencies were kept away from the president and left to the departments where they belonged with the cabinet heads. Thus the staff collectively had far less power than it had under Roosevelt. At the same time, it was expanded as new agencies were added to the Executive Office, including the National Security Council and the Council of Economic Advisers.

Routinization as a process within the presidency was already under way, but it was not allowed to stifle the flexibility that is so necessary to insure the president will control the key informational and decision-making structures of his office. As Neustadt has written:

> Truman's methods in the White House followed forms somewhat like Eisenhower's to results somewhat like Roosevelt's. In theory Truman was as much committed as was Eisenhower to straight lines and tidy boxes on the organizational chart, and to "completed staff work." But in practice Truman had more feel for personalities than jurisdictions, and his instinct was to improvise arrangements around problems rather than to work through fixed procedures. In dealing with his staff he set no precise lines of demarcation or of hierarchy; those he did establish he was likely to ignore. . . . His office was decked out with many of the trappings of what later became known as a staff system, but he himself, remained incurably informal and accessible. . . . Although Truman rather frowned on Roosevelt's methods and would not have dreamed of fostering disorder for its own sake, his accessibility and personal decisiveness combined to furnish him—under the table, so to speak—with information in his mind and choices in his hands.[47]

Every morning Truman held a ten o'clock meeting with a dozen or so of his aides to go over the business of the day, receive reports, and issue instructions on matters the president had decided the night before. Truman also held regularly scheduled separate meetings with the secretary of defense, secretary of state, the chairman of the Democratic National Committee, the National Security Council, and the Democratic leaders of Congress. He met twice weekly with the full cabinet. These latter sessions were primarily for general discussion of problems facing the administration rather than for dealing with specific problems of the departments. Truman dealt with the cabinet secretaries on an individual basis on those questions. He also held weekly news conferences. Matt Connelly, the president's appointments secretary, divided Truman's day into fifteen-minute segments, as had been done for Roosevelt, for meetings with the many people who had to speak to the president. Truman, too, learned best through conversation and thus was willing to see virtually any cabinet member, aide, mayor, governor, or member of Congress who requested an appointment, and usually within forty-eight hours of the request. For a president who was so accessible, it was impossible to become a prisoner of his staff.

Dwight Eisenhower brought the first real hierarchy to the White House staff system. The most frequently cited reason for this was his long experience in the military where the chain of command system was standard operating procedure. In theory, intelligence and obedience were to flow smoothly up to the top, and orders down to the bottom where they were to be executed. Eisenhower had his greatest success and made his reputation as a staff general rather than as a leader of troops in the field. The organization of vast armies, along with the supplies and equipment they needed, demanded centralization of control rather than allowing individuals (no matter how talented) to run off and fight battles on their own. This was Eisenhower's forte, and his own experience proved to him that this was the way to insure that the commander could efficiently oversee the entire operation.

The formalized system that emerged placed Sherman Adams immediately under Eisenhower as assistant to the president. Adams really functioned as chief of staff for the president, a position that no aide had fulfilled for FDR or Truman. Now one man had virtually total determination over everybody and everything allowed into the Oval Office. The only exceptions to this were the scheduled weekly meetings with the National Security Council, the leaders of Congress, the cabinet, and one hour a week briefings from the chairman of the Joint Chiefs of Staff and the secretary of defense. John Foster Dulles simply ignored Adams and went in any time he wanted to see the chief, and Ike's close friend in the cabinet, Secretary of the Treasury George Humphrey, entered through a back door. Although Eisenhower had an appointments secretary, the real decisions as to who got in were made by Adams.[48] The rest of the staff, too, reported to Adams rather than to Eisenhower, with each given fixed responsibility for a particular subject matter. Since the president hated to read long reports, Adams insisted that they be condensed to a single page. Even then, unless they required a presidential decision, Ike did not want to see them. Only those memos that dealt with problems that could not be solved on a lower level and which carried recommendations for action passed Adams's inspection. "OK, S.A." had to be penned on each paper which reached the chief executive's desk. Ike returned them with a simple "yes" or "no" of his own. Thus Adams largely controlled access and the flow of information to the president.[49]

Perhaps more than any other chief executive, Eisenhower utilized his cabinet as a policy advisory institution. It was given a secretariat headed by a "secretary to the cabinet" to handle the agenda and paperwork generated by its meetings. Eisenhower expected the cabinet secretaries to run their own departments and not bother him with the details of their work. Domestic and foreign policy questions were the ones he believed the people elected him to deal with. The difficulty with this was that, because of his screening and staff system, he was generally the last person in the administration to become aware of problems. Most of the details were filtered out at a lower level, and he could not intervene to shape many situations before they had reached a point of no return. Neustadt feels that he unnecessarily limited his choices in this way.[50] So much authority was delegated to lighten the chief executive's work load that crucial decisions were of necessity made by others. When a person can determine the information as well as the options that are presented for consideration to another, then that person takes on real power in his or her own right. Unfortunately for Eisenhower, he did not reach outside his own formal structure to avoid the built-in isolation that comes from overreliance on staff. Ike did not usually even read daily newspapers, only clippings in which Adams felt he would be interested.

More and more special assistants were added to the White House to deal with specific areas, such as atomic energy, disarmament, public works, economic policy, and so on. Staffs had to be provided for all of the committees and for the specialists, with the result that the White House Office expanded to around 400 (up from 279 under Truman). Routine patterns and ways of doing things were the goals, so that everybody would know exactly what his or her function was and who had responsibility for any given problem. There is no doubt that the system was what Eisenhower desired, and it fit the needs of the kind of presidency he intended to operate.

Kennedy pledged in his election campaign to "get the country moving again," and he attempted to organize his staff system to do just that. He abolished the chief of staff position and substituted himself as traffic cop, determining who got into his office. Aides, among whom there was little formal hierarchy, had open access to their chief. As an admirer of Roosevelt (and a student of Neustadt's *Presidential Power*), Kennedy sought to minimize formal structures and permanent assignments as much as possible. Specialities did of course exist (such as press relations, congressional relations, speechwriting, national security, and so forth), but the president dismantled much of the superstructure that Eisenhower had added to the cabinet, National Security Council, and other bodies. As a result, he could get by with fewer top aides in the elite corps of "special advisers," "assistants to," and the like than Eisenhower had employed.

The president himself did not hesitate to circumvent the formal channels of government. Like Roosevelt, he sought to reach out for ideas and information wherever they could be found. He encouraged his staff to do the same thing, for he also shared with Roosevelt a profound distrust of the bureaucracy. Aides were utilized to "prod, double-check, and bypass" the permanent government.[51] The cabinet as an advisory institution was again played down, although some of its individual members, such as Robert McNamara, were influential. It met as a body only infrequently. The result was that the staff became more powerful than any in history up to that point. Most of his key aides had been with Kennedy for a considerable period of time. He believed he knew their strengths and weaknesses and delegated power and authority accordingly. Several tended to the arrogant side and did not hesitate to let others know they spoke for the president. Carl Hayden, dean of the Senate, is said to have remarked that he wished some of them had at least run for sheriff so they would be as expert at politics as they fancied themselves.

Kennedy pretty much expected the cabinet secretaries to be able to handle their own affairs. They, like his staff, could readily get appointments with their boss or call him on the phone, but the more usual process was to feed ideas or suggestions through his aides. Within this fluid situation several key advisers operated. Kenneth O'Donnell handled appointments, arranged trips, and acted as liaison with the Democratic National Committee and local party organizations. He also gave advice on policy questions in his ten to twenty visits with the president each day. The special counsel was Ted Sorensen, who wrote speeches, helped formulate legislative programs and the budget, briefed the president before press conferences, and participated in policy decisions. McGeorge Bundy filled the newly created position of special assistant for national security affairs. He screened the State Department and CIA cables for information of which the president had to be aware and advised on foreign policy issues. The assistant for congressional relations was Larry O'Brien, who had five assistants of his own to help him with this duty. This is one of the offices that was enlarged and strengthened under Kennedy. The press secretary was Pierre Salinger. Arthur Schlesinger, Jr., sat in on some kinds of policy questions and acted as contact with the intellectual community to stimulate innovative proposals. And of course in almost every area of importance, President Kennedy sought the advice of his brother Robert.[52]

Although the Kennedy staff was powerful, the president did not confine himself to it for either advice or information. He read newspapers (though he could become angry at them, as when he canceled a subscription to the *New York Herald Tribune*), questioned reporters, called lower-level officials on the phone, and met with individual members of Congress. He was a voracious reader of reports from the agencies, but he knew that each of them had its own clients, interests, and special viewpoints. Despite this constant effort at "openness," there remained the capacity for self-delusion that comes from being set apart from ordinary constraints and wielding vast power. Since everyone in the White House jumps when the chief executive makes a suggestion, there is a tendency to believe that the rest of the world is subject to the same kind of control. The disastrous Bay of Pigs invasion forced the administration to take a close look at the information and advice it was receiving and seek new ways to keep in contact with reality.

Lyndon Johnson sought to emulate his hero Franklin Roosevelt in the White House. He tried to control everything in the government and everyone around him. Government, however, had been vastly enlarged since the days of the New Deal, and Johnson's talent for controlling men did not match FDR's. While Roosevelt was able to inspire intense and permanent loyalty in those who served him (despite his manipulations), Johnson instead was faced by a large turnover of worn-out and disillusioned aides. He did manage to centralize in his office policy origination as no president had been able to do before him. "Under the direction of Special Assistant Joseph A. Califano, the White House staff assumed the paramount role in setting the framework for legislative and administrative policy making."[53] The departments could not be counted on to provide the kind of innovative ideas Johnson wanted or to turn ideas into policies with a unique Johnson stamp, and thus the task force device under the Johnson aides was utilized. He began his administration like a whirlwind. Johnson was everywhere, seeing everybody, trying to do everything, open and accessible to any and all who wanted to consult with him.

As things began to go badly and the Vietnam War came to occupy more and more of his time, however, the staff structure became more formalized and rigid. Fewer aides and outsiders had access to him, but many were glad to stay out of range of the famous Johnson temper. Marvin Watson became the president's appointments secretary and acted as gatekeeper to protect Johnson's time. Even some of his top staffers, such as McGeorge Bundy and Bill Moyers, were on occasion forced to go through Watson as a form of punishment when they displeased their boss. Johnson still preferred to get information verbally rather than in written form, however, so he did continue to see a large number of people. Many of these meetings were used to reinforce "consensus" within the Johnson team rather than as genuine open forums to explore alternatives. The technique was to poll those present after the president had reached a decision to make sure all concurred with his judgment. Few dared risk the chief's fury by opposing him, as is revealed by this quote from Chester Cooper in *The Lost Crusade:*

> During the process I would frequently fall into a Walter Mitty-like fantasy: When my turn came I would rise to my feet slowly, look around the room and then directly at the President, and say very quietly and emphatically, "Mr. President, gentlemen, I most definitely do *not* agree." But I was removed from my trance when I heard the President's voice saying, "Mr. Cooper, do you agree?" And out would come a "Yes, Mr. President, I agree."[54]

The staff was greatly enlarged from Kennedy's day, but unlike his predecessor Johnson begrudged them any recognition for their achievements. When the most talented among them left, one by one, Johnson raged at their betrayals. For instance, he said that Bill Moyers, who he claimed had been like a son to him, had only used the president to advance his own career: "Well, Lyndon Johnson wasn't stupid, he knew what Moyers had been doing, he read the clips, and why was it that his press secretary's image kept getting better and better, but Johnson's image got worse and worse?"[55] When stories appeared in the press to the effect that Jack Valenti was his chief aide, the president had Valenti's office moved further away from the Oval Office and forced him to go through Watson for an appointment when he wanted to see the president. Only two of the twelve top aides appointed after the 1964 election lasted to the end of Johnson's term in January 1969.[56] LBJ refused to limit his attention to broad policy questions but rather insisted on becoming involved in the details of management. Bill Moyers felt that he became overly immersed in these details: "He wanted to know as much as he could about what was going on in the implementation of his programs, and he became so involved in the operation of those programs that he usurped, unintentionally perhaps, the managerial responsibilities of the Cabinet."[57]

Despite his constant efforts to keep informed, his surge of activity, and his long working hours, Johnson became progressively more isolated in the White House. By all accounts he continued to believe that opposition to the war was shared by only a small minority of college students, radicals, and the establishment media. "The people" were on his side. He raged at the three television sets he kept in his office and at the daily newspapers he read when they carried stories unfavorable to his administration. He badgered his press assistants to change his image. Johnson's style, his intolerance of criticism, and his habit of listening primarily to sycophants assured that he would lose touch with reality once he was enclosed in the presidential mantle of authority.

Richard Nixon sought to restore system and order to the operation of the White House. He did not want to become as straightjacketed as Eisenhower had been by his staff, but at the same time he sought to avoid what he considered to be the pitfalls of the competing and disorganized fiefdoms of aides in the Kennedy and Johnson administrations. Since Nixon, unlike the other presidents discussed, preferred to get most of his information in written rather than verbal form, he arranged his staff accordingly. At the apex of the structure he created was the chief of staff position, a role first occupied by H. R. (Bob) Haldeman and later by Alexander Haig. The job of the chief of staff was to insure that the president had large blocks of time to himself so he could make the decisions that only the president can make. At the same time Haldeman and Haig were charged with seeing to it that Nixon got all of the relevant information and "options" needed for making those decisions. During the first years of his administration, the president participated frequently in meetings of the National Security Council, the Domestic Council, the Urban Affairs Council, and the Republican congressional leadership. Decisions were not reached at these meetings; instead Nixon used them to explore alternatives, one of which would be chosen by the president himself in solitude.

As the years progressed, Nixon became less and less accessible to all but his closest aides and friends. Before two years were up, Walter Hickel, secretary of the interior, complained that he had been able to see the president privately only twice in fifteen months. He blamed the "Berlin Wall" (Haldeman and Ehrlichman) for isolating the president from members of his own cabinet. In fact, only three of the many cabinet secretaries who came and went during Nixon's five and a half years in the White House had ready access to the chief executive. These three—John Mitchell, John Connally, and Henry Kissinger—were men whose advice Nixon valued. Outside of these three, however, Haldeman (and to a lesser degree Ehrlichman) decided whether or not a cabinet secretary's business was important enough to disturb the chief. Partially as a result, there was more turnover in these positions than in any previous administration. Altogether there were thirty separate cabinet appointments, surpassing the previous record of twenty-six set in Grant's eight years in office. Not one lasted the entire five years of Nixon's incumbency. There were four attorneys general (two of whom were later indicted for crimes), three secretaries of labor, three secretaries of defense, three secretaries of the treasury, three secretaries of commerce, three secretaries of health, education, and welfare, two secretaries of state, two secretaries of agriculture, two secretaries of housing, two secretaries of transportation, and two secretaries of the interior. (One postmaster general served before that office was taken out of the cabinet.)

Immediately after the 1972 landslide reelection, Nixon (through Haldeman) informed the members of his administration that he expected their resignations, not all of which he would accept. Over the years most of the prominent figures in the cabinet who had independent political support of their own were replaced by men largely without bases of power upon which they could fall back. His first cabinet had included personal friends, such as Mitchell, Finch, and Rogers. These too were gone in the later cabinet. In introducing the first group of people selected to head the departments, Nixon had said that they were "men of extra dimension" and "independent thinkers" who could give him competing advice and counsel. There is little evidence he consulted personally at all (except on the rarest of occasions) with the people who succeeded his original cabinet. Many citizens had difficulty in even remembering the names of Frederick Dent, James T. Lynn, Claude Brinegar, or Peter Brennan. With little power of their own, under secretaries appointed from the White House staff to keep a watch on the departments, and the OMB overseeing the execution of policy, most secretaries were almost totally excluded from policy making within their areas of jurisdiction. They were reduced to the status of administrators for the White House. Paradoxically, as the attention of the president and his top aides came to focus nearly completely on Watergate-

related matters, the departments gained a measure of independence (except from the OMB), which they had not experienced in
years.

Estimates of the size of the Nixon staff varied greatly. As
mentioned, specialists were borrowed from the departments and
continued on the department budgets even as they worked for
the president. In addition, the figures varied depending on which
agencies were counted as belonging to the Executive Office of the
President. The CIA officially reports directly to the chief executive, but its 15,000 members are not attributed to the Executive
Office. The Associated Press, drawing on monthly reports published by the Civil Service Commission, reported that the Executive Office staff more than doubled in Nixon's first four years,
from 1,748 to 3,562 employees. Charles E. Jacob put the figure at
4,716 in 1973, while Thomas Cronin found 5,395 people working
for the president in that year.[58] Since the AP figures are the lowest,
reliance on them should provide a safe minimal estimate. This is
the growth they cite: Franklin Roosevelt operated with a White
House staff (the elite corps of advisers, assistants, counselors, and
so on) of 51 men prior to World War II; under Harry Truman this
number increased to 243; by December 1972, 606 people were
employed by Nixon in the White House Office. Similarily, the
Executive Office contained 1,100 additional employees under
Truman, 1,500 under Kennedy, and reached 1,700 with Lyndon
Johnson. Kissinger's National Security Council staff more than
doubled to 80 people, John Ehrlichman employed 50 in the
Domestic Council, and the Office of Telecommunications Policy
had 69 employees, while 79 served the Office of Science and
Technology, 68 the Council on Environmental Quality, 58 the
Council of Economic Advisers, and 689 the Office of Manage-
ment and Budget.[59]

With a staff of that size, it is clearly impossible for the president
to oversee personally the activities of even the people who work
directly for him, much less serve as an efficient "chief administrator" for the 2.5 million civilian employees of the departments. A
president could spend all of his time just supervising his own
staff. But for a president who disliked seeing most employees
personally, the problem was compounded. Thus Nixon delegated
vast amounts of power and authority to his close aides to speak in

his behalf and to act as his surrogates in managing the White House and the agencies beyond. Even high-level White House people were excluded. For example, John Dean, legal counsel for Mr. Nixon and the person put in charge of "containing" Watergate, only rarely saw the president until the cover-up began unraveling. Dean began work in the White House in July of 1970, but as his testimony before the Senate Watergate Committee makes clear, this did not mean he had access to the president. Senator Gurney questioned Dean about why he had not reported Liddy's break-in plans to Mr. Nixon directly as soon as he learned of them in January and February of 1972:

> Senator Gurney: At this particular time, Mr. Dean, were you not the Counsel for the President: Was that not your job?
>
> Mr. Dean: That was my title and that was my job.
>
> ....
>
> Senator Gurney: Why did you not go back to the President and tell him about this hair-raising scheme?
>
> Mr. Dean: Well, I did go back, but I did not have access to the President, as I think I explained. I went to Mr. Haldeman.
>
> Senator Gurney: Did you try to gain access to the President?
>
> Mr. Dean: Senator, I did try. I had never been in to the President or called by the President before. My reporting channel was through Mr. Haldeman. [60]

Thus in more than a year and a half, the counsel to the president had not seen his client. Other staffers reported similar experiences.

Attorney General Elliot Richardson and Deputy Attorney General William Ruckelshaus were not allowed to see or talk on the phone with Nixon in the crucial five days in October 1973 when the president was deciding to fire Special Prosecutor Cox. Instead, they had to deal with Alexander Haig. Only when Richardson threatened to resign was an appointment arranged. After the firing, Ruckelshaus was asked if he had attempted to warn Nixon beforehand of the "firestorm" that would occur if the president went through with his intentions. The reply was that he had not seen Mr. Nixon or talked to him for the nearly five months he had served as acting FBI director and deputy attorney general.

Such a system guarantees vast authority to those who control access to the chief executive. Alexander Butterfield, who served for more than four years as one of Haldeman's aides and as deputy assistant to the president, testified before the House Judiciary Committee's impeachment inquiry that "Haldeman was the alter ego. Haldeman was almost the other President. I can't emphasize that enough." He went on to estimate that Haldeman saw the president at least seven times more frequently than anyone else, including Henry Kissinger and John Ehrlichman.[61] Butterfield claimed that Haldeman was not a decision maker but simply an "implementer" of Nixon's decisions, but he failed to see the obvious control that a gatekeeper exercises by including or excluding the people and information upon which a president bases his decisions. Presidents, like other decision makers, tend to act on what is in front of them. The person who can determine what gets to the president's desk can effectively set the agenda for action. The presidential transcripts also make it clear that Haldeman's and Ehrlichman's advice was frequently solicited. Other aides, as well as cabinet members, submitted their reports and requests for audiences with the president through these two top staffers. Frequently such reports were summarized for Nixon by Haldeman and Ehrlichman. Even the best intentioned of aides are subject to judgmental errors in deciding what should get through and what should be excluded as extraneous to presidential needs. In addition, written reports cannot convey the intensity of a position, cannot answer questions, and cannot provide further elaboration of the points they make. Only face to face conversations with advocates can do that.

Nor did Nixon read the newspapers for himself as other presidents had done. Instead a daily news summary was prepared for him by an aide, Patrick Buchanan, along with a staff of four. Each summary contained four or five sections, totaling around thirty-five pages altogether. One section contained an edited UPI and AP wire service report, another dealt with what had been said about the administration on the radio and TV news and talk shows, the third contained a news summary from several East Coast morning newspapers, and the fourth section was a digest of analyses and editorials from around fifty papers across the country. The final part of the summary was a report on how thirty to thirty-five magazines and newsletters were covering particular issues (such as Vietnam, Watergate, the China trip, and so on). A cartoon report was included in the back.[62] Once again, the judgments of aides about what should reach the president's eyes were substituted for his own independent search for information. It may never be discovered just how objective these summaries were, but William Safire, himself a former Nixon speechwriter, indicates that those who prepared the news briefings sought to "think positively" by including whatever praise for the president they could find. This in itself could have a distorting effect if Nixon were led to believe that at least half of his reviews were favorable. To quote Safire on the job of Mort Allin, who prepared the summaries in the last days of the administration: "In the old days, Mort could balance a blast with a bouquet, send a cheery cartoon along with the Herblockages. But during the siege, as in Water torture, he was doomed to the day-after-day production of the dreariest daily publication in America, and he hated every moment of it."[63] When aides hate to give their chief an objective report on what is happening in the country, the president is almost sure of losing touch with reality.

Since presidential assistants have gathered enormous power of their own in recent administrations, their selection and supervision become crucial matters for the chief executive's attention. In such a large group of people, it is nearly impossible to insure against making one or more bad appointments. Thus careful observance of their work and setting the proper examples for their conduct are important parts of a president's job. Gerald Ford was asked in his first press conference if he intended to set up a code of ethics for the executive branch. His answer was direct and to the point and illustrates a truism about all administrations: presidential aides generally take their cues from the person at the top. "The code of ethics that will be followed will be the example that I set," said Ford.[64]

Staffers who have had experience in the political process have an advantage in that they understand the traditions of the institutions of government and the comity which is necessary if the process is to function smoothly. They learn the limits of acceptable behavior on the part of each branch of government. And they understand that political opposition does not make one an enemy. Richard Nixon, a man of vast political experience himself, selected a staff almost totally devoid of any training in government. Haldeman had managed the Los Angeles branch of the advertising firm of J. Walter Thompson before coming to the White House as the president's chief of staff. Ehrlichman (the president's chief domestic adviser) was a Seattle lawyer specializing in real estate and an old college classmate of Haldeman's. Dwight Chapin (the president's appointment secretary), had worked for Haldeman at J. Walter Thompson. Ron Ziegler (Nixon's press secretary) had been employed at Disneyland and J. Walter Thompson. Among the other Thompson alumni were Bruce Kehrli, the White House secretary; Larry Higby, Haldeman's chief deputy; and Kenneth Cole, the director of the Domestic Council. Gordon Strachan had been a lawyer with Nixon's firm in New York. Egil Krogh, Jr., had worked as a lawyer with Ehrlichman in Seattle. Jeb Magruder had been in advertising and management and ran a small cosmetics firm of his own before joining the administration. Most of these people had worked in Nixon's election campaigns as advance men or in other capacities but had not served in any governmental positions themselves.

Even John Mitchell, whose advice the president frequently sought, had spent most of his career as a bond lawyer in New York and, except for managing Nixon's 1968 campaign, had limited political experience. Thus the example that Nixon set and how he viewed the rest of the government was of the utmost importance to the people who served him. They had no independent basis for judgments of their own about what a president or his staff can legitimately do. Without brilliance, or philosophies of their own to guide them, or experienced senior staffers who could rein in their zeal, the young men brought into the administration did what the young sometimes do—they went to excess. The climate within which White House aides worked was one of total loyalty to the man at the top and willingness to do anything to serve him. Charles Colson, a senior White House staffer, announced that he would "walk over his grandmother to reelect Richard Nixon." The example these young people had to follow was made clear by several incidents. One occurred in May 1970 when a group of antiwar student demonstrators marched through the financial district of New York City. As policemen watched, they were set upon and beaten by a group of hard-hatted construction workers. Within three weeks Peter J. Brennan, president of the Building and Construction Trades Council of New York, was invited to the White House where Nixon posed in a hard hat that had been presented to him. Later the president named Brennan to the cabinet as his secretary of labor. John Dean testified that Nixon became furious on one occasion when he looked out his office window and saw a lone man with a large sign across the street in Lafayette Park. Nixon ordered the sign removed, even though no law had been broken. Dean goes on: "When I came out of Mr. Higby's office, I ran into Mr. Dwight Chapin who said that he was going to get some 'thugs' to remove that man from Lafayette Park. He said it would take him a few hours to get them, but they could do the job."[65] What sorts of lessons must have been learned by junior staffers from these examples?

There were intense group pressures to conform to the notion that any activity which advanced the cause of the president was justified. Senator Baker questioned Bart Porter, a young aide, on this point:

> Senator Baker: At any time did you ever think of saying: I do not think this is quite right, this is not quite the way it ought to be. Did you think of that?
>
> Mr. Porter: I think most people would probably stop and think about that.
>
> Senator Baker: Did you?
>
> Mr. Porter: Yes, I did.
>
> Senator Baker: What did you do about it?
>
> Mr. Porter: I did not do anything.
>
> Senator Baker: Why didn't you?
>
> Mr. Porter: In all honesty, probably because of the fear of group pressure that would ensue, of not being a team player.[66]

Jeb Stuart Magruder tells of being ordered by the president to spread the word that an unfriendly correspondent was a Communist and an agent of the Rumanian government. "I didn't waste any time in soul-searching—I'd already seen, in one month in the

White House, that those assistants who tried to second guess the President's judgments didn't last long in his favor."[67] Magruder blames the atmosphere thus created for many of the problems experienced by the Nixon administration:

> We had a tendency, from inside the beseiged White House, to lump all our critics together—all journalists were enemies, all Vietnam critics were radicals. If Haldeman had talked more to our critics, and seen that they weren't all radicals or revolutionaries, it might have made a difference. As it was, there was too little fresh air blowing through the White House, and we all tended to become caught up in the "enemies" mentality.[68]

Once it is possible to dismiss all critics as enemies, then it is unnecessary to pay any attention to their advice or to the competing information that they may have to offer. The result is that an administration becomes totally isolated and dependent upon its own rather distorted view of reality.

Following are a few of the views of those who worked in the Nixon White House:

> I never really questioned whether what he [the President] wanted done was right or proper. . . . I have thought a lot about what happened to me in the White House, what may have happened to others and why. It troubles me, because I now realize how easy it is for even strong and well disciplined men to lose their perspective under pressure. I had one rule—to get done that which the President wanted done. . . . As a member of the White House staff . . . sensitivity gave way to expediency. . . . [Charles Colson, special counsel to the president][69]

> I had a lot to learn about government. I didn't know a liberal from a conservative. I didn't understand that Congress made the laws and the executive executed them. [Fred Malek, deputy director of the OMB][70]

> They [Haldeman, Ehrlichman, Colson] isolated him from the people, from members of Congress whose counsel was essential to him, and planted in his mind a distrust of his own Cabinet officers. . . . In leading him down the path to disaster, by substituting dishonesty and deceit for truth and openness, they built a wall about him—in the guise of a more efficient staff operation—that shut him off from loyal friends whose contrary views might weaken their influence over him. . . .

[Senior assistants] began to hide facts from the President on matters both large and small. . . . [The President] denied himself the opportunity for a cross-fertilization of ideas which any successful executive needs. . . . [After 1970] most of the President's advisers who had real political experience and talent found that they were allowed little or no access to him. . . . He withdrew from friends and ideas and delegated still more power to the selected few. [Herbert Klein, director of communications][71]

The disaster that befell the Nixon presidency should come as no surprise in light of these comments from observers who themselves served in high-level positions within the system.

It takes any administration a year or two to establish routine patterns and develop characteristic ways of handling the problems that are laid on its doorstep and for relationships between the president and his key aides to become fixed. Thus it is impossible at this writing to specify fully all of the operating patterns in Gerald Ford's White House. Initially, at least, it appears that the president intends to maintain a much more open and flexible system than Nixon did. At the apex of the staff are nine assistants who have daily access to the president. Each of these in turn has deputies who have the same authority and access in the absence of the president's assistants. This arrangement was described as "pure Jerry Ford" by Donald Rumsfeld, who oversees White House operations, staff coordination, and recruitment for the president. (The old title of chief of staff has been abolished.) Henry Kissinger remains as presidential assistant for national security affairs as well as secretary of state. Ron Nessen serves as press secretary. James T. Lynn directs the Office of Management and Budget. John O. Marsh, Jr., is the counselor to the president and supervises the offices of Congressional and Public Liaison. Robert T. Hartman deals with political matters and speechwriting, Philip Buchen is the president's lawyer and also does political work, and William Seidman is responsible for economic affairs. Finally, James M. Cannon, a former Rockefeller aide, has been named executive director of the Domestic Council as well as a presidential assistant. Most of these aides resemble Ford in their social and political outlooks: conservative and Republican. Many were former colleagues in the House of Representatives or are old friends from Michigan. In this Ford has followed the pattern of his predecessors.

In an attempt to guard against overdependence on the views of those in the White House, Ford meets from time to time with a group of friends and advisors with no formal governmental positions. Supposedly, they have no axes of their own to grind. However, these men, whose judgment the presidents trusts, tend to share Ford's major policy viewpoints and provide little challenge to his basic philosophy.

President Ford's operating style has not changed much since leaving the House of Representatives. He puts in eighteen-hour days, with few large blocks of time reserved for reflection or planning. Rather, his time is divided among countless meetings with cabinet officials, aides, members of Congress, friends, and political leaders and formal committee sessions. In this he resembles Roosevelt and Truman rather than Nixon. He has also taken some steps to guard against the development of an "imperial" mentality in the White House. Titles are being abolished, the use of limousines curtailed, and fewer aides invited on the presidential jet. The formal trappings surrounding the president himself, however, have not been reduced, and Ford is traveling (though not to private estates) as much as Nixon did.[72]

The most influential aides to emerge early in the new administration were Rumsfeld, Hartman, Seidman, and Marsh. Henry Kissinger continued to play the dominant role in foreign affairs, serving as virtually the only voice the president listened to. Jerry terHorst, Ford's first appointment as press secretary, resigned over the pardon the president granted to Richard Nixon. TerHorst said that he had been "misled" by those around Ford into giving out false stories to the effect that such a pardon was not under consideration. Some observers saw both the pardon and the attempt to make decisions in secret and keep them from other key aides as an indication that the White House had already begun to close in around Ford. After a month of almost universal praise from Congress, the press, and the people, with ringing endorsements for his judgments and policies in his ears, it may have been that he, like his predecessors, misjudged the public sentiment. By most accounts the president was surprised at the intensity of the negative reaction to his decision. For the first time he heard boos in public. In any case, terHorst was the first aide within memory who publicly said he resigned because of a policy disagreement with his chief. Such a reaction, if it became common practice, could have the effect of forcing presidents to canvas all segments of opinion before annoucing their decisions.

Problems with the Staff System

It is true, as many have pointed out, that a president is limited by what one man can do; that cabinet officers and other members of the executive branch have interests different from that of the chief executive; that leaders in Congress, private interest groups, and the press have power of their own to thwart the policies of the president in various areas. But he still commands more power than any of them singly, and even more than most of them in combination. In his own branch he appoints to office, removes, organizes, reorganizes, shuffles, promotes, demotes, bestows favors and attentions, or scowls and ignores. Every rumor about who has his attention, sees him frequently, was invited to travel on the presidential jet, or received a note from the boss is immediately spread through the grapevine and in the press. Such a person, presumed to have the president's ear and favor, is likely to gain influence enabling him to exercise power of his own. Thus a president's judgments about people, about the correct subordinates for each position (especially among his top staff), are perhaps the most critical decisions he must make early in his administration. But he must be held accountable for his selections and their actions, and he must superintend their activities.

It may be that the president and his aides are frustrated many times by the power of others. But the democratic process, the system of checks and balances and separation of powers set up by the Constitution, were all designed to frustrate the unitary exercise of authority. Over the years, the limitations imposed upon him have eroded. The point is this: the president has immense power and so do his aides. Today the office is not the narrowly defined and prescribed one of history, but is instead unrivaled among the world's executive leaders.

In a sense, the president has to be protected from the presidency. Staffers surrounding him who are part of the office suffer many of the same limitations that beset the chief himself—they tend to be elevated above, and isolated from, political reality. In the words of Irvin Janis, chief executives who become dependent on an "inner circle of advisers and set up group norms that encourage unanimity" may fall victim to the dangers of "group-think," with disastrous consequences for the nation as well as the administration.[73] Thus the advice and help aides are able to give the chief executive is limited by their own positions. Melvin Laird, perhaps aware of this, said he did not want to join the Ford administration because any president needs a friend on the outside who can stand back and give objective counsel. In addition to this, the aspirations of aides may affect the independence of judgment that any president needs. As Patrick Anderson has said of White House staffers:

> The one factor almost all of them have shared is uncommon ambition, a thirst for power and glory, even reflected power and glory, and a willingness to sacrifice friends, family, and personal health, often to suffer personal and political humiliation, in order to satisfy their ambitions.[74]

Objectivity and dissent are difficult to foster among ambitious staffers who believe (rightly or wrongly) that they have to mirror their chief's every view if they are to remain in power. Fawning sycophants give poor advice.

Another conundrum that besets the modern presidency arises from the very growth of the institution itself. Over the years the office has come to resemble in many ways the organizations it was designed to circumvent because of their supposed inability to deal with problems:

> The Presidency has become a large, complex bureaucracy itself, rapidly acquiring many dubious characteristics of bureaucracies in the process: layering, overspecialization, communication gaps, interoffice rivalries, inadequate coordination, and an impulse to become consumed with short-term, urgent operational concerns at the expense of thinking systematically about the consequences of varying sets of policies and priorities and about important long-range problems.[75]

Alfred de Grazia has nicely summed up the true plural nature of the office: "The President is a Congress with a skin thrown over him."[76] Although viewed as a single man, the presidency is in reality many people. What frequently is not recognized is that the urge to "let the president do it" means in fact that the president's staff will be given new responsibilities. He can do virtually nothing by himself. He already has so many duties that additional ones can only add to the White House bureaucracy which acts in his name.

The office will remain large as long as the problems with the cabinet secretaries and departments mentioned in this chapter continue. It will expand if each new crisis brings demands for presidential solutions, if secrecy remains a consuming passion, and if Congress continues to renounce its own responsibility as a full partner in the governmental process.

NOTES

1. See, for example, James David Barber, *The Presidential Character* (Englewood Cliffs, N.J.; Prentice-Hall, 1972); Erwin C. Hargrove, *Presidential Leadership: Personality and Political Style* (New York: Macmillan, 1966); Tom Wicker, *JFK and LBJ: The Influence of Personality upon Politics*, (Baltimore: Penquin, 1968).

2. George Reedy, *The Twilight of the Presidency* (New York: New American Library, 1970), p. 26.

3. Marcus Cunliffe, *American Presidents and the Presidency* (New York: American Heritage, 1968), pp. 42, 43.

4. The story was first reported some years after the incident, and its authenticity is doubted by some. See, for instance, Dumas Malone, *Jefferson and His Time*, IV, *Jefferson the President* (Boston, Little, Brown, 1970), p. 29.

5. For the following advantages, plus additional perquisites, see Dan Cordtz, "The Imperial Lifestyle of the U.S. President," *Fortune*, 88, no. 4 (October, 1973) 143–147, 220–224; *U.S. News and World Report*, 27 January 1969, pp. 32–34; *Newsweek*, 20 August 1973, pp. 30–31; Reedy, chap. 1, *passim*.

6. Philippa Strum, *Presidential Power and American Democracy* (Pacific Palisades, Calif.; Goodyear, 1972), p. 74.

7. Philip Shabecoff, in *New York Times*, 1 January 1974.

8. *Newsweek*, 20 August 1973, pp. 30–31.

9. Cordtz, pp. 220–221.

10. Shabecoff.

11. Associated Press news release, 26 November 1973.

12. *New York Times*, 23 March 1974.

13. Shabecoff.

14. "Additional Taxable Income Because of the Expenditure of Federal Funds at the President's Properties at San Clemente and Key Biscayne," table from the joint committee staff, reprinted in the *New York Times*, 4 April 1974.

15. Cordtz, *passim*.

16. *New York Times*, 25 May 1974.

17. Jack Anderson, "Tax Issue Closing in on Nixon," *Daily Idahonian*, 8 March 1974.

18. Cordtz, p. 224.

19. "Examination of President Nixon's Tax Returns for 1969 through 1972," staff report (No. 93–966) prepared for the Joint Committee on Internal Revenue Taxation, 93rd Cong., 2nd Sess., 3 April 1974.

20. Cordtz, p. 144.

21. *U.S. News and World Report*, 27 January 1969, pp. 32–34.

22. Shabecoff.

23. Theodore H. White, *The Making of the President 1968*, (New York: Anthenum 1969), pp. 428, 434.

24. Quoted in Fred I. Greenstein, "What the President Means to Americans," in *Choosing the President*, ed. James D. Barber (Englewood Cliffs, N.J.: Prentice-Hall, 1974), p. 141.

25. *Time*, 19 August 1974, pp. 27, 32-33.

26. George Reedy, *The Presidency in Flux* (New York: Columbia University Press, 1973), p. 11.

27. Reedy, *Twilight*, pp. 36-37.

28. Charles Frankel, *High on Foggy Bottom*, (New York: Harper & Row, 1968), p. 78.

29. These points are made in Frankel, chap. 7.

30. David Halberstam, *The Best and the Brightest* (New York: Random House, 1969), p. 437.

31. Robert F. Kennedy, *Thirteen Days* (New York: Norton, 1969), pp. 33, 112.

32. Theodore C. Sorensen, *Decision Making in the White House* (New York: Columbia University Press, 1963), p. 71.

33. Henry Fairlie, "Thoughts on the Presidency," *The Public Interest*, no. 9 (Fall 1967), 32.

34. Cited in Patrick Anderson, *The President's Men* (Garden City, N.Y.: Doubleday 1968), p. 53.

35. For an analysis of cabinet selection criteria see Richard F. Fenno, *The President's Cabinet* (New York: vintage, 1959), pp. 51–87.

36. Richard E. Neustadt, *Presidential Power* (New York: Wiley, 1960), p. 39. Much of the following concerning the "five masters" relies on this source.

37. Cited by Neustadt, p. 39.

38. Marriner S. Eccles, *Beckoning Frontiers* (New York: Knopf, 1951), p. 336, quoted in Neudstadt, p. 42.

39. Edward S. Corwin, *The President: Office and Powers*, 4th rev. ed. (New York: New York University Press, 1957), p. 301.

40. Patrick Anderson., pp. 54–55.

41. *Report of the President's Committee on Administrative Management* (Washington, D.C.: GPO 1937), p. 5.

42. *Ibid.*, p. 5.

43. Mary Costello, "Presidential Reorganization," *Editorial Research Report of Congressional Quarterly*, 11, no. 2 (11 July 1973), 528.

44. Quoted in Charles E. Jacob, "The Quest for Presidential Control: Innovation and Institutionalization in the Executive Branch," paper read at the annual meeting of the American Political Science Association, New Orleans, La., September 1973, p. 4.

45. Arthur M. Schlesinger, Jr. *The Coming of the New Deal* (Cambridge, Mass.: Riverside, 1959), p. 515–525.

46. *Ibid.*, pp. 527–528.

47. Neustadt, pp. 171–172.

48. Herbert S. Parmet, *Eisenhower and the American Crusades* (New York: Macmillan 1972), chap. 22.

49. Dorothy B. James, *The Contemporary Presidency*, 2nd ed. (Indianapolis: Pegasus, 1974), pp. 155–156.

50. Neustadt, p. 159 and *passim*.

51. Patrick Anderson, p. 195.

52. Joseph Kraft, "Kennedy's Working Staff," *Harper's*, December 1962, reprinted in *The Modern Presidency*, ed. Nelson Polsby (New York: Random House, 1973), pp. 146–151.

53. Norman C. Thomas and Harold L. Wolman, "Policy Formulation in the Institutionalized Presidency: The Johnson Task Forces," in *The Presidential Advisory System*, ed. Thomas E. Cronin and Sanford D. Greenberg (New York, Harper & Row, 1969), p. 127.

54. Cited in James D. Barber, *The Presidential Character* (Englewood Cliffs, N.J.: Prentice-Hall, 1972), p. 82.

55. Halberstam, p. 640.

56. Richard T. Johnson, *Managing the White House* (New York: Harper & Row, 1974), pp. 178–179.

57. An interview with Bill Moyers by Hugh Sidey, reprinted in *Inside the System*, ed. Charles Peters and John Rothchild (New York: Praeger, 1973), p. 41.

58. Associated Press news dispatch, in the *Daily Idahonian*, 8 December 1972; Jacob, p. 4; Thomas E. Cronin, "The Swelling of the Presidency," *Saturday Review of the Society*, 1, no. 1 (December 1973), 30.

59. Associated Press news dispatch, in the *Daily Idahonian*, 8 December 1972.

60. Testimony of John W. Dean, "Presidential Campaign Activities of 1972," *Hearings Before the Select Committee on Presidential Campaign Activities*, Senate, 93rd Cong., 1st Sess., June, 1973, Book 4, pp. 1353-1354. Hereafter called *Hearings*.

61. *New York Times*, 25 July 1974.

62. Telephone interview with Patrick Buchanan, December 1970.

63. William Safire, "Last Days in the Bunker," *New York Times Magazine*, 18 August 1974, p. 6.

64. *Weekly Compilation of Presidential Documents*, 10, no. 35 (2 September 1974), 1070.

65. *Hearings*, p. 917.

66. *Ibid.*, p. 648.

67. Jeb. S. Magruder, *An American Life* (New York: Atheneum, 1974), p. 55.

68. *Ibid.*, p. 101.

69. *New York Times*, 22 June 1974.

70. *New York Times*, 13 August 1974.

71. *New York Times*, 25 August 1974.

72. For a good early treatment of Ford's White House operation, see John Hersey, "The President," a special issue of the *New York Times Magazine*, 20 April 1975. Hersey spent a full week with the president, sitting in on almost all meetings he attended. The only exceptions were sessions devoted to national security matters.

73. Irving L. Janis, *Victims of Groupthink* (Boston: Houghton Mifflin, 1972), p. 191.

74. Patrick Anderson, p. 3.

75 Cronin, "The Swelling of the Presidency," p. 34.

76. Alfred de Grazia, *Republic In Crisis* (New York: Federal Legal Publications, 1965), p. 72.

5

Reforms

Many people still argue that America needs a strong and vigorous presidency. It is difficult for the 535 men and women of Congress to provide the continuous and unified national leadership that is a requirement of modern industrial society. Even those nations unburdened by superpower status do not have legislatures capable of exercising such leadership. But Watergate has proven one thing: even though Richard Nixon may have been an aberration in the White House, aberrations can and do occur there. Surely the next time a president is tempted to go beyond the parameters of acceptable behavior, he will not be foolish enough to tape record his own culpabilities. For without those tapes Nixon would almost certainly have served as President until January 20, 1977. Nor can the United States depend upon electing "good" people for its salvation; even men of the best intentions have been subject to the lapses of judgment that come when the office isolates an incumbent from political reality.

Criticism of the presidency predates the adoption of the Constitution. Throughout its existence, commentators have offered innumerable suggestions for change in the size, shape, and scope of the office's powers. Some believed that the institution had too much power and was implicitly a threat, while others saw its shortcomings in the opposite direction. It is the latter school of thought that won the adherence of most liberal scholars in recent decades. The picture, however, is more complicated than this, for some drew a distinction between foreign affairs (where they argued that the president had too much power) and domestic affairs (where he had too little). With the Vietnam War and

Watergate, the critique of the institution focused once again on the dangers inherent in the ascendant presidency. The errors of judgment, the mistaken policies, and the seemingly inexplicable lapses in the political acumen of recent incumbents have led many liberals to seek ways to guard against the potential abuses they see inhering in the office.

Some of the solutions offered seek not only to protect the people from the president but also to insure that the president will be able to avoid the snares that have trapped his predecessors. Chief executives, too, have an interest in making the right decisions. They want not only to be popular in their own times but to be remembered as great presidents by history. A few reforms have already come about and others are likely to be enacted. Many proposals, however, will never get beyond the stage of talking. Although Watergate was the most traumatic occurrence ever to befall the institution, it seems unlikely that the more extreme proposals calling for constitutional revision will pass Congress and the state legislatures. They are of interest, however, because they illustrate the extent of dissatisfaction with the office as it is presently constituted. Unless the more modest reforms succeed, pressure may build for more drastic modifications in the way the United States is governed. This chapter begins with an examination of some of the proposals that require constitutional amendments and then turns to changes that could be implemented either through law or merely by alterations in the way the office has been conducted in recent years. It also examines some of the objections that have been voiced with regard to these proposals, and the possible consequences of their adoption.

Change in the Term of Office

The Virginia plan at the Consitutional Convention proposed a single seven-year term for the chief executive. This, like other provisions, was the subject of compromise among the delegates. The result was a term of four years, with no limitation on the number of terms a person could serve. In what some analysts have seen as a posthumous slap at Franklin Roosevelt's four elections, the Twenty-second Amendment was added to the

Constitution in 1951, prohibiting any person from being elected more than twice. The length of time a president should serve is still not a settled question for many of those interested in the office. The most frequent proposal for change is to that of a single six-year term, as advocated by Jackson, Polk, Harrison, Cleveland, and Taft. Modern presidents like Lyndon Johnson and Richard Nixon also have suggested that six years might be the ideal length of service. Clearly the motives for such a change are mixed; some seek thereby to limit the president, others to increase his power, and still others to take the office as much as possible out of politics.

Many of the Watergate abuses were connected with Nixon's reelection campaign of 1972. An argument can be made that, if the president had not been eligible to run again, the bugging of Democratic headquarters, the illegal campaign contributions, and the misuse of governmental agencies to try to cover up White House involvement would never have occurred. (The plumbers' activities and other horrors were not related to the election, of course.) It is doubtful whether the president or his subordinates would have undertaken such activity on behalf of Spiro Agnew or any other candidate of the president's party. Senator Mike Mansfield, majority leader of the Senate (and no friend of the imperial presidency) has written:

> There is no more compelling argument for this proposal than that which says every step must be taken that serves to divorce the office of the presidency from the arena of the political campaign. A single term of six years—or five or seven—would assist such an end. . . . With a single six year term, gone would be the charge, however invalid, that a president uses his power to appoint to achieve political ends and to pave the way for his own reelection. For that matter, too, it would help offset the charge that political considerations enter into decisions involving such crucial areas as foreign and economic policy.[1]

An additional set of reasons for the six-year term centers upon the vital question of time. Without having to concentrate on his own reelection, this reasoning goes, a chief executive could devote his full energies to solving the problems of the country. As Jack Valenti, an aide to former President Johnson, put it:

Each passing month makes it more apparent that the man who holds that office has to deal with problems so monstrous, so disruptive, so resistant to permanent solution that the re-election process is no longer suitable. The President cannot be allowed to be directed from his hard duties and even harder decisions by the so called normalcies of politics and reelection.[2]

A variation on this "time" theme is that the present four-term is too short for a president to enact his program and get it firmly underway. By the time a new chief executive is inaugurated in January, the current fiscal year is already half over, and planning for the next one is well under way. A new president will at most be able to affect minor changes until he has the opportunity to submit a full budget of his own. It is well into his second year, then, before the governmental agenda bears the full stamp of the new president. By then he has to begin thinking about his reelection. Rexford Tugwell proposes a nine-year term (unless the president is rejected by sixty percent of the voters after three years) to get around this dilemma.[3]

Proponents of a six-year term maintain that it would allow the full implementation of a president's program and relieve him of reelection worries. Moreover, the second four-year term, as currently permitted, has not been very fruitful in terms of major policy enactment by chief executives. Most of Theodore Roosevelt's, Woodrow Wilson's, Franklin Roosevelt's, and Lyndon Johnson's innovative programs were enacted in their first few years in office. It can be argued that by the end of six years an administration has used up its creative thrust as well as its political clout, and it is usually downhill after that. To those who maintain that a single term of office would make a new incumbent a lame duck immediately upon election, defenders of the six-year term point out that the identical status exists currently for a president who is reelected. Since any new chief executive has favors he can bestow, the diminution of power that besets all administrations may not set in sooner under one system than another.

Some of those who oppose a single six-year term cite the lame duck problem. Others base their case on the ground that it is inherently undemocratic to try to take the presidency out of politics. Reedy argues that presidents are most effective only when they understand the political process and are immersed in it. Isolation from the reality of politics is what has led recent incumbents into making faulty decisions. Unless they can practice the art of politics successfully, their programs do not stand much chance of passage. Most of the successful chief executives, like Jackson, Lincoln, and the two Roosevelts, engaged in politics to the hilt and relished every moment of it. It was those presidents who shunned politics, or who lacked the necessary skills, who were failures in meeting their obligations.[4] It makes as much sense to criticize presidents for "playing politics" as it does to criticize quarterbacks for playing football. In a democratic political system, politics is the name of the game.

Similarly, those who oppose a single six-year term see an unstated assumption of distrust for the people and Congress lying behind this proposal. The desire for a long term without the possibility of reelection seems to take for granted the notions that a president liberated from politics would be able to accomplish what he knew was best for the country and that democratic elections are impediments to good government.[5] Many of those who are against long single terms also oppose the Twenty-second Amendment as a violation of a fundamental principle of democracy: that the electorate has the right to select for office any person it wishes, and for as many terms as it wishes.

A Plural Executive

The contention that the president is overburdened with responsibilities is widespread in the literature of politics (although it is probably vastly exaggerated). The listing of his tasks as chief of his political party, legislative leader, commander in chief, head of state, chief administrator, foreign policy overseer, and so on reminds the reader that even under the current system much of the work is delegated to subordinates. Holding these aides accountable, or even kowing who they are, has proven a difficult matter in recent years. Since a president cannot spend sufficient time to carry out all of his duties, there have been some suggestions that he be relieved of those duties not crucial for the president personally to carry out. This would free his time to concentrate on those things that only he can do, such as supervise foreign policy, exercise legislative leadership, and direct the military forces of the country.

Rexford Tugwell's proposed new constitution provides for two vice-presidents to be elected with the president, one of whom would be designated as first successor should the president die or become incapacitated. The job of these two people would be to relieve the chief executive of the managerial, regulatory, and custodial duties that he presumably can no longer perform effectively anyway. The chancellors of foreign, financial, military, and legal affairs would be responsible to the vice-president for general affairs. Chancellors of other departments would be responsible to the vice-president for internal affairs, at the president's discretion.[6] Administrative duties and the chore of following up on decisions to see that they are implemented in the departments would then be much more efficiently handled than at present, it is argued. At the same time the president should be able to function full time as a policy maker in the really crucial areas of governmental concern. Responsibility would also be easy to pinpoint.

Herman Finer would carry the process further. He proposes electing a president and eleven vice-presidents every four years. The figure eleven is seen as the minimal number of people who can handle the major departments of government and still function as a small collective advisory body. Some of the vice-presidents would not be assigned to specific departments but rather would serve as deputies to the president concerned with general policy and counseling areas. To be eligible to serve as president or vice-president, a person would have to be either currently a member of Congress (and would resign upon selection) or to have at least four years experience in one of the two houses. This would not only insure practical political experience in the executive but would serve to improve the caliber of those who seek election to the Congress as well, Finer reasons. The president under this system would determine the order of succession among the vice-presidents.[7]

What is the desired gain from restructuring the executive in this fashion? Primarily insurance against the overburdening of one person and the institutionalization of collective decision making. To quote Finer:

A one-man executive has not the brains, the vision, the patience or the mental and physical capabilities to draw intellectual and spiritual nourishment from a multitude of sources . . .

Talent and character are amply provided by twelve men, and collective responsibility assures the presence of these qualities. . . .

Assuming that the President and his cabinet have served together for some time, cabinet members would be fully involved in the work of Congress, their political party, and in the cabinet itself, and better prepared to assume greater responsibility by succession.[8]

Under the Finer plan the president and his cabinet would function as the leadership group for Congress and actually sit in the House of Representatives. This would not only tie the executive and legislative branches together but would serve as a mechanism for holding the president accountable. It would also insure against the political isolation that besets modern chief executives. Finally, the president and his cabinet could resign and call new elections. In such a case the president and his vice-presidents would face the electorate, but so would all members of both the House and Senate. The presidential term would be four years, unless another resignation took place.

Finer, like a long line of American political scientists (including Woodrow Wilson), has admired the British system of government. Some, such as the members of the Committee on Political Parties of the American Political Science Association, have set forth proposals that are designed to incorporate into the American system as much as possible of the British model without having to change the Constitution.[9] Others have questioned the feasibility or desirability of such changes. Critics such as Austin Ranney point out, for example, that it is difficult to adopt another country's political system, much less only a portion of that system.[10] That is, majority rule democracy (at the expense of currently protected minority rights), responsible and disciplined parties, coherent and ideologically distinct party platforms, and local party structures subordinate to national ones are integral parts of cabinet government as practiced in Great Britain. Citing A. Lawrence Lowell approvingly, Ranney concludes that "American parties are the way they are because they are entirely appropriate to the kind of government the American people want."[11]

There is little chance in the near future for the massive restruc-turing of the governmental and political systems that would be necessary to achieve the reforms mentioned. Liberals who saw in these proposals a way to strengthen the president against a recalcitrant Congress now search for means to limit him.[12] Nor would Congress be likely to give up its own leadership structure and independent status to be joined more closely to the executive. Presidential ability to dissolve Congress, along with concurrent four-year terms for all elective federal officials, are not measures designed to win the legislative heart. In addition, under the Finer plan, the Senate would become a subordinate body to the House, giving up its power over treaties and appointments and its voice in overriding vetoes. Finally, the American people are probably not ready to buy the whole package of collective leadership and responsibility or the attendant restructuring of the party system. Despite revulsion over Watergate, there seems to be little demand for wholesale alteration in the Constitution, which remains for many almost an icon.

Regardless of the improbability of achieving collective leader-ship in the United States, it is a measure of the appeal of the idea that new proposals designed to promote it continually emerge. Barbara Tuchman suggests a six-person "directorate" elected on a party ticket for a period of six years. Each member would serve for one year as chairperson.[13] Harvey Wheeler, although he fails to specify the number of people he would like to see at the head of the executive branch, says that "there is need for a plural executive, for collective leadership. . . . What we know of large scale organization in industrial and corporate life is that the plural-executive or collective leadership approach has been effective."[14] Proponents of the plural executive can go all the way back to the New Jersey plan at the Constitutional Convention for historical legitimation of the concept. As eminent a founding father as Edmund Randolph decried the unitary executive as "a foetus of monarchy."

One of the difficulties in convincing Congress and the people that a plural executive is desirable is that a strong case can still be made for a single person holding the top job and exercising wide authority. To those who wished a weak president, Hamilton answered, "A feeble executive implies a feeble execution of the government," and Polsby and Wildavsky more recently have reminded the critics that "it is not feasible to limit the damage Presidents can do without also limiting the good they can do."[15] Critics of all the collegial executive plans make another point: that the parties in seeking votes may well try to offer the electorate a "balanced" ticket rather than searching for the most qualified candidates. Tuchman's six-person directorate or Finer's eleven vice-presidents might be chosen as much for their "representativeness" as for their talents (like the cabinet today). Thus the parties may feel compelled to choose persons from the various geographical regions, ethnic and racial groups, religious denominations, occupations, philosophical persuasions, and sexual identifications. The result may not be much different from the current system. Whether the argument against the plural executive is persuasive is left for the reader to judge. Even many who seek to guard againt a recurrence of the abuses of recent years do not find the spreading and blurring of responsibility to be the solution. In any case, since constitutional amendments are the least likely remedies, it is well to consider proposals more easily adopted.

Bringing Congress into the Cabinet

Even before the autonomous waging of the Vietnam War by Presidents Johnson and Nixon, many critics had begun to worry about the danger of allowing the chief executive to operate independently of the legislature. Thus observers of the office sought various mechanisms for tying the president and Congress closer together. Edward S. Corwin proposed a new type of cabinet composed of department heads, members of regulating bodies, and congressional leaders. The latter would be drawn from a "Joint Legislative Council" chosen and removable by the two houses of Congress.[16] The purpose of including members of Congress would be to build up the power and influence of the cabinet as a genuine advisory body (which it is not today because of the dependence of department secretaries on the president). The primary job of the legislative members would be "first, to control presidential whim and, secondly, to provide the sort of consensus that is now lacking, though popular government inherently needs it, especially in an era of stress and uncertainty."[17]

Corwin and Louis Koenig felt this proposed new cabinet could be brought about without a constitutional amendment. Rather, such a body would be established by "compact" between the two branches. The president's obligation would be to consult with the cabinet on all important issues before making final decisions. For its part, Congress would organize itself to guarantee that it would consider and act (one way or the other) on every legislative proposal sent to it by the president—and within a reasonable period of time. The constitutional powers of neither branch would be reduced by such a plan. One objective would be to minimize "the occasions for autocratic courses and irresponsible pronouncements by the President." This would be achieved by "maximizing the availability of the lawmaking power."[18]

Critics of the various proposals to tie Congress and the president together in a collective decision-making process make a number of points. There is no guarantee that including senior members of Congress (and they almost certainly would be members of long experience) in executive decisions would produce less precipitous or dangerous action. For instance, Robert Kennedy reported that, when President Kennedy informed the leaders of his decision to "quarantine" Cuba during the missile crisis, "many Congressional leaders were sharp in their criticism. They felt that the President should take more forceful action, a military attack or invasion, and that the blockade was far too weak a response."[19] On other occasions a conservative "Joint Legislative Council" with the right to participate in decisions might have formed a serious obstacle to the president's sending of troops to enforce civil rights laws and court decisions in the South.

When Congress is controlled by one poitical party and the executive branch by the other (and this was the case during most of Eisenhower's and all of Nixon's and Ford's service in the White House), additional problems arise. Neither the Republican nor the Democratic party is internally unified on policy issues, and merely including some congressional party members in the cabinet will not necessarily "provide consensus" or "reduce antagonism" as envisioned by this plan. In fact, Amlund argues, tension within the system may be increased as new power relationships are developed.[20]

Revitalization of the Cabinet and Limitation of Staff

Another suggestion aimed at increasing accountability within the executive branch without going to the election of a plural executive or bringing in congressional members is to reverse the present lowly state of the cabinet. Although no president has found that body to be an entirely satisfactory institution, certain steps could be taken to revitalize it while at the same time reducing the power and influence of the staff. Much of the criticism of the presidents since Roosevelt has centered on the inordinate control they have allowed their staffs to accumulate. Since aides are not elected, approved by the Senate, or generally subject to questions by either house of Congress, there has been little check on their activities. Each new chief executive has sworn to reverse this trend, but, for many of the reasons discussed in Chapter 4, little has come of these pledges. With the staff abuses revealed by Watergate, and the widespread realization that close aides suffer the same isolation that presidents do, there may finally be a real attempt to alter the situation.

The first step would be to reduce the number of people in the White House Office and the Executive Office of the President. This in itself would force the remaining staff to rely more heavily upon the regular departments to get their work done. Merely limiting the budget for presidential aides, however, would not accomplish the goal unless there also were a prohibition on "borrowing" staff from other agencies. Such a limitation on the size of his staff would force a president to think carefully about the utilization of his aides; one would hope that he could not afford to let large numbers of them spend their time on extraneous matters such as "screwing our enemies" or on public relations campaigns. Surviving staff in the White House Office would be authentic personal advisers, rather than a separate operating branch of government protected from the system of checks and balances.

Although there is little probability that the American president's staff will (or could) be reduced to the size of its British counterpart, it is interesting to note that Britain gets by with far fewer aides at the top level of the executive. A Cabinet Secretariat (or Cabinet Office) was first created in 1916 under Lloyd

George to keep track of the agenda and decisions of the cabinet. In recent years, Harold Wilson doubled the size of the secretariat to around a hundred civil servants drawn from the regular departments. Their job is to give expert advice in areas such as economic affairs, social policy, and foreign affairs. Within this body there is a smaller central policy review staff. All of these people serve the cabinet as well as the prime minister.[21]

In addition to the secretariat, there is also the No. 10 Office to help the prime minister exclusively. Its members include a press secretary and one assistant, a foreign policy specialist, a "Principal Private Secretary and his assistant," an expert on the House of Commons (who helps the prime minister with his speeches and the questions he faces before that body), and "a person to keep the diary and a rather separate official whose sole task is Church and other patronage."[22] Harold Wilson added one new ingredient to this staff, a personal political office to respond to his constituency and political mail. Thus a British prime minister is expected to get by with eight or nine personal aides. Despite the comparatively minuscule size of this staff, it is still a source of worry to some observers:

> There are elements of danger in that some modern Prime Ministers have had something like a private court in which they live, a body of confidants giving advice in a sympathetic manner so that Premiers become cut off from other sections of the government and their party and unduly reliant on this one source of advice.[23]

The American chief executive has more duties than his equivalent in the British system, but there is probably still much room for reduction in the rather bloated condition of the Executive Office. Essential services could still be provided by a staff half the size of the current one.

One way to keep the presidency from constantly growing is to limit the creation of new agencies within the Executive Office. Among the agencies added in the last ten years are the Domestic Council, the Office of Consumer Affairs, the Special Action Office for Drug Abuse Prevention, the Office of Telecommunications Policy, and the Energy Policy Office. Congress has perhaps been as guilty, continually expecting the president to deal with each new "crisis" as it arises. Thus, for instance, the Council of Economic Advisors, the National Security Council, and the Council on Environmental Quality all are in the Executive Office of the President because Congress put them there through legislation. As Thomas Cronin has said, "Congress should curb its own impulse to establish presidential agencies and to ask for yet additional reports and studies from the President. In the past Congress has been a too willing partner in the enlargement of the presidency."[24]

Nor are Congress and an expansionist presidency alone to blame for the continuing growth of the office. Especially important here are interest groups. Since many of the important governmental decisions are made in the presidency, more and more groups seek representation within its structure so they can have a hand in determining policy and a voice close to the chief executive's ear. No longer is lobbying Congress or departments a guarantee of sufficient "input" into the programs of government. Even during the outcry over the "imperial presidency" in the last months of the Nixon administration, the call for expansion went on. In June 1974 the National Academy of Sciences proposed that a new "Council for Science and Technology" be created by Congress and attached to the president. The Academy concluded that "science and technology can fully serve the Federal Government—and the nation—only if adequate means are included within the staff structure of the Executive Office of the President."[25]

Once established in the White House (or anywhere else in the bureaucracy for that matter), agencies tend to take on lives of their own. In this area, however, President Nixon had in 1973 dismantled the old Office of Science and Technology, the Presidential Science Advisory Committee, and the position of White House science advisor which had been created in the Eisenhower days. Many scientists viewed Nixon's action as a "demotion" of their specialities (as well as their influence) and strenuously objected. Dr. George B. Kistiakowsky, who had served as science advisor to President Eisenhower, suggested a new agency with many of the same roles as the old groups but with more power. Under this proposal, a Council on Science and Technology would have the authority to examine the budget requests of all agencies (such as the National Security Agency, the Defense Department, the CIA, and the Space Agency) where scientific or technological issues were involved. In this respect the new agency would be on a relative par with OMB, with disputes between the two taken directly to the president.[26] There is no doubt that presidents need competent scientific advice over a wide range of problems. But the illustration is used here to remind the reader of the importance groups themselves attach to having significant influence over decisions that they see as affecting their interests. More and more this means being represented on the staff of the president. President Ford, yielding to pressure from the scientific community, announced in the summer of 1975 that a new science advisers' office would be attached to the White House. It will have a staff of ten to fifteen and a budget of between $1 million and $1.5 million.

One of the reasons for the growth of the staff in recent years is that many issues cannot be neatly contained within the bounds of a single department, as Roosevelt observed. Environmental concerns, for example, involve the Agriculture; Interior; Health, Education, and Welfare; Transportation; Treasury; and Commerce Departments and many other agencies and bureaus as well. A host of sometimes conflicting federal programs is administered within this fragmented bureaucracy. The impulse to make sense out of this confusion results in attempts to centralize overall direction in the White House. Thus, when an energy shortage threatens the United States, a new Energy Policy Office is created as part of the Executive Office of the President. This has led one observer to write:

> There is really no other way to run the government. The more the government does, the more there must be a central body to coordinate its workings. The major issues of the day—such as the economy, race, cities, foreign policy, balance of payments—are not divisible into neat parcels to be distributed among the various Cabinet departments. . . . The White House, and its executive arm, the Office of Management and Budget, must bring them together. . . . The power to coordinate is power indeed.[27]

As it is, nine departments and twenty agencies have one or more education programs, and seven departments and eight agencies deal with health programs.[28]

Added to this obvious need for coordination is the distrust

presidents and their staffs have displayed toward the traditional civil servants in the departments. They are viewed either as inefficient and recalcitrant or as overcommitted to traditional ways of doing things. Only by having a function performed directly under the control of the president (or in a newly created and staffed "independent" agency) do those in the White House see an opportunity to evade the stifling hand of the bureaucrats. As Elizabeth Drew points out, it is not so much that the departments are full of "enemies" as it is that those who administer programs tend to believe in them and resist either change or abolition of policies.[29]

Despite the very real problems with reorganization of the executive branch, it is probably a necessary step if some of the functions performed in the White House are to be returned to the departments. The obvious example is coordination of the multiplicity of programs administered in the various agencies. Since separate departments today are incapable of resolving conflicts over competing claims for money and jurisdiction, the OMB and White House aides and councils have had to referee the disputes and make final decisions. With fewer, consolidated departments, strengthened cabinet secretaries should be able to broker the internal interests of their agencies and relieve White House staffers of this power. (This assumes, of course, that such departments would be entrusted to people of genuine stature and competence.) It is also possible that cabinet members would gain a measure of independence from the interest groups and clients served by their departments. If they had to contend with the profusion of cross pressures from competing demands, their role as advisers to the president (rather than merely as advocates of particular interests) may be enhanced. All of this should mean a reduced need for aides and councils in the Executive Office of the President.[30]

Increased authority for cabinet members would also mean that cabinet posts would be more attractive to independent and competent people. Cabinet secretaries are not as subject to the isolation that plagues the president and his staff, and greater reliance upon the former group should open up informational channels and give the chief executive a better view of reality. Department heads have to appear before Congress, both for initial confirmation and later to justify budget requests and to explain policy. Walter Hickel, whose appointment to be secretary of the interior was opposed by many environmentalists, said his confirmation hearings were an education for him. Later many of the decisions he made as secretary were applauded by the same groups that had originally fought his nomination. Not only do cabinet secretaries learn from Congress, but they tend to be more open to the press as well. As Hickel himself pointed out, this gives them a fairly accurate reading of the public mood. If they are utilized by the president for their knowedge, better decisions could emerge from the executive branch.[31]

Senator Walter Mondale of Minnesota has suggested an additional way to upgrade the cabinet while at the same time increasing the checks on the administration's policies. Mondale's proposal calls for a periodic "question-hour" of department heads. The idea itself is based on the British practice and has been promoted off and on in the United States since the early days of the Republic. Under the Mondale plan, these sessions before Congress would be televised live to the nation. This could have a number of effects. Presidents would probably want to select secretaries to represent them who were capable of an articulate defense of the administration; they would seek men and women of competence and stature, rather than just those willing to follow the orders of White House aides. The people themselves would become better informed about their government's policies and might be encouraged to try to influence decisions. If this were the case, "special interests" could lose some of their influence. The practice would also acquaint more of the voters with the legislative branch and their own representatives. More attention paid to Congress may increase expectations from that branch, enhancing its role as a participant in the decision-making process. Hasty and secret decisions made by a small coterie in the White House might decrease if office holders had to defend those decisions under hard questioning in a public arena. Finally, as Richard Neustadt has written, such appearances would put some distance between cabinet members and the president and "so make them more important to him, in the very act of making them perform independently."[32]

The danger Neustadt sees in this proposal is that by distancing the cabinet members from the president, their status might be diminished as well. Power in recent decades has rested in proximity to the chief executive. A further caveat is that Congress is not guaranteed of a favorable response by the viewers. This may be especially true if a comparison is drawn on the one hand between an attractive and articulate president (Kennedy, for example) and "Senator Klaghorn" types on the other. Many members of Congress who fear just such a reaction have opposed televising congressional sessions. Long debate preceded the decision to allow cameras into the Judiciary Committee's impeachment hearings, and although events denied the full House the opportunity to hear the case, the leadership had been drawing up strict rules governing the use of television. Specifically, cameras were to be focused solely on the well of the House or on the representative speaking. The fear was that roving cameras would catch members talking to each other, reading newspapers, or snoozing. Evidently the leadership had little confidence in its own membership, even during one of the most critical matters ever presented to the House.

Mondale has also proposed that senior White House staffers be subject to the same requirement of senatorial confirmation that applies to the cabinet and a host of lesser officials. After all, it is argued, many, if not most, of the important decisions in the executive branch are made by the president and these aides. Yet Congress has no check upon them as it does upon the heads of departments, no way of holding them accountable. As a first step, a new law requires senatorial confirmation of the director and deputy director of the Office of Management and Budget. Life and death control over many programs rests with these two officials.

In its search for solutions, the Senate Select Committee on Presidential Campaign Activities (the Watergate Committee) commissioned a panel of the prestigious National Academy of Public Administration to make recommendations for avoiding future abuses of power on the part of the executive branch. In perhaps the most extreme proposal of this sort, the panel suggested that the White House staff be limited to approximately fifteen top aides supported by not more than fifty professional employees. This latter group would be covered by the Hatch Act, which prohibits political activity by federal civil servants. The presidency would be stripped of all "special purpose" agencies not specifically concerned with providing staff assistance to the president. In their place, Congress could authorize the creation of a number of temporary offices of secretarial rank outside the Executive Office of the President. These secretaries would be subject to senatorial confirmation and would be available to the president to take on temporary assignments calling for interdepartmental coordination. Finally, in the words of the panel, "The function of the Executive Office, particularly the Office of Management and Budget, should be to assist the President, not to be the general manager of the Executive Branch."[33] Perhaps because its members feared such a radical departure from the accustomed way of governing the United States, this proposal was not among the final recommendations of the Watergate Committee.

Reform in Justice

Some of the White House "horrors" were connected to the Justice Department. One attorney general, John Mitchell, was charged in two separate Watergate-related cases—the Vesco affair and participation in the cover-up of Watergate, and was convicted for the latter offense. Another attorney general, Richard Kleindienst, pleaded guilty to "failure to testify fully" about orders he had received from Nixon himself to drop an antitrust case against International Telephone and Telegraph. Other activities that raised the question of the quality of justice in the United States included wiretapping without court order, political trials against so-called radical groups, the use of *agents provocateurs*, selective prosecution of tax cases, special divisions set up in the Justice Department to go after specified groups of people, secret FBI files on citizens innocent of any crime, the firing of Special Prosecutor Cox when he refused to cease pursuing evidence against the president (and the resulting resignations of Richardson and Ruckelshaus when they would not fire Cox), and the use of high Justice Department officials, such as Mitchell and Robert Mardian, to participate in the president's reelection campaign. Mitchell had been Nixon's campaign manager in the 1968 election as well, which raised the question of the propriety of utilizing a political operative as the nation's chief law enforcement officer. In this, however, Nixon was merely following a long line of precedent. Harding named his campaign manager, Harry Daugherty, to be attorney general. Similarly, Truman chose Howard McGrath, Eisenhower named Herbert Brownell, and Kennedy selected his brother Robert. All had directed presidential campaigns.

One of the most cherished ideals of the American political system is that this country has a government of laws, not men. Justice applies equally to all, regardless of status. Thus many people see the performance of the system of justice as the linchpin of freedom. If that system becomes politicized; if in the name of national security or any other rationale government bends or perverts the laws for its own purposes, then democracy is in peril. For, as Justice Brandeis wrote:

> Decency, security, and liberty alike demand that government officials shall be subjected to the same rules of conduct that are commands to the citizen. In a government of laws, existence of the government will be imperiled if it fails to observe the law scrupulously. Our government is the potent, the omnipresent, teacher. For good or for ill, it teaches the whole people by its example. Crime is contagious. If the government becomes a lawbreaker, it breeds contempt for the law; it invites every man to become a law unto himself; it invites anarchy. To declare that in the administration of the criminal law that the end justifies the means—to declare that the government may commit crimes in order to secure the conviction of a private criminal—would bring terrible retribution.[34]

Although the Justice Department under Nixon was not the first to bring federal justice into question (for instance, consider Robert Kennedy's efforts to "get" Jimmy Hoffa and the wiretaps on Martin Luther King's telephone), the revelations of lawbreaking in the Nixon administration resulted in several proposals aimed at insuring that justice would not again become a matter of politics.

"Who will investigate the investigators, and who will prosecute the prosecutors?" are ancient questions. Public pressure and distrust of the Justice Department's handling of the Watergate investigation resulted in the appointment of a special prosecutor for that case. Nixon's tapes make clear the dimensions of the problem. Assistant Attorney General Henry Petersen had been conducting the case for the Justice Department, and his performance was the subject of the following exchange between John Dean and the President in the famous March 21 meeting:

> Dean: There is no doubt that I was totally aware of what the Bureau was doing. I knew what witnesses were going to be called. I knew what they were asked, and I had to.
>
> President: Why did Peterson play the game so straight with us?
>
> Dean: Because Peterson is a soldier. He kept me informed. He told me when we had problems, where we had problems and the like. He believes in you and he believes in this administration. This administration has made him. I don't think he has done anything improper, but he did make sure that the investigation was narrowed down to the very, very fine criminal thing which was a break for us. There is no doubt about it.[35]

Later, in a conversation about the investigation with John Ehrlichman on April 16, Nixon asserted, "I've got Peterson on a short leash."[36]

To insure against any future president keeping the Justice Department "on a short leash" when investigating wrongdoing, former Senator Sam Ervin proposed removing the attorney general from the cabinet and the Justice Department from the executive branch. Other proposals include giving the White House counsel's functions to Justice (former Supreme Court Justice Arthur Goldberg); removing the FBI from Justice (Senator Robert Byrd); and taking the department out of politics by requiring the attorney general or his deputy and three assistant attorneys general to be of a different political party from the president, along with a prohibition against appointing campaign managers to the Justice Department (former Attorney General Ramsey Clark).[37]

The panel from the National Academy of Public Administration suggested that the attorney general be divorced from politics by prohibiting him from advising the president on political or personal matters. The chief executive would be able to appoint only the top eleven officials in the department, while all U.S. attorneys (now patronage posts) would become part of a career legal service. The conflict in roles for the department between being the government's chief prosecutor and also the major screening and recommending body for federal judges would be resolved by taking the department out of the judicial selection process. To insure a vigorous effort to weed out political miscreants, an office of permanent special prosecutor would be created to handle all cases involving alleged wrongdoing by governmental officials. This office would also be in charge of election fraud cases. A nonpartisan appointment, confirmation by the Senate, and a fixed term of at least six years would promote independence from the political process.[38] Thus would the panel definitively answer the questions of who would investigate the investigators and who would prosecute the prosecutors.

The final recommendations that emerged from the Senate Watergate Committee included modified acceptance of the panel's suggestions in this area. The committee called for the establishment of a "permanent office of public attorney" to deal with criminal cases where there was a conflict of interest within the executive branch. An ombudsman function would allow the public attorney to investigate the administration of justice in the executive branch and to follow up complaints and charges about matters involving the conduct of the departments and regulatory agencies. It would have full power to gain access to executive records. To insure that the office would be taken out of politics, appointment would be made by the judicial branch, with confirmation by the Senate. A fixed term, (for example, five years) would prohibit the removal of the public attorney for political reasons.[39]

Clearly the suggestions aimed at removing the administration of justice from politics have wide appeal. But the advocates of these various plans should be aware that politics pervades every institution—governmental, educational, occupational, or religious. Simply removing the attorney general or the Justice Department from the nexus of presidential influence does not remove the institution from politics; it merely changes the arena. Perhaps the central question to ask with regard to a special prosecutor is whether the United States needs a permanent Office of Public Attorney free from political control. Admiration for Special Prosecutor Cox (who did not prove immune to presidential removal) or Special Prosecutor Jaworski (who, because of special circumstances, did) should not blind proponents to the potential danger of such an office. There is no guarantee that men of such stature would always fill the role. Nor is there any guarantee that a future independent special prosecutor would devote his energies to holding "dangerous" presidents accountable for their mistakes. The fear most commonly expressed is of the possibility of someone like Joseph McCarthy holding the office and being immune from removal or political control. McCarthy was denied access to personnel records of executive branch employees, and liberals applauded. It was ultimately the political process that finished him. A McCarthy as special prosecutor tomorrow may decide that "Communists" (or homosexuals, or militants, or other unpopular groups) are dangerous and thus must be exposed and ferreted out of the federal government. There are already several "independent" agencies in Washington, D.C., but as the presidential transcripts make clear, this did not deter the president and his men from manipulating the Securities and Exchange Commission, the Federal Communications Commission, or other such bodies. Most of these agencies also have a history of identifying with the interests of those they supposedly regulate. There is no assurance that this would not occur in this instance as well.

"Politics" does not necessarily imply evil or corruption. It is one method of holding officials accountable. To remove the attorney general or the Justice Department from the executive branch may mean a loss of accountability to the people through the political process. The department prosecutes a wide range of cases, from civil rights abridgments through antitrust cases to ordinary criminal violations. What recourse would a progressive president (or Congress) have if an independent attorney general decided that his agency should concentrate its resources on radical groups and largely neglect the vigorous enforcement of civil rights statutes? Since resources are always limited, political judgments of this sort are constantly being made. With an independent Justice Department, however, such decisions would be beyond the control of officials elected by the people. Just because the wrong political decisions may have been made in recent administrations does not mean that all political decisions are bad. For instance, the decision to go after organized crime for the first time in a massive, integrated fashion was a political decision. Nor would electing an attorney general provide a viable solution. To elect candidates based on their promises to emphasize areas of the law seems to be a sure way of guaranteeing that the Bill of Rights, the Fourteenth Amendment, and unpopular Supreme Court decisions will go largely unenforced. The Constitution needs more insulation from popular whim than this.

There is little doubt that, even had the Justice Department been an independent agency headed by a presidential nominee as attorney general when Nixon took office in 1969, Nixon could have successfully named John Mitchell to that post. Mitchell seems not to have cared much what the people thought of him one way or the other. In this sense he was what some critics want an "independent" attorney general to be—oblivious to his own political career (though obviously Mitchell was not apolitical in the sense of lacking a particular philosophy or bias for and against certain groups of people). Total immunity from public pressures, then, does not insure against the abuse of office. Elliot Richardson, on the other hand, seems to have been very concerned with his reputation and chances for a further political career. He resigned from office rather than jeopardize either. A prohibition against the appointment of "politicians" to the position may be the wrong solution to the problem.

A compromise proposal that seems to make sense would be to leave the Justice Department and the attorney general within the executive branch and to create special prosecutors only when circumstances (such as Watergate) call for them. The newly created Federal Elections Commission could be entrusted with enforcement of strengthened election laws. Within broad guidelines set down by Congress, the president should continue to set policy for where the resources of the Department of Justice will be concentrated. Congress can increase its role in the process by the passage of laws and by closer attention to the budget requests of the divisions within the department (for example, FBI, Civil Rights, Antitrust, and so on)—adding here, trimming there, as it determines necessary. Further more, Congress can insure that all top appointees to the department are frequently reminded of the oath of office that all federal officials must take. That is, loyalty is to the Constitution of the United States, not to the president. The educative function of Congress can thus be strengthened if it exercises the will to do so. Finally, to restore a measure of popular confidence in the impartiality of justice, the attorney general and his lieutenants should be barred from any participation in political campaigns. This should include a ban on appearances at conventions, the making of partisan speeches for candidates, and serving as political advisers to the president. U.S. attorneys should be selected through a career system, and judges screened elsewhere in the political system.[40]

The Strengthening of Congress

Rexford Tugwell has written that "to reform the legislature has always been the most obvious way to a better government; but it has been the one reform that nothing has been done about."[41] In the last few years, a number of proposals have aimed at doing just that. Most, however, have as their goal the strengthening of Congress, without necessarily reforming it. Even some recent critics of the presidency fear that a newly powerful but unreformed legislative branch would be capable of more harm than good. As Marcus Cunliffe has said, "If the alternative to executive dominance were legislative dominance, few Americans would welcome the prospect."[42] Nevertheless, it is now widely recognized that some measure of adjustment between the branches must be attained if the system of checks and balances is to have any meaning in the last quarter of the twentieth century.

Foreign policy was the first governmental activity to be dominated by presidents. It is also perhaps the most sensitive. It is difficult to construct devices to keep presidents from abusing power, as in unilateral waging of war, secret commitments to various countries around the world, or covert operations against selected "unfriendly" regimes, without at the same time crippling the secrecy, initiative, and unity that are sometimes necessary for the successful maintenance of peace and the furtherance of American interests. The virtually imperial manner in which presidents since Truman have conducted foreign policy, however, has led to several attempts to assure congressional (and especially senatorial) participation in the framing of that policy. The removal of Richard Nixon did not signal that a full partnership in foreign affairs between Congress and president was about to be reached. In his first address to a joint session of the legislature Ford said:

> Throughout my public service, starting with wartime naval duty under the command of President Franklin D. Roosevelt, I have upheld all our Presidents when they spoke for my country to the world. I believe the constitution commands this. I know that in this crucial area of international policy I can count on your firm support.[43]

The president failed to cite the provision of the Constitution that "commands" such support. Nor did he specify if in his view there were any limitations to the scope of activities in which the president could speak for the country.

Chapter 2 contained a discussion of the War Powers Act that passed over President Nixon's veto in 1973. It remains to be fully tested to see if any significant increase in Congress's control over war making has been achieved or whether in the heat of crisis things will be done pretty much the way they have been in the past. Ford's unilateral handling of the *Mayaguez* affair indicates that not much has changed. In another area, Congress is at work on efforts to prohibit the president from circumventing by the use of executive agreements the constitutional requirement of senatorial advice and consent on treaties. Conservative members of Congress first undertook to move in this direction in the early 1950s. With the Vietnam War and the discovery of several secret agreements between the United States and various foreign governments (including Vietnam), liberal members took over the fight in the 1960s and 1970s. Senators complained that the role of treaties and executive agreements had become reversed—the former are now used mainly for minor or technical matters while the latter deal with substantive issues affecting vital national interests. Arthur Schlesinger, Jr., cites figures showing that in 1930 the United States entered into 20 treaties and only 9 executive agreements. By 1971 there were 17 new treaties but 214 executive agreements.[44]

Among the treaties senators were asked to vote on were ones dealing with shrimp, copyrights, stamp collections, issues of protocol, the preservation of cultural artifacts, and extradition. The subjects of many of the executive agreements were not made public, but some dealt with the establishment and maintenance of military bases, the stationing of nuclear weapons, and military assistance.[45] Congress did not get to vote on these. In 1972 a law went into effect that requires all new executive agreements to be transmitted to both houses of Congress within sixty days of their conclusion. At a minimum, Congress wanted to be informed about what commitments the president was making in the name of the United States. Former Senators Ervin and Fulbright would take the process a step further and give Congress the right to veto any executive agreement within sixty days. What Schlesinger and others hope for is a return to the comity which formerly existed between the branches. Congressional approval of foreign bases and troop commitments, along with frequent consultation and review, would not hamper the effective execution of policy but would strengthen the checks on the president.[46] There is little doubt that any president will do whatever he deems necessary to protect the nation in times of genuine crisis. In such instances the Congress and people will affirm that action and in fact rally around him. The real question is routinized powers during noncrisis periods. Emergency powers of the chief executive must be restricted to genuine emergencies and not remain available for everyday use as a president determines. There should be automatic expiration dates on all such emergency power statutes invoked.

Frequent consultation between the president and a "watchdog" committee of Congress is probably not enough to insure control of the CIA, another foreign policy instrument, though it is obviously preferable to no consultation at all. Senator Fulbright has maintained that such meetings usually turn into briefings, with the CIA or White House aides doing the talking and senators and representatives listening. If the meeting takes place in the White House, the results are even less satisfactory because of the psychological barriers created by the president's status as chief of state as well as head of government. He thus must be treated with respect and deference rather than subjected to hard questioning. "One does not contradict Kings in their palaces or Presidents in the White House," Fulbright has said.[47] And, in the words of Katzenbach, watchdog committees "have generally done more 'dogging' than 'watching.'"[48]

The dangers of personalization of power were emphasized more than thirty years ago by Edward S. Corwin. The trend has vastly accelerated since then. Programs and policies are deemphasized, while personal relationships and personalities are stressed in foreign policy. A danger in this is that programs are not institutionalized but rather depend on specific persons being in power. Thus today few foreign countries want to deal with lower officials in the State Department—they want to talk to Henry Kissinger. Secrecy and unpredictability become the supreme virtues, so that the leaders can present Congress and the people with *faits accomplis* rather than allowing them to participate in policy formulation. The State Department, the electorate, and members of the House and Senate are expected to be passive observers or enthusiastic applauders as each startling bombshell is detonated—whether the announcement concerns a China trip, détente with the Soviet Union, or the unleashing of *schrecklichkeit* against North Vietnam. Personalized leaders such as Nixon and Kissinger tend to deal best with their counterparts in the rest of the world. This usually means dictators in the Communist countries or in the West. Thus America's relations were warm with the leaders in the USSR, China, Greece, Pakistan, Egypt, and South Vietnam, but deteriorated with democracies in India and Japan as well as with most allies in Western Europe.[49] (This is not to deny that the very real divergence of interests between the United States and other democracies does not play a significant role in relationships.)

It may be argued that the president must continue to provide leadership, establish priorities, and set forth proposals in foreign policy, but that these must be open to discussion and criticism both by the public and Congress. Obsessive secrecy must give way to candor and a broadening of participation in decisions. This would entail at a minimum public airing of views by those who now set policy— whether they are in the State Department, the White House, or the National Security Council. The use of executive privilege to prohibit aides from testifying before Congress should be minimized. Much more information must be declassified. Congress itself should be more willing to participate in hard choices—even knowing that some decisions will be unpopular with the electorate back home.[50] The wisdom of the cut-off of aid to Turkey and the Jackson Amendment to the trade agreement with the Soviet Union may be debated, but at least they are indications that Congress has begun to reassert itself.

One factor that affects the ability of Congress to participate meaningfully in setting both foreign and domestic policy is the control of information. Today the legislative branch is almost totally dependent upon the executive for the facts and reports upon which legislators must base their decisions. A first step has been taken to strengthen the Freedom of Information Act to provide Congress with access to materials critical to its work. An increase in expert staff is also needed, as is computer capacity to analyze the information it possesses. Currently senators and representatives must use much of their limited staff on constituency matters in order to be reelected. In one area at least Congress has voted to equip itself with better resources. It recently created the Office of Technological Assessment to conduct studies and to give the legislative branch a competing source of information. Thus on such matters as SSTs, space shuttles, air pollution effects, rapid transit, the use of solar energy, the effects of pesticides, and the like, Congress will not be so dependent on the executive branch as in the past. It would be counterproductive, however, to try to duplicate the vast bureaucracy of the Executive Office or of the departments. Thus the most critical matter is to make the executive branch responsive to congressional requests. Congress, which passes the laws, has a constitutional right to demand the full cooperation of all federal employees in supplying information, studies, reports, and testimony.

As Thomas Cronin has pointed out, Congress itself is in large measure responsible for its present lowly estate. Presidents haven't had to seize power—Congress has marched down the Hill to present it to the chief executive on a silver platter.[51] To paraphrase Mao, power comes from the barrel of a budget. The reform act passed in 1974 could go a long way toward reestablishing Congress's power of the purse if Congress does not shirk from its responsibilities by passing them back to the president and the Office of Management and Budget. Besides having its own budget office, Congress could require OMB to consult as yearly requests for funds are processed. Executive privilege has no place here. The additional reforms of 1975 and the modification of the system whereby chairmanships were automatically awarded to the most senior members should further strengthen Congress's ability to meet the challenge of governing in the last quarter of the twentieth century.

One other step that could lead to a strengthened legislative branch is to broaden congressional access to the people through television. Today no one person or institution can compete with the president in gaining the attention of the citizens and thus setting the agenda of the nation. Broadcasts are used to rally support, mute opposition, and generate public pressure for initiatives that the president announces. He has almost total control over his own appearances, including the timing, frequency, and format. News broadcasts and "specials" dealing with the opposition cannot match the president's command of the media. Party leaders and members of Congress are totally dependent upon the broadcasters for the coverage they receive. To provide a partial remedy, the authors of a report commissioned by the Twentieth Century Fund recommend that Congress permit cameras to broadcast specially scheduled prime time evening sessions at least four times a year. The most important matters facing Congress and the nation would be discussed and debated at these sessions, and, to give Congress the same chance at a wide audience that the president enjoys, all three networks would broadcast coverage simultaneously. "Equal time" provisions of the law would be suspended for these telecasts.[52] Additionally, the National Committee of the opposition party would have an automatic right to choose a representative to reply to any presidential address made within ten months prior to a presidential election or within ninety days of a congressional election.

What of the expressed fears of some members of Congress that the legislative branch would suffer in the public eye if its sessions were broadcast? Some fragmentary evidence now exists that tends to refute this idea. A study by Bradley Greenburg and Charles Atkin commissioned by the Corporation for Public Broadcasting found that high school pupils in Florida who were randomly selected to view televised sessions of the state legislature generally wound up much more favorably disposed to that institution than control groups who did not view these sessions. For the group exposed to the programs, interest in state politics was significantly increased: they talked more about politics with friends and parents; increased their reading about the legislature in newspapers; were more favorably impressed with the intelligence, trustworthiness, and hard work of legislators; and significantly increased their knowledge about the Florida legislature.[53] The Senate Watergate hearings exposed millions of viewers for the first time to the national legislature and created several new household names in the process. Even as large a group as the thirty-eight-member House Judiciary Committee favorably impressed the electorate. In April 1974 (before the televised impeachment hearings got underway) a Gallup poll found that only 30 percent of the people approved of the way Congress was handling its job. By August of that year, however, this had increased to 48 percent. The shift took place among every major group and in every region of the country. Favorable responses went up a minimum of 8 percent and a maximum of 38 percent for the various groups surveyed.[54] Thus exposure and publicity may significantly improve the image of Congress. A fuller use of television could increase public expectations of that branch and give it added weight in its struggles with the executive. Perhaps fewer people would believe that only the president can, and should, deal with the problems confronting society.

Demythologizing the Presidency

Expectations about what a president is able to achieve are vastly inflated. The people now tend to hold the chief executive responsible for most of the difficulties that beset the body politic. Presidents, knowing this, feel that they cannot begin to master these problems unless they centralize power closely in a few hands where they can directly supervise the setting of policy. They are unlikely to be willing to give power to Congress, the states, or the bureaucracy when the people expect presidential solutions. Since it would be dangerous to give presidents the power to solve all the nation's problems, as is now expected, the alternative is to change the expectations.

The process could begin in the White House itself. If unrealistic public expectations contributed to the failures of recent chief executives, many of them helped create their own subsequent unpopularity by needlessly inflating hopes about what they could accomplish. Exaggerated rhetoric by candidates, and later by incumbents, feeds the already distorted view of the office. John Kennedy, running for the presidency in 1960, was guilty of this sanctification of the dream: "Upon him alone converge all the needs and aspirations of all parts of the country, all departments of the government, all nations of the world."[55] Lyndon Johnson promised the people guns and butter and continually saw the "light at the end of the tunnel" in Vietnam. Richard Nixon swore to end inflation without increasing unemployment, bring the war to a close (it took him longer to achieve this than the entire period of American involvement in World War II), and restore respect to the presidency. Richard Neustadt, writing more than fifteen years ago, said that unrealistic expectations were the chief enemies of presidential prestige.[56] Thus a successful president must teach reality to the people; he must not artifically inflate expectations beyond the capacity of institutions to deliver. Although it may be true that people need dreams and aspirations beyond their immediate grasp to strive for, repeated failure and unrealistic hopes breed disillusionment.

The public, too, on its part needs a more realistic conception of the presidency. Alfred de Grazia has said that "much of the difficulty with the institution . . . is the overlay of myth and magic on the President," and that "it is up to each generation to contain him."[57] If it is to be able to contain him, the electorate must be able to distinguish between the reality and the myth of the office. This would entail a clearer understanding of which elements of the presidency are historical magnifications and which are accurate descriptions. A less idealized and romanticized version presented in our textbooks and in the media could go a long way toward modifying the socialization patterns of recent generations that have been the basis of many of the current expectations of the office. Less deification would result in less empowerment of any person who happened to hold the office. There is some evidence that "the textbook presidency" is already undergoing modification.[58]

De Grazia discusses several particulars of the presidential image that he considers to be myths. First of all, there is the view of the president as executive. The presidency and the executive branch have been personalized in the being of the president. Gerald Ford, in his first speech to Congress, reminded his listeners of his corporate status: "Under the Constitution, I now belong to the executive branch. The Supreme Court has even ruled that I am the executive branch, head, heart, and hand."[59] Until scandal brought it to light, little was publicly known about the vast bureaucracy that makes up the presidency. More commonly, a listing of the roles of the president conveyed the impression that he personally managed foreign affairs, headed his political party, took care that the laws were faithfully executed, commanded the armed forces, acted as chief legislator, and so on ad infinitum. The previous chapter should remind the reader that the presidency is many people—around five thousand under Richard Nixon. In many cases the president's staff will make important decisions in his name, screen his information, and control access to his office. The presidency is no less a collective than Congress, and the desire to turn over a problem to the president results in its being turned over to aides.

A second myth that de Grazia attacks is that of the president as champion of the majority (on other occasions the champion of the minority). As the "great engine of democracy," "the American peoples' one authentic trumpet," he is seen as the representative of all of the people. This naturally encourages the desire to take power away from Congress (which is attacked as selfish and parochial in its outlook) and give it to the president. In some cases the president may be extremely popular and doing what the people want done; in others he may completely misread the public sentiment. Do his acts by definition serve society? Almost every policy he pursues will please some and make others unhappy. In the course of his incumbency, he is almost sure to act in the interests of some groups more than others. His successor may reverse these preferences. Which was the champion of the people?

The president as advocate of the public interest is a myth closely related to that of the president as the representative of the entire people. It, too, largely hangs on his method of selection compared with that of Congress, as well as on his central role in the political system.[60] The role of the chief executive as advocate of the public interest (compared with Congress's representation of local interests) can be traced through Andrew Jackson, Teddy Roosevelt, and Woodrow Wilson to the present. Because most historians have judged the actions of these presidents to be the correct ones, and because strong presidents championed the kinds of policies that liberal scholars favor, most of the literature of politics assumed that the actions of future strong presidents would also be in the public interest. Only conservatives tended to assume that Congress could represent that interest.[61] To an extent it depends upon whose ox is being gored.

Part of the reason for viewing the president as the custodian of the public interest is his command of the foreign policy and military establishments. That "single voice" with which the United States speaks is his. National security has become preeminently identified with the office, and to question his decisions strikes many as treasonous. His pronouncements have seemed to be *ex cathedra*. In an age when total war is a possibility, it is easy to extend that conception to internal affairs as well. President Nixon sought to defend himself at home by pointing to the dangers of weakening the presidency when he was so needed to bring peace to a troubled world. When Alexander Haig conveyed Nixon's order to fire the special prosecutor to Elliot Richardson, he said, "your Commander-in-Chief orders you." Much of the plumbers' activity was justified in terms of national security. And keeping information from Congress or actually lying to that body is, it has sometimes been claimed, even warranted under the circumstances. That a president's policies do not always define the public interest should become clear from these examples.

A fourth common belief that de Grazia sees as a myth is that the president is the center of responsibility and initiative in the American political system. The most famous expression of that myth was the sign on Harry Truman's desk: "The buck stops here." Although it may be true that people tend to blame chief executives for failures in the system (even many beyond his control), this is not because most presidents willingly accept such responsibility. One would have to go back beyond recent memory to find an example of a chief executive saying to the people, "I was wrong," or "I goofed today," or "My policies in this area were 180 degrees off." Presidents, being only human, are glad to take credit when things work out and the people are happy. But

blunders are generally attributed to others. The blame is sometimes put on Congress—for failing to pass the executive's program, or passing it with provisions the chief did not ask for.
Sometimes blame is attributed to economic interests—such as
greedy businessmen or labor unions or Arab oil sheiks. Occasion-
ally a president's aides are even singled out for criticism—as when
they keep those with competing advice or vital information from
him. (In the case of Watergate, President Nixon at first publicly
accepted "responsibility" but then proceded to lay the blame on
overzealous staffers.) Even those who disagree with a president's
program are blamed for its lack of success, as when the protesters
against the Vietnam War were credited with strengthening Ha-
noi's will to resist and thus with prolonging the war. And so the
buck is passed more frequently than it stops in the Oval Office. In
addition, giving the president increased responsibilities for dealing with the country's problems must mean in fact the parceling
off of those duties to subordinates. He is "responsible" for them in
name only.

One final element of the presidential myth that de Grazia
attacks is the notion that only the president has the time and
ability to react quickly to any situation when the demand arises.[62]
Congress is often pictured as wasting time in extended hearings
and prolonged debate while the chief executive merely has to
issue orders to get things done. Richard Neustadt has effectively
demonstrated that orders have only a limited applicability even in
the executive's own domain, and that they are frequently counterproductive. Here, as in other areas, the trading of advantages
and bargaining are as necessary as they are in congressional
relationships.[63] In addition, a president "wastes" time in perhaps
more ways than Congress does. Formal and ceremonial chores,
along with routine tasks such as signing letters, laws, and documents, eat into the same twenty-four-hour day imposed on all
mortals.

Where presidents do respond with "speed and dispatch" is
generally in "emergency" situations, such as the sending of troops
to trouble spots or the ordering of relief supplies for disaster
areas. De Grazia maintains that it is unwarranted to generalize
from these instances to the belief that action is as swift in all
situations. Opposing viewpoints must be reconciled, often within

the president's own official family, before many actions can be taken. Hasty action without wide consultation, fact gathering, and sufficient reflection has often proven unwise, as in the Bay of Pigs invasion and the Tonkin Gulf incident. In the latter case, Congress proved how rapidly it can act during crises, and in the process also demonstrated that it would have been a virtue to delay, debate, and seek more and better information than that which prompted the president to act. It is the tendency to view virtually every problem as a crisis which has added so many powers to the presidency.

Other elements of the presidential myth have been discussed earlier. Notable among these is that the president always has more, and better, information than others in the political system on most crucial issues. Also problematic is the notion of the "lonely" and "overburdened" status of the person who occupies the Oval Office. Pictures of President Kennedy on a solitary stroll on the beach with the brooding ocean in the background or of President Nixon lost in reflection at the window of his office, help convey this popular image. So do innumerable stories in the press. But as should now be clear, the president is only as solitary as he chooses to be. He is surrounded by staff and can call in virtually anyone in Washington, D. C., whenever he desires. As for overwork, he can keep or delegate as many of the duties of office as he pleases, as Dwight Eisenhower proved. George Reedy has written: "Despite the widespread belief to the contrary . . . there is far less to the presidency in terms of essential activity, than meets the eye. The psychological burdens are heavy, even crushing, but no president ever died of overwork and it is doubtful whether any ever will." [64] Eisenhower, essentially a happy man who allowed his aides (and especially Sherman Adams) to bear much of the workload, suffered a heart attack in office. Yet Herbert Hoover put in crushing hours on the job—and survived for thirty years afterwards. And Lyndon Johnson, who had had a heart attack as majority leader of the Senate, escaped the presidency without a recurrence of the problem. The danger in this myth is that it leads to the desire to pamper the incumbent and fulfill his every whim—thus leading to the removal of the president from constraints imposed upon others.

There remains but one myth about presidential power to be mentioned here. It is called by Arthur Larson the "greater-includes-the-less concept" of the presidency.[65] This is closely related to the myth of the president as executive (as exemplified in President Ford's citation of the Supreme Court to the effect that "I am the executive branch"). Recent presidents have acted as if this were true, relegating many of the functions of the departments to the Executive Office of the President. But each agency of the federal government was established by congressional statute; each exercises those powers alloted to it by Congress. When executive officials are sworn in, they take an oath to uphold the Constitution and laws of the United States, not the president. Impoundment is but one very obvious illustration of how recent chief executives have believed that an act of Congress can be negated by a presidential decision. More than two dozen court decisions, including one by the Supreme Court, have now refuted this idea. Congress and administrators as well must now begin to see that spending is not the only area where the law delegates authority to lower-ranking officials that is not subject to presidential discretion.

Once myths have been identified, is it wise to try to destroy them? Do they have a certain efficacy and serve vital functions for the society? Several very serious scholars of the presidency believe it would be dangerous to take the myth and magic away from the office. John Cogley, senior fellow at the Center for the Study of Democratic Institutions and editor of the *Center Magazine,* said at a recent conference on the presidency:

> Maybe we are getting to the point where all of us would like to demythologize the Presidency. I don't. I think we need myth, and I think we need symbol. I don't think we could live without it, even if we wanted to. We just aren't that rational. Happily we're too human for that. We will either live by the myth that has served us fairly well for almost two hundred years, or we will probably find a much worse one.[66]

And Edwin Guthman, at the same conference, reminded his listeners that "in this country the Presidency is the one national office that we have. We don't have a national religion; we don't have a national education system. We have a President."[67]

These authorities tend to assume that a personification of America, especially in the body of one living person, is a requisite for the successful continuance of a unified society. This, however, may be open to serious question. If a symbol of national unity is needed, Americans have many to choose among. Icons abound, and they do not suffer the frailties of mortal men. There is the flag, the Fourth of July, the Declaration of Independence, the Constitution, the Bill of Rights, the American eagle, the goals of freedom and equality, and a free democratic political system. Surely these are important elements when people think of why they are proud of their country. If an embodiment of the abstraction "America" is necessary, if heroes help weld a society together, then once again there are many from which to choose. There are George Washington, Thomas Jefferson, Patrick Henry, Abraham Lincoln, Woodrow Wilson, Franklin Roosevelt, Martin Luther King, and many others. That they are all dead is to their advantage in serving as heroes: they are safely past making future mistakes. Their feet of clay are now buried in that soil, beyond the reach of all but the revisionist historians. Deification suits dead presidents better than live incumbents. Even popes must wait for their elevation to sainthood until sufficient time has passed to prove them worthy of canonization.

It is unhealthy to focus needs, desires, expectations—and hatreds—so heavily on one politician subject to vast fluctuations in popularity. If he is the symbol—the embodiment of unity— then it is dangerous to criticize him. This is the problem, recognized two hundred years ago, of making one person both the head of government and the head of state. Henry Fairlie, a British observer of the presidency, wrote a few years back: "The Presidency seems to me to be a seed bed for, and already to have in it some of the seeds of, the most refined of all absolutist systems: Caesaropapism."[68] The United States has combined the temporal power of the government with the spiritual authority of the nation. Popes are elected by their colleagues in the College of Cardinals: once crowned their authority comes from God. In the Byzantine Empire, the emperor was elected by the "Christian Commonwealth," which had the right to take the throne away as well. But once crowned he became the viceroy of God. "His power having been given to him from below, the Emperor then exercised it as being confirmed from above. It was a brilliant device."[69] Recent presidents, too, have in some cases behaved as if their grant of power from the electorate (the *ascending* theory of government) conferred upon them the absolute divine right to make decisions for the people (the *descending* theory of government). This has been especially true in the expanding area of "national security." When questioned about the legal justification for the secret bombing of Cambodia, an assistant secretary of state replied: "The justification is the re-election of President Nixon." This comes perilously close to the claim of Louis XIV, "*l'état, c'est moi.*"

It is hard to hold gods responsible; their actions are beyond the judgments of mortals. Recall a quote from Chapter 3: "Every President's right to our loyalty is non-forfeitable. Whether we voted for him or not, he is entitled to it for as long as he discharges the awesome responsibility of that office, regardless of the charges against him."[70] In a way, it is like the problems Christians have had in understanding God's ways: famine, infant mortality, plague, pestilence, and war don't have to be explained, only accepted. So too with presidents for many people: they know more than we do; we must accept their judgments; it's our duty to obey.

Divinity carries with it the imputation of infallibility. Not only is there a danger in a large percentage of the electorate accepting this notion, but it may be even more pernicious if presidents themselves come to believe it. The acclaim of the masses, the deference presidents receive from fellow politicians, and the reverential treatment afforded them by their staffs—all reinforce the idea. This makes it very difficult to admit mistakes, to reverse policies once the presidential prestige has become committed to a particular course of action. Even in the face of mounting evidence that a policy or strategy is not working, a president may convince himself that just a little more time, a few thousand more troops, or fuller support in Congress or from the people will demonstrate the correctness of his decisions. If people today are too foolish to appreciate the wisdom of the president, then surely history will accord him ultimate vindication.

Institutions qua institutions should not command respect and obedience in a democracy. It is only the successful and representative performance of those institutions that is worthy of deference. The notion that constituted authority (such as the president) is due allegiance simply because it is authority was rejected by the patriots who died at Bunker Hill and by those who wrote the Declaration of Independence. Thus the record, the performance of Washington, Lincoln, or Roosevelt is revered; that of Buchanan, Grant, Harding, or Hoover is not. (Although it is true that character and personalities of some presidents have themselves become subjects of myths and reverence, this has happened generally only to those whose record in office merited the praise due great men.) In recent years presidents have been behaving as if merely holding the office qualifies them for the automatic loyalty of the people. The sooner citizens and presidents alike return to the realization that there is no transfiguration, no transubstantiation of flesh and blood that occurs when a person takes the presidential oath, the sooner everyone involved will again be able to view the office as merely being occupied by a politician temporarily exercising power for the people.

A mature and well-educated political community does not require a personification of its institutions. Although some scholars worry about the effects of demythologizing the presidency, America survived Fillmore, Pierce, Buchanan, Andrew Johnson, Grant, Hays, Arthur, Taft, Harding, Coolidge, and Hoover. In recent years it even survived Lyndon Johnson and Richard Nixon. (If it is true that only the president can serve as the embodiment of the nation, how is it that millions of people distrusted both Johnson and Nixon but remained loyal Americans?) People got up in the morning, went to their farms, factories, and schools, attended church, engaged in their routine activities, and, to an extent that still bewilders political scientists, ignored politics. If they felt their institutions under attack, at least part of this was due to the unnecessary confusion of the fate of their country with the fortunes of the man in the White House.

A first step in reversing the tendency of the last forty years to magnify the expectations of the office would be more realistic, less romanticized history and political science treatments of the presidency in textbooks. There is a need to take Lincoln out of the politician who is currently president. More emphasis on the contributions to society of various groups, social movements, economic factors, and notable members of Congress would give a more balanced and accurate interpretation of events in the United States. It is difficult to treat these subjects in a simplified fashion but not impossible. The next step must come from the media. By not focusing on Congress, the press continues to allow that branch to behave irresponsibly. By its overconcentration on the presidency, it helps enlarge and glorify that institution. Most particularly, the attention given to any president as a man helps further the personalization of authority. (One of the earliest criticisms of Jerald terHorst's performance as Ford's first press secretary was that he didn't pay enough attention to details—such as what color suit the president was wearing.) It may be said that the press only gives the people what they want, but to a large degree it has created its own demand.

A bloated White House press corps is partially responsible for the current glut of excessive detail that inundates citizens. If there is no story, no "hard" news, they still must report some work being tended to each day. In a sense the White House press corps has become part of the White House public relations flak corps. One partial remedy might be to move the press out of the White House. If reporters paid less attention to the man and more to his policies, programs and proposals, the electorate would be better informed. It is condescending to treat American citizens as if they were capable of assimilating nothing more complicated than movie star gossip. What is needed is more investigative reporting and fewer human interest stories. More reporters like Jack Anderson, Carl Bernstein, Bob Woodward, Clark Mollenhoff (and even Dan Rather) showing less reverence toward the presidency is one way to insure that officials will be held accountable for their actions. It may also mean less inflation of ordinary men into persons whose every activity, no matter how banal, must be worthy of front page coverage.

Governor Daniel Evans of Washington has proposed a way to keep the president in touch with the ordinary people of the country and at the same time let him live a private life of his own while keeping the press informed. Evans would have the president agree to a regular weekly press conference "in exchange for the privilege of going abroad in the land with relative freedom and flexibility."[71] The freedom and flexibility refer to moving about without hundreds of reporters tagging along and creating a "media event" every time the chief executive sets foot outside of the White House gates. Such an arrangement should allow a president to listen to the people on a regular basis and to live a more ordinary life himself. This too would be advantageous. A regularly scheduled press conference would also guarantee that the press would be able to put important questions to the president in a timely fashion. A more human but also a more responsive presidency could result by paying less attention to the president.

The task of creating a "life-size" presidency is a difficult one. Michael Novak suggests moving the president out of the White House and moving in a new chief of state who would perform the ceremonial and symbolic functions for the nation.[72] Most other countries in the world have separated the responsibility for conducting the affairs of government from those of state. Thus prime ministers do not personify the national identity: that function is left to the king, queen, or president. Rarely do the heads of state wield significant political or governmental authority. Even the Soviet Union has seen the necessity of dividing powers in this way. Without creating a new official in the United States or amending the Constitution to provide for a separate position, certain steps could be taken to relieve the president of the inordinate amount of power and independence he draws from the symbolism of his office.

There is no constitutional provision requiring that only the president be allowed to engage in the rituals of nationhood or perform the ceremonies of independence. These could be divided among various federal officials. The speaker of the House of Representatives could light the nation's Christmas tree on the lawn of the Capitol; the majority leader of the Senate could throw out the first baseball of the season; the chief justice could purchase the first Easter Seal and be photographed with the poster child; Congress could proclaim Thanksgiving (with an appropriate message to the people); foreign heads of state could be greeted jointly by the leaders of all three branches of government—symbolizing the unity of the American people that exists despite the separation of power. Medals for heroes, televised Fourth of July speeches recalling the nation's greatness, and other rituals could be similarly rotated among the leaders of government. It would be a healthy thing for the American people to become more familiar with the other two branches of government and at the same time reduce the magic of the presidency. It would create a set of peers for the chief executive in the public mind, and also perhaps in the minds of presidents.

Conclusion

Until recent years there was widespread satisfaction among scholars and the public with the institution of the presidency. Those who called for reforms generally sought to strengthen the office at the expense of the federal bureaucracy, Congress, or the states. It was these latter institutions that stood in the way of modern, effective, and democratic government, according to most observers. A series of strong, progressive presidents had proven that the "executive impulse" was not only an inevitable but a desirable trend. The reforms called for today generally seek to limit the power of the executive, to check his independent activities by revitalizing the historic mechanisms which have been allowed to rust, or to devise new means of holding presidents accountable. Others scholars, however, saw in this a danger of going too far, of fantasizing about the capabilities of other institutions to provide the necessary leadership in a twentieth-century democracy. Some years ago Clinton Rossiter wrote that the presidency has been "one of the few truly successful institutions created by men in their endless quest for the blessings of free government."[73] To cripple the office because of the presidencies of Lyndon Johnson and Richard Nixon would be to deny the American people of the kind of government that has served them so well in the past, and that is necessary to provide dynamic leadership in the future. The problem was with the men not the office, according to this view.

But too much has happened in recent years to be attributable solely to the personality failings of recent incumbents. The office itself, the institution, seemed to magnify what was worst in presidents and to minimize the political acumen that has enabled them to rise to power. Lyndon Johnson had been an enormously successful majority leader, perhaps the most successful that the Senate had ever known. And Richard Nixon was noted for his meteoric rise, his pragmatism, and his ability to overcome defeat with ultimate triumph. Both won electoral victories of massive proportions. Yet each somehow managed to lose control of events and become their victims rather than their masters. A reexamination of the presidencies of other modern chief executives has indicated that Johnson and Nixon were not the creators of new tendencies but rather were reapers of fruit, the seeds of which had been sown by their predecessors. To assure the people responsible government and to protect the president from the presidency seems to call for a rethinking of some of the conventional wisdom of the last forty years.

Many more reforms than those covered in this book have been proposed. Some are essential if the system is to be both revitalized and held in check. Perhaps the single most desirable improvement would be a regeneration of the political parties and the restoration of them to meaningful participation in the selection of candidates and the operation of government. Third-party movements can also play a significant role in requiring governors to pay attention to the people. Citizen politics, such as Common Cause and Ralph Nader's raiders, have demonstrated that the individual citizen can participate between elections and have a significant impact. Electoral reforms and public financing of elections for every official at the federal level would reduce the impact of money on determining policy and, perhaps, improve both Congress and the presidency. Proposed laws, such as those limiting wiretaps and imposing closer regulation on intelligence agencies, would help protect political liberties.

Laws alone, however, will not insure responsive and accountable government. As Thomas Jefferson said two hundred years ago, "Eternal vigilance is the price of liberty." Fundamentally, what is needed is an aware and questioning citizenry. A mature and educated people should be able to survive as a society without the deification of its executive. Less reverence and awe and a little less splendor in the White House would contribute toward bringing the presidency back to earth. Stripping the office of many of its ceremonial functions would still leave vast governmental powers in the hands of the president, but without the color of religious authority. The people may expect fewer miracles and not continually be disappointed with the current incumbent. Finally, the concentration of attention on the majesty and pageantry of the office has allowed organized interests to gain their demands essentially outside the public's vision. Presidential appointments to the courts, the independent agencies, and the federal bureaucracy significantly affect the lives of every American. So too do the activities of congressional committees and of the permanent government. When people's attention is focused solely on the man in the White House, they are misled into believing that they are witness to the essence of government. Actually they see only the drama and not the substance. A democracy owes more to its citizens.

NOTES

1. Mike Mansfield, "Case For a Six-Year Term" *Spokesman Review*, 4 June 1973 (copyright 1973, *Los Angeles Times*).

2. Jack Valenti, "The Case for a Six-Year Presidency," *Saturday Review*, 3 August 1968, p. 13.

3. Rexford Tugwell, "Constitution for a United Republic of America," Version XXXVII, *Center Magazine*, 3, no. 5 (September/October 1970), 30.

4. George E. Reedy, "Should the Constitution be Amended to Provide for a Single Six-Year Presidential Term?" *Congressional Digest*, 51 (March 1972), 93.

5. See, for example, Arthur M. Schlesinger, Jr., "The Runaway Presidency," *Atlantic Monthly*, 232, no. 5 (November 1973), 47.

6. Tugwell, p. 31.

7. Herman Finer, *The Presidency* (Chicago: University of Chicago Press, 1960), pp. 302–313.

8. Ibid., pp. 302, 310, 313.

9. Committee on Political Parties of the American Political Science Association, *Toward a More Responsible Two-Party System* (New York: Rinehart, 1950).

10. Austin Ranney, "Toward a More Responsible Two-Party System: A Commentary," *American Political Science Review*, 45, no. 2 (June 1951), 488–499.

11. *Ibid.*, p. 495.

12. See Nelson W. Polsby and Aaron B. Wildavsky, *Presidential Elections*, 3rd ed. (New York: Scribner, 1971), chap. 4.

13. Barbara Tuchman, "Should We Abolish the Presidency?," *New York Times*, 13 February 1973.

14. Harvey Wheeler, "The Powers of the Presidency," *Center Magazine*, 4, no. 1 (January/February 1971), 11.

15. Alexander Hamilton, *The Federalist*, No. 70; Polsby and Wildavsky, p. 230.

16. Edward S. Corwin, *The President: Office and Powers*, 2nd ed. (New York: New York University Press, 1941) p. 361.

17. Edward S. Corwin and Louis W. Koenig, *The Presidency Today* (New York: New York University Press, 1956) p. 95. For a more complete explication of the plan see Corwin, *A Constitution of Powers in a Secular State* (Charlottesville, N.C.: Michie, 1951), pp. 73–82.

18. Corwin and Koenig, cit. pp. 95–96.

19. Robert F. Kennedy, *Thirteen Days* (New York: Norton, 1969), p. 53.

20. Curtis A. Amlund, *New Perspectives on the Presidency* (New York: Philosophical Library, 1969), p. 52.

21. Gwendolen M. Carter, *The Government of the United Kingdom*, 3rd ed. (New York: Harcourt Brace Jovanovich, 1972), pp. 125–126.

22. John P. Mackintosh, *The British Cabinet*, 2nd ed. (London: Methuen 1968), p. 509.

23. *Ibid.*, p. 510.

24. Thomas E. Cronin, "The Swelling of the Presidency," *Saturday Review of the Society*, 1, no. 1 (February 1973), 36.

25. "Report Proposing a New Science Council in Office of President," *New York Times*, 27 June 1974.

26. Walter Sullivan, *New York Times*, 11 June 1974.

27. Elizabeth Drew, "Reports and Comment: Washington," *Atlantic Monthly*, 231, no. 2 (February 1973), 8.

28. Robert C. Toth, "Federal Bureaucracy Will Resist Reform," *Spokesman Review*, 3 December 1972 *(copyright 1972, Los Angeles Times)*.

29. Drew, p. 12.

30. Cronin, p. 36.

31. Walter J. Hickel, "The Need for No-Men," *New York Times*, 9 October 1973.

32. Richard E. Neustadt, "The Constraining of the President," *New York Times Magazine*, 14 October 1973, p. 117.

33. "Panel's Report: Too Much Centralization of Power," *Washington Post*, 21 March 1974.

34. Mr. Justice Brandeis in dissent in *Olmstead v. United States*, 277 U. S. 438 (1928).

35. *Submission of Recorded Presidential Conversations to the Committee on the Judiciary of the House of Representatives by President Richard M. Nixon, April 30, 1974* (Washington, D.C.: GPO, 1974), p. 185.

36. *Ibid.*, p. 941.

37. A good summary of these proposals is contained in Victor S. Navasky, "The Politics of Justice," *New York Times Magazine*, 5 May 1974, pp. 19, 48–50, 52–54, 58, 63.

38. *Washington Post*, 21 March 1974.

39. *The Final Report of the Select Committee on Presidential Campaign Activities*, Senate, 93rd Cong., 2nd Sess., Report no. 93-981 (June 1974), pp. 96–100.

40. Some of these proposals are discussed in Navasky; Theodore C. Sorensen, "Justice Department Reform," *New York Times*, 30 June 1974; Harry McPherson, "The System Worked, but Can It Be Improved?" *New York Times*, 25 April 1974.

41. Tugwell, p. 21.

42. Marcus Cunliffe, "A Defective Institution?" *Commentary*, 45, no. 2 (February 1968), 27–33.

43. Address to the Congress," August 12, 1974, *Weekly Compilation of Presidential Documents*, 10, no. 33, (19 August 1974), 1033.

44. Arthur Schlesinger, Jr., *The Imperial Presidency* (Boston: Houghton Mifflin, 1973), p. 313.

45. *Ibid.*

46. *Ibid.*, pp. 311–316.

47. Statement of J. William Fulbright, "Separation of Powers," *Hearings Before the Subcommittee on Separation of Powers of the Committee on the Judiciary*, Senate, 90th Cong. 1st Sess., 19 July 1967, Part 1, pp. 41–53.

48. Nicholas de B. Katzenbach, "Foreign Policy, Public Opinion and Secrecy," *Foreign Affairs*, 52, no. 1 (October 1973), 15.

49. See Thomas L. Hughes, "Foreign Policy: Men or Measures," *Atlantic Monthly*, 234, no. 4 (October 1974), 48–60; Anthony Lake, "An End to Either/Or," *New York Times*, 12 August 1974.

50. Katzenbach, pp. 14–18.

51. Thomas E. Cronin, "Making the Presidency Safe for Democracy," *Center Magazine*, 6, no. 5 (September/October 1973), 30.

52. Newton Minow, John B. Martin, and Lee Mitchell, *Presidential Television, A Twentieth Century Fund Report* (New York: Basic Books, 1973), p. 161.

53. Reported in John G. Stewart, "The Possible Impact of Broadcast Coverage of Congress on Teaching American Government," *DEA News*, no. 3 (Fall 1974), p. 1.

54. Gallup poll reported in *New York Times*, 28 August 1974.

55. Speech delivered to the National Press Club, January 14, 1960. Reprinted in Robert S. Hirschfield, ed., *The Power of the Presidency*, 2nd ed. (Chicago: Aldine, 1973), p. 133.

56. Richard E. Neustadt, *Presidential Power* (New York: Wiley, 1960), p. 106.

57. Alfred de Grazia, *Republic In Crisis* (New York: Federal Legal Publications, 1965), p. 70. The myths dealt with in the present work are discussed in chap. V of *Republic in Crisis*.

58. Thomas E. Cronin, "The Textbook Presidency and Political Science," paper prepared for delivery at the American Political Science Association meeting, Los Angeles, California, September 7–12, 1970.

59. *Weekly Compilation of Presidential Documents*, p. 1030.

60. De Grazia, p. 79.

61. See, for example, Willmore Kendall, "The Two Majorities," *Midwest Journal of Political Science*, 4 (November 1960), 317–345.

62. De Grazia attempts to destroy other myths about the president as well, including the "republicanism of the Presidents," "the freedom boss" syndrome, and the "trustee of the nation" myth. The interested reader is referred to chap. V of *Republic in Crisis*.

63. Neustadt, Presidential Power, p. 106.

64. George Reedy, *The Twilight of the Presidency* (New York: Mentor, 1970), p. 31.

65. Arthur Larson, "Some Myths about the Executive Branch," *Center Magazine*, no. 5 (September/October 1974), 53–60.

66. John Cogley in a panel discussion on the presidency, reported in *Center Magazine*, 27, no. 5 (September/October 1974), 36.

67. *Ibid.*, p. 47.

68. Henry Fairlie, "Thoughts on the Presidency," *The Public Interest*, no. 9 (Fall 1967), p. 44.

69. *Ibid.*, pp. 45–46.

70. *Los Angeles Times*, 28 October 1973.

71. Evans's proposal is reported in David Broder's column in *Washington Post*, 4 September 1973.

72. Michael Novak, *Choosing Our King* (New York: Macmillan, 1974), pp. 262–269.

73. Clinton Rossiter, *The American Presidency*, 2nd ed. (New York; Harcourt, Brace & World, 1960), p. 15.

APPENDIX

Presidents of
the United States

<table>
<tr><td></td><td></td><td>TERM</td></tr>
<tr><td>1.</td><td>George Washington (1732–99)</td><td>1789–1797</td></tr>
<tr><td>2.</td><td>John Adams (1735–1826)</td><td>1797–1801</td></tr>
<tr><td>3.</td><td>Thomas Jefferson (1743–1826)</td><td>1801–1809</td></tr>
<tr><td>4.</td><td>James Madison (1751–1836)</td><td>1809–1817</td></tr>
<tr><td>5.</td><td>James Monroe (1758–1831)</td><td>1817–1825</td></tr>
<tr><td>6.</td><td>John Quincy Adams (1767–1848)</td><td>1825–1829</td></tr>
<tr><td>7.</td><td>Andrew Jackson (1767–1845)</td><td>1829–1837</td></tr>
<tr><td>8.</td><td>Martin Van Buren (1782–1862)</td><td>1837–1841</td></tr>
<tr><td>9.</td><td>William Henry Harrison (1773–1841)</td><td>1841</td></tr>
<tr><td>10.</td><td>John Tyler (1790–1862)</td><td>1841–1845</td></tr>
<tr><td>11.</td><td>James K. Polk (1795–1849)</td><td>1845–1849</td></tr>
<tr><td>12.</td><td>Zachary Taylor (1784–1850)</td><td>1849–1850</td></tr>
<tr><td>13.</td><td>Millard Fillmore (1800–74)</td><td>1850–1853</td></tr>
<tr><td>14.</td><td>Franklin Pierce (1804–69)</td><td>1853–1857</td></tr>
<tr><td>15.</td><td>James Buchanan (1791–1868)</td><td>1857–1861</td></tr>
<tr><td>16.</td><td>Abraham Lincoln (1809–65)</td><td>1861–1865</td></tr>
<tr><td>17.</td><td>Andrew Johnson (1808–75)</td><td>1865–1869</td></tr>
<tr><td>18.</td><td>Ulysses S. Grant (1822–85)</td><td>1869–1877</td></tr>
<tr><td>19.</td><td>Rutherford B. Hayes (1822–93)</td><td>1877–1881</td></tr>
<tr><td>20.</td><td>James A. Garfield (1831–81)</td><td>1881</td></tr>
<tr><td>21.</td><td>Chester A. Arthur (1830–86)</td><td>1881–1885</td></tr>
<tr><td>22.</td><td>Grover Cleveland (1837–1908)</td><td>1885–1889</td></tr>
<tr><td>23.</td><td>Benjamin Harrison (1833–1901)</td><td>1889–1893</td></tr>
<tr><td>24.</td><td>Grover Cleveland (1837–1908)</td><td>1893–1897</td></tr>
<tr><td>25.</td><td>William McKinley (1843–1901)</td><td>1897–1901</td></tr>
<tr><td>26.</td><td>Theodore Roosevelt (1858–1919)</td><td>1901–1909</td></tr>
<tr><td>27.</td><td>William Howard Taft (1857–1930)</td><td>1909–1913</td></tr>
</table>

28. Woodrow Wilson (1856–1924)   1913–1921
29. Warren G. Harding (1865–1923)   1921–1923
30. Calvin Coolidge (1872–1933)   1923–1929
31. Herbert Hoover (1874–1964)   1929–1933
32. Franklin Delano Roosevelt (1882–1945)   1933–1945
33. Harry S Truman (1884–1972)   1945–1953
34. Dwight D. Eisenhower (1890–1969)   1953–1961
35. John F. Kennedy (1917–63)   1961–1963
36. Lyndon B. Johnson (1908–73)   1963–1969
37. Richard M. Nixon (b. 1913)   1969–1974
38. Gerald R. Ford (b. 1913)   1974–

Constitutional Provisions
Pertaining to the President

ARTICLE I

Section 2. The House of Representatives . . . shall have the sole Power of Impeachment.

Section 3. The Senate shall have the sole Power to try all Impeachments. When sitting for that Purpose, they shall be on Oath or Affirmation. When the President of the United States is tried, the Chief Justice shall preside: And no Person shall be convicted without the Concurrence of two thirds of the Members present.

Judgment in Cases of Impeachment shall not extend further than to removal from Office, and disqualification to hold and enjoy any Office of honor, Trust or Profit under the United States: but the Party convicted shall nevertheless be liable and subject to Indictment, Trial, Judgment and Punishment, according to law.

Section 7. Every Bill which shall have passed the House of Representatives and the Senate, shall, before it become a Law, be presented to the President of the United States; If he approve he shall sign it, but if not he shall return it, with his Objections to that House in which it shall have originated, who shall enter the Objections at large on their Journal, and proceed to reconsider it. If after such Reconsideration two thirds of that House shall agree to pass the Bill, it shall be sent, together with the Objections, to the other House, by which it shall likewise be reconsidered, and if approved by two thirds of that House, it shall become a Law. But in all such Cases the Votes of both Houses shall be determined by Yeas and Nays, and the Names of the Persons voting for and against the Bill shall be entered on the Journal of each House respectively. If any Bill shall not be returned by the President within ten Days (Sundays excepted) after it shall have been presented to him, the Same shall be a Law, in like

271

Manner as if he had signed it, unless the Congress by their Adjournament prevent its Return, in which Case it shall not be a Law.

Every Order, Resolution, or Vote to which the Concurrence of the Senate and House of Representatives may be necessary (except on a question of Adjournment) shall be presented to the President of the United States; and before the Same shall take Effect, shall be approved by him, or being disapproved by him, shall be repassed by two thirds of the Senate and House of Representatives, according to the Rules and Limitations prescribed in the Case of a Bill.

ARTICLE II

Section 1. The executive Power shall be vested in a President of the United States of America. He shall hold his Office during the Term of four Years, and together with the Vice President, chosen for the same term, be elected, as follows

Each State shall appoint, in such Manner as the Legislature thereof may direct, a Number of Electors, equal to the whole Number of Senators and Representatives to which the State may be entitled in the Congress: but no Senator or Representative, or Person holding an Office of Trust or Profit under the United States, shall be appointed an Elector.

°The Electors shall meet in their respective States, and vote by Ballot for two Persons, of whom one at least shall not be an Inhabitant of the same State with themselves. And they shall make a List of all the Persons voted for, and of the Number of Votes for each; which List they shall sign and certify, and transmit sealed to the Seat of the Government of the United States, directed to the President of the Senate. The President of the Senate shall, in the Presence of the Senate and House of Representatives, open all the Certificates, and the Votes shall then be counted. The Person having the greatest Number of Votes shall be the President, if such Number be a Majority of the whole Number of Electors appointed; and if there be more than one who have such Majority, and have an equal Number of Votes, then the House of Representatives shall immediately chuse by Ballot one of them for President: and if no Person have a Majority, then from the five highest on the List the said House shall in like Manner chuse the President. But in chusing the President, the Votes shall be taken by States, the Representation from each State having one Vote; A quorum for this Purpose shall consist of a Member or Members from two thirds of the States, and a Majority of all the States shall be necessary to a Choice. In every Case, after the Choice of the President, the Person

°Altered by Twelfth Amendment.

having the greatest Number of Votes of the Electors shall be the Vice-President. But if there should remain two or more who have equal Votes, the Senate shall chuse from them by Ballot the Vice President.

The Congress may determine the Time of chusing the Electors and the Day on which they shall give their Votes; which Day shall be the same throughout the United States.

No Person except a natural born Citizen, or a Citizen of the United States, at the time of the Adoption of this Constitution, shall be eligible to that Office who shall not have attained to the Age of thirty-five Years, and been fourteen Years a Resident within the United States.

°In case of the Removal of the President from Office, or of his Death, Resignation or Inability to discharge the Powers and Duties of the said Office, the Same shall devolve on the Vice-President, and the Congress may be Law provide for the Case of Removal, Death, Resignation or Inability, both of the President and Vice-President, declaring what Officer shall then act as President, and such Officer shall act accordingly, until the Disability be removed, or a President shall be elected.

The President shall, at stated Times, receive for his Services a Compensation, which shall neither be increased nor diminished during the Period for which he shall have been elected, and he shall not receive within that Period any other Emolument from the United States, or any of them.

Before he enter on the Execution of his Office, he shall take the following Oath or Affirmation:—"I do solemnly swear (or affirm) that I will faithfully execute the Office of President of the United States, and will to the best of my Ability, preserve, protect and defend the Constitution of the United States."

Section 2.   The President shall be Commander in Chief of the Army and Navy of the United States, and of the Militia of the several States, when called into the actual Service of the United States; he may require the Opinion, in writing, of the principal Officer in each of the executive Departments, upon any Subject relating to the Duties of their respective Offices, and he shall have power to grant Reprieves and Pardons for Offences against the United States, except in Cases of Impeachment.

He shall have Power, by and with the Advice and Consent of the Senate, to make Treaties, provided two thirds of the Senators present concur; and he shall nominate, and by and with the Advice and Consent of the Senate, shall appoint Ambassadors, other public Ministers and Consuls, Judges of the Supreme Court, and all other Officers of the United States, whose Appointments are not herein otherwise provided for, and which shall be established by Law; but the Congress may by Law vest the Appointment of such inferior Officers, as they think proper,

°Altered by Twenty-fifth Amendment.

in the President alone, in the Courts of Law, or in the Heads of Departments.

°The President shall have Power to fill up all Vacancies that may happen during the Recess of the Senate, by granting Commissions which shall expire at the End of their next Session.

Section 3. He shall from time to time give to the Congress Information of the State of the Union, and recommend to their Consideration such Measures as he shall judge necessary and expedient; he may, on extraordinary Occasions, convene both Houses, or either of them, and in Case of Disagreement between them, with Respect to the Time of Adjournment, he may adjourn them to such Time as he shall think proper; he shall receive Ambassadors and other public Ministers; he shall take Care that the Laws be faithfully executed, and shall Commission all the Officers of the United States.

Section 4. The President, Vice-President and all civil Officers of the United States, shall be removed from Office on Impeachment for, and Conviction of, Treason, Bribery, or other High Crimes and Misdemeanors.

AMENDMENT 12°°

The Electors shall meet in their respective states and vote by ballot for President and Vice-President, one of whom, at least, shall not be an inhabitant of the same state with themselves; they shall name in their ballots the person voted for as President, and in distinct ballots the person voted for as Vice-President, and they shall make distinct lists of all persons voted for as President, and of all persons voted for as Vice-President, and of the number of votes for each, which lists they shall sign and certify, and transmit sealed to the seat of the government of the United States, directed to the President of the Senate;—The President of the Senate shall, in the presence of the Senate and House of Representatives, open all the certificates and the votes shall then be counted;—The person having the greatest number of votes for President, shall be the President, if such number be a majority of the whole number of Electors appointed; and if no person have such majority, then from the persons having the highest numbers not exceeding three on the list of those voted for as President, the House of Representatives shall choose immediately, by ballot, the President. But in choosing the President, the votes shall be taken by states, the representation from each state having one vote; a

°Altered by Seventeenth Amendment.
°°Ratified July 27, 1804.

quorum for this purpose shall consist of a member or members from two-thirds of the states, and a majority of all the states shall be necessary to a choice. And if the House of Representatives shall not choose a President whenever the right of choice shall devolve upon them, before °the fourth day of March next following, then the Vice-President shall act as President, as in the case of the death or other constitutional disability of the President.—The person having the greatest number of votes as Vice-President, shall be the Vice-President, if such number be a majority of the whole number of Electors appointed, and if no person have a majority, then from the two highest numbers on the list, the Senate shall choose the Vice-President; a quorum for the purpose shall consist of two-thirds of the whole number of Senators, and a majority of the whole number shall be necessary to a choice. But no person constitutionally ineligible to the office of President shall be eligible to that of Vice-President of the United States.

AMENDMENT 20°°

Section 1. The terms of the President and Vice-President shall end at noon on the 20th of January, and the terms of Senators and Representatives at noon on the 3d day of January, of the years in which such terms would have ended if this article had not been ratified; and the terms of their successors shall then begin.

Section 3. If, at the time fixed for the beginning of the term of the President, the President elect shall have died, the Vice-President elect shall become President. If a President shall not have been chosen before the time fixed for the beginning of his term, or if the President elect shall have failed to qualify, then the Vice-President elect shall act as President until a President shall have qualified; and the Congress may by law provide for the case wherein neither a President elect nor a Vice-President elect shall have qualified, declaring who shall then act as President, or the manner in which one who is to act shall be selected, and such person shall act accordingly until a President or Vice-President shall have qualified.

Section 4. The Congress may by law provide for the case of the death of any of the persons from whom the House of Representatives may choose a President whenever the right of choice shall have devolved upon them, and for the case of the death of any of the persons from whom the Senate may choose a Vice-President whenever the right of choice shall have devolved upon them.

°Altered by Twentieth Amendment.
°°Ratified July 23, 1933.

AMENDMENT 22°

Section 1.   No person shall be elected to the office of the President more than twice, and no person who has held the office of President, or acted as President, for more than two years of a term to which some other person was elected President shall be elected to the office of the President more than once. But this Article shall not apply to any person holding the office of President when this Article was proposed by the Congress, and shall not prevent any person who may be holding the office of President, or acting as President, during the term within which this Article becomes operative from holding the office of President or acting as President during the remainder of such term.

AMENDMENT 25°°

Section 1.   In case of the removal of the President from office or of his death or resignation, the Vice-President shall become President.

Section 2.   Whenever there is a vacancy in the office of the Vice-President, the President shall nominate a Vice-President who shall take office upon confirmation by a majority vote of both Houses of Congress.

Section 3.   Whenever the President transmits to the President pro tempore of the Senate and the Speaker of the House of Representatives his written declaration that he is unable to discharge the powers and duties of his office, and until he transmits to them a written declaration to the contrary, such powers and duties shall be discharged by the Vice-President as Acting President.

Section 4.   Whenever the Vice-President and a majority of either the principal officers of the executive departments or of such other body as Congress may by law provide, transmit to the President pro tempore of the Senate and the Speaker of the House of Representatives their written declaration that the President is unable to discharge the powers and duties of his office, the Vice-President shall immediately assume the powers and duties of the office as Acting President.

Thereafter, when the President transmits to the President pro tempore of the Senate and the Speaker of the House of Representatives his written declaration that no inability exists, he shall resume the powers and duties of his office unless the Vice-President and a majority of either the principal officers of the executive department or of such other body as Congress may by law provide, transmit within four days to the President pro tempore of the Senate and the Speaker of the House of Representatives their written declaration that the President is unable to discharge

° Ratified February 27, 1951.
°° Ratified February 10, 1967.

the powers and duties of his office. Thereupon Congress shall decide the issue, assembling within forty-eight hours for that purpose if not in session. If the Congress, within twenty-one days after receipt of the latter written declaration, or, if Congress is not in session, within twenty-one days after Congress is required to assemble, determines by two-thirds vote of both Houses that the President is unable to discharge the powers and duties of his office, the Vice-President shall continue to discharge the same as Acting President; otherwise, the President shall resume the powers and duties of his office.

Bibliography

Following are some of the significant works on the presidency and the executive branch of government. Obviously the list is merely suggestive. Some valuable sources, such as the papers of the various presidents, are not included. Most biographies are also excluded.

BOOKS

Acheson, Dean. *Present at the Creation*. New York: Norton, 1969.

Alley, Robert. *So Help Me God: Religion and the Presidency, Wilson to Nixon*. Richmond: John Knox Press, 1972.

Allison, Graham. *Essence of Decision: Explaining the Cuban Missile Crisis*. Boston: Little, Brown, 1971.

Alsop, Stewart. *The Center: People and Power in Washington*. New York: Harper & Row, 1968.

Anderson, Patrick. *The President's Men*. Garden City, N.Y.: Doubleday, 1968.

Barber, James D. *The Presidential Character*. Englewood Cliffs, N.J.: Prentice-Hall, 1972.

Berger, Raul. *Executive Privilege*. Cambridge, Mass.: Harvard University Press, 1974.

―――. *Impeachment*. Cambridge, Mass.: Harvard University Press, 1973.

Brant, Irving. *Impeachment*. New York: Knopf, 1972.

Brown, Stewart. *The American Presidency: Leadership, Partisanship and Popularity*. New York: Macmillan, 1966.

Burns, James. *The Deadlock of Democracy*. Englewood Cliffs, N.J.: Prentice-Hall, 1963.

―――. *Presidential Government*. Boston: Houghton Mifflin, 1965.

Chayes, Abram. *The Cuban Missile Crisis*. New York: Oxford, 1974.

Clark, Leon P. *Lincoln: A Psycho-Biography*. New York: Scribners, 1933.

Chamberlain, Lawrence. *The President, Congress and Legislation*. New York: Columbia University Press, 1946.

Chase, Harold, and Allen Lerman. *Kennedy and the Press*. New York: Thomas Y. Crowell, 1965.

Cochran, Bert. *Harry Truman and the Crisis Presidency*. New York: Funk & Wagnalls, 1973.

Commager, Henry S. *The Defeat of America*. New York: Simon and Schuster, 1974.

Cornwall, Elmer. *Presidential Leadership of Public Opinion*. Bloomington: Indiana University Press, 1965.

Corwin, Edward. *The President, Office and Powers*. New York: New York University Press, 1957.

Cronin, Thomas, and Sanford Greenberg, eds. *The Presidential Advisory System*. New York: Harper & Row, 1969.

Cunliffe, Marcus. *The American Heritage History of the Presidency*. New York: American Heritage, 1968.

David, Paul T., Ralph Goldman, and Richard Bain. *The Politics of National Party Conventions*. Rev. ed. Washington, D.C.: Brookings, 1964.

Davis, James W., *Presidential Primaries: Road to the White House*. New York: Thomas Y. Crowell, 1967.

Destler, I. M. *Presidents, Bureaucrats, and Foreign Policy*. Princeton, N.J.: Princeton University Press, 1972.

Downs, Anthony, *Inside Bureaucracy*. Boston: Little, Brown, 1967.

Dunn, Delmer. *Financing Presidential Campaigns*. Washington, D.C.: Brookings, 1972.

Edinger, Lewis. *Political Leadership in Industrialized Societies*. New York: Wiley, 1967.

Fairlie, Henry. *The Kennedy Promise: The Politics of Expectations*. Garden City, N.Y.: Doubleday, 1973.

Fenno, Richard *The President's Cabinet*. Cambridge, Mass.: Harvard University Press, 1959.

Finer, Herman. *The Presidency, Crisis and Regeneration*. Chicago: University of Chicago Press, 1960.

Fisher, Louis. *President and Congress*. New York: Free Press, 1972.

Flash, Edward. *Economic Advice and Presidential Leadership: The Council of Economic Advisers*. New York: Columbia University Press, 1965.

Frankel, Charles. *High on Foggy Bottom*. New York: Harper & Row, 1968.

Freud, Sigmund, and William Bullitt. *Thomas Woodrow Wilson: Twenty-Eighth President of the United States, A Psychological Study*. New York: Avon, 1967.

George, Alexander, and Juliette George. *Woodrow Wilson and Colonel House*. New York: John Day, 1956.

Goldman, Eric. *The Tragedy of Lyndon Johnson*. New York: Knopf, 1969.

Graber, Doris. *Public Opinion, the President, and Foreign Policy*. New York: Holt, Rinehart and Winston, 1968.

Grundstein, Nathan. *Presidential Delegation of Authority in Wartime*. Pittsburgh: University of Pittsburgh Press, 1961.

Halberstam, David. *The Best and the Brightest*. New York: Random House, 1972.

Hargrove, Erwin C. *Presidential Leadership: Personality and Political Style*. New York: Macmillan, 1966.

Harris, Richard. *Decision*. New York: Dutton, 1971.

Herring, E. Pendleton. *Presidential Leadership*. New York: Farrar & Rinehart, 1940.

Hilsman, Roger. *The Politics of Policy Making in Defense and Foreign Affairs*. New York: Harper & Row, 1971.

Hobbs, Edward. *Behind the President*. Washington, D.C.: Public Affairs Press, 1954.

Hoopes, Townsend. *The Limits of Intervention*. New York: McKay, 1969.

Hoxie, R. Gordon. *The White House: Organization and Operations*. New York: Center for the Study of the Presidency, 1971.

Hughes, Emmet. *The Living Presidency*. New York: Coward, McCann and Geoghegan, 1973.

——. *The Ordeal of Power*. New York: Atheneum, 1963.

James, Dorothy B. *The Contemporary Presidency*. New York: Pegasus, 1974.

Janis, Irving. *Victims of Groupthink*. Boston: Houghton Mifflin, 1972.

Javits, Jacob. *Who Makes War*. New York: Morrow, 1973.

Kallenback, Joseph E. *The American Chief Executive: The Presidency and the Governership*. New York: Harper & Row, 1966.

Keogh, James. *Nixon and the Press*. New York: Funk & Wagnalls, 1972.

Kennedy, Robert F. *Thirteen Days*. New York: Norton, 1968.

Kessel, John. *The Domestic Presidency*. N. Scituate, Mass.: Duxbury Press, 1975.

Koenig, Louis. *The Chief Executive*. Rev. ed. New York: Harcourt Brace Jovanovich, 1975.

Laski, Harold. *The American Presidency*. New York: Grosset & Dunlap, 1940.

McConnell, Grant. *The Modern Presidency*. New York: St. Martin's, 1967.

——. *Steel and the Presidency*. New York: Norton, 1963.

McGinniss, Joe. *The Selling of the President, 1968*. New York: Trident Press, 1969.

Mann, Dean, and Jameson Doig. *The Assistant Secretaries: Problems and Processes of Appointment.* Washington, D.C.: Brookings, 1965.

Marcy, Carl. *Presidential Commissions.* New York: King's Crown, 1945.

May, Ernest, ed. *The Ultimate Decision.* New York: George Braziller, 1969.

Mazlish, Bruce. *In Search of Nixon: A Psychohistorical Inquiry.* New York: Basic Books, 1972.

Miller, Merle. *Plain Speaking.* New York: Berkley, 1973.

Minnow, Newton, John Martin, and Lee Mitchell. *Presidential Television.* New York: Basic Books, 1973.

Moos, Malcolm. *Politics, Presidents, and Coattails.* Baltimore: Johns Hopkins, 1952.

Morgan, Edward, et al. *The Presidency and the Press Conference.* Washington, D.C.: American Enterprise Institute for Public Policy Research, 1971.

Mueller, John. *War, Presidents and Public Opinion.* New York: Wiley, 1973.

Nathan, Richard. *The Plot That Failed: Nixon and the Administrative Presidency.* New York: Wiley, 1975.

Neustadt, Richard. *Presidential Power.* New York, Wiley, 1960.

Nixon, Richard. *Six Crises.* Garden City, N.Y.: Doubleday, 1962.

Novak, Michael. *Choosing Our King.* New York: Macmillan, 1974.

Pierce, Neal. *The People's President.* New York: Simon and Schuster, 1968.

Polsby, Nelson. *Congress and the Presidency.* 2nd ed. Englewood Cliffs, N.J.: Prentice-Hall, 1971.

Pollard, James F. *The Presidents and the Press: Truman to Johnson.* Washington, D.C.: Public Affair Press, 1964.

Pomper, Gerald. *Nominating the President: The Politics of Convention Choice.* Evanston, Ill.: Northwestern University Press, 1966.

Popper, Frank. *The President's Commissions.* New York: Twentieth Century Fund, 1970.

Reedy, George. *The Presidency in Flux.* New York: Columbia University Press, 1973.

———. *The Twilight of the Presidency.* New York: World, 1970.

Rossiter, Clinton. *The American Presidency.* Rev. ed. New York: Harcourt Brace Jovanovich, 1960.

———. *Constitutional Dictatorship.* Princeton, N.J.: Princeton University Press, 1948.

———. *The Supreme Court and the Commanderer-in-Chief.* Ithaca, N.Y.: Cornell University Press, 1951.

Sayre, Wallace, et al. *Voting for President: The Electoral College and the American Political System.* Washington, D.C.: Brookings, 1970.

Schlesinger, Arthur M., Jr. *The Imperial Presidency.* Boston: Houghton

Mifflin, 1973.

———. *A Thousand Days: John F. Kennedy in the White House.* Boston: Houghton Mifflin, 1965.

Schubert, Glendon. *The Presidency in the Courts.* Minneapolis: University of Minnesota Press, 1957.

Scigliano, Robert. *The Supreme Court and the Presidency.* New York: Free Press, 1971.

Sherwood, Robert E. *Roosevelt and Hopkins.* New York: The Universal Library, 1948.

Sickels, Robert. *Presidential Transactions.* Englewood Cliffs, N.J.: Prentice-Hall, 1974.

Sorensen, Theodore. *Decision-Making in the White House.* New York: Columbia University Press, 1963.

———. *Watchman in the Night.* Cambridge, Mass.: M.I.T. Press, 1975.

Sundquist, James. *Politics and Policy: The Eisenhower, Kennedy, and Johnson Years.* Washington, D.C.: Brookings, 1968.

Taft, William H. *Our Chief Magistrate and His Powers.* New York: Columbia University Press, 1916.

Thomas, Norman C., and Hans Baade. *The Institutionalized Presidency.* Dobbs Ferry, N.Y.: Oceana Publications, 1972.

Tugwell, Rexford. *The Enlargement of the Presidency.* Garden City, N.Y.: Doubleday, 1960.

———. *How They Became President.* New York: Simon and Schuster, 1965.

West, J. B. *Upstairs at the White House.* New York: Warner, 1974.

White, Theodore. *The Making of the President, 1960.* New York: Atheneum, 1961.

———. *The Making of the President, 1964.* New York: Atheneum, 1965.

———. *The Making of the President, 1968.* New York: Atheneum, 1969.

———. *The Making of the President, 1972.* New York: Atheneum, 1973.

Williams, William A. *Some Presidents, Wilson to Nixon.* New York: New York Review Books, 1972.

Wills, Garry. *Nixon Agonistes.* Boston: Houghton Mifflin, 1971.

Wilson, Woodrow. *Constitutional Government in the United States.* New York: Columbia University Press, 1908.

Wise, David. *The Politics of Lying.* New York: Random House, 1973.

Young, Donald. *American Roulette: The Vice-Presidency.* New York: Viking, 1974.

ARTICLES

Burns, James. "Don't Go Too Far." *The Center Magazine,* 7, no. 5 (September–October 1974).

Carey, W. D. "Presidential Staffing in the 60's and 70's." *Public Administration Review*, 29, no. 5 (September 1969).

Cooper, J., and G. Bombardier. "Presidential Leadership and Party Success." *Journal of Politics*, 30, no. 4 (November 1968).

Cornwell, Elmer, Jr. "Presidential News: The Expanding Public Image." *Journalism Quarterly*, 36, no. 3 (Summer 1959).

Cronin, Thomas. "Everybody Believes in Democracy Until He Gets to the White House." *Law and Contemporary Problems*, 35, no. 3 (Summer 1970).

———. "The Swelling of the Presidency." *Saturday Review of the Society*, 1, no. 1 (February 1973).

Edelman, Murray, and Rita Simon. "Presidential Assassinations: Their Meaning and Impact on American Society." *Ethics*, 79, no. 3 (April 1969).

Fairlie, Henry. "The Lessons of Watergate." *Encounter*, 43, no. 4 (October 1974).

———. "Thoughts on the Presidency." *The Public Interest*, no. 9 (Fall 1967).

Falk, Stanley L. "The National Security Council Under Truman, Eisenhower, and Kennedy." *Political Science Quarterly*, 79, no. 3 (September 1964).

Greenstein, Fred I. "The Impact of Personality on Politics: An Attempt to Clear Away Underbrush." *American Political Science Review*, 61, no. 3 (September 1967).

———. "Popular Images of the President." *American Journal of Psychiatry*, 122, no. 5 (November 1965).

Groth, Alexander. "Britain and America: Some Requisites of Executive Leadership Compared." *Political Science Quarterly*, 85, no. 2 (June 1970).

Henry, L. L. "Presidential Transitions: The 1968–69 Experience in Perspective." *Public Administration Review*, 29, no. 5 (September 1969).

Johannes, John R. "Where Does the Buck Stop? Congress, President, and the Responsibility for Legislative Initiation." *Western Political Quarterly*, 25, no. 3 (September 1972).

Kallenbach, Joseph. "The Presidency and the Constitution: A Look Ahead." *Law and Contemporary Problems*, 35, no. 3 (Summer 1970).

Long, N. E. "Reflections on Presidential Power." *Public Administration Review*, 29, no. 5 (September 1969).

Mansfield, Harvey. "Reorganizing the Federal Executive Branch: The Limits of Institutionalization." *Law and Contemporary Problems*, 35, no. 3 (Summer 1970).

Morrow, W. L. "Legislative Control of Administrative Discretion: The

Case of Congress and Foreign Aid." *Journal of Politics*, 30, no. 4 (November 1968).

Moynihan, Daniel. "The Presidency and the Press." *Commentary*, 51, no. 3 (March 1971).

Mueller, J. E. "Presidential Popularity from Truman to Johnson." *American Political Science Review*, 64, no. 1 (March 1970).

Neustadt, Richard E. "Approaches to Staffing the Presidency: Notes on FDR and JFK." *American Political Science Review*, 57, no. 4 (December 1963).

———. "Presidency and Legislation: Planning the President's Program." *American Political Science Review*, 49, no. 4 (December 1955).

———. "Presidency and Legislation: The Growth of Central Clearance." *American Political Science Review*, 48, no. 3 (September 1954).

———. "The Presidency at Mid-Century." *Law and Contemporary Problems*, 21, no. 4 (Autumn 1956).

Rogin, Michael, and John Lottier. "The Inner History of Richard Milhous Nixon." *Trans-Action*, 9, nos. 1–2 (November–December 1971).

Schick, Allen. "The Budget Bureau That Was: Thoughts on the Rise, Decline, and Future of a Presidential Agency." *Law and Contemporary Problems*, 35, no. 3 (Summer 1970).

Seligman, Lester G. "The Presidential Office and the President as Party Leader." *Law and Contemporary Problems*, 21, no. 4 (Autumn 1956).

Sigel, Roberta S. "Image of a President: Some Insights into the Political Views of School Children." *American Political Science Review*, 62, no 1 (March 1968).

———. "Image of the American Presidency: Part II of an Exploration into Popular Views of Presidential Power." *Midwest Journal of Political Science*, 10, no. 1 (February 1966).

Stokes, Donald E. "Some Dynamic Elements of Contests for the Presidency." *American Political Science Review*, 60, no. 1 (March 1966).

Thomas, Norman. "Presidential Advice and Information: Policy and Program Formulation" *Law and Contemporary Problems*, 35, no. 3 (Summer 1970).

———, and Harold Wolman. "Presidency and Policy Formulation: The Task Force Device." *Public Administration Review*, 29, no. 5 (September 1969).

Tugwell, R. G. "Historians and the Presidency: An Essay Review." *Political Science Quarterly*, 86, no. 2 (June 1971).

Weisberg, H. F., and Jerrold Rusk. "Dimensions of Candidate Evaluation." *American Political Science Review*, 64, no. 4 (December 1970).

Weiss, S. L. "American Foreign Policy and Presidential Power." *Journal of Politics*, 30, no. 3 (August 1968).

Willner, A. R., and D. Willner. "The Rise and Role of Charismatic Leaders." *The Annals*, 358 (March 1965).

Wildavsky, Aaron. "The Goldwater Phenomenon: Purists, Politicians, and the Two-Party System." *Review of Politics*, 27, no. 3 (July 1965).

———. "The Two-Presidencies." *Trans-Action*, 4, no. 4 (December 1966).

Index

Abplanalp, Robert, 167
Acheson, Dean, 100
Acting president, 276–77
Adams, John, 24, 28, 89, 159
Adams, John Quincy, 28
Adams, Larry, 68
Adams, Sherman, 199, 256
Advisory councils, 74–75
Agnew, Spiro, 132, 146
Agriculture, Department of, 187–88
Ailes, Roger, 145
Alien and Sedition Acts (1798), 27
Allin, Mort, 210
Amlund, Curtis A., 231–32
Anderson, Jack, 170, 261
Anderson, Patrick, 217
Antideficiency Acts, 65, 66
Antilobbying Law, 78
Appropriations: emergency, 70; im-
  poundment of, 64–70; see also Im-
  poundment of appropriations
Appropriations Committee (House),
  63
Arterton, F. Christopher, 149–51
Arthur, Chester A., 28
Atkin, Charles, 250
Attorney(s) general: as campaign
  managers, 239–40; depoliticization
  of, 241–45

Bagdikian, Ben, 144
Ball, George, 180
Bank of the United States, 18
Bernstein, Carl, 261
Berger, Victor, 27
Bill of Rights, 244
Brandeis, Louis D., 240
Brennan, Peter, 186, 206, 212
Bret, Jane, 142
Brezhnev, Leonid, 171
Brinegar, Claude, 206
British monarchy, 10–12
Broadcast media: congressional use of,
  250–51; presidential use of, 128–44;
  see also Television
Brownell, Herbert, 240
Brownlow Committee, 56
Buchanan, James, 28, 89
Buchanen, Patrick, 137, 209
Buchen, Philip, 183, 214
Budget, federal: congressional reforms

projected, 49; control of expendi-
  tures, 61, 63; presidential control,
  225; presidential manipulation, 64–73
Budget and Accounting Act (1921), 55
Budget reforms of 1974, 63–64, 70, 73
Bundy, McGeorge, 83, 202, 203
Bureau of the Budget, 56–57, 194; see
  also Office of Management and Bud-
  get
Burger, Warren, 92
Burns, James MacGregor, 4
Butterfield, Alexander, 209
Butz, Earl L., 187
Buzhardt, J. Fred, 183
Byrd, Harry, 48
Byrd, Robert C., 241

Cabinet: and Congress, 230; Jackson's
  "kitchen," 18; under Kennedy, 202;
  limitations of structure, 193, 235;
  origins, 13; reforms, 230–33; selec-
  tion, 185–86; and special interest
  groups, 234, 237
Cabinet government, British type, 228,
  232
Cabinet heads: Congressional confir-
  mation, 237; under Nixon, 91, 206;
  obligations of, 187, 190; presidential
  appointment of, 189–91; White
  House staff versus, 181–92, 236
Califano, Joseph A., 203
Cambodia, intervention into, 71, 96, 99,
  101, 120, 140
Campaign promises, 251–52
Cannon, James N., 214
Carlucci, Frank, 192
Carson, Johnny, 131
Cato (George Clinton), 10
Caulfield, John, 192
Center for Political Research, 79
Center for the Study of Democratic
  Institutions, 257
Central Intelligence Agency (CIA), 83,
  86, 207
Chapin, Dwight, 211
Chief of state, distinct from executive
  officer, 262
Church, Frank 96, 98
Civil Rights Act (1964), 67
Civil service careerists, 188–89
Clark, Ramsey, 241

287

Clawson, Ken W., 137
Clay, Henry, 17
Cleveland, Grover, 28
Clinton, George, 10
Cogley, John, 257
Cole, Kenneth, 211
Colson, Charles, 87, 91, 134-35, 211, 213
Commander in chief, presidential role as, 9-11, 42-43, 99-105, 273; see also War powers
Commerce, Department of, 187
Committee on Administrative Management, 193
Committee on Public Information, 26
Committee to Re-elect the President, 139
Common Cause, 264
Congress: abdication of power by, 6, 249; administrations' discrediting of, 60; belief in dominance for, 17; budgetary role of, 55-56, 61-64, 71; budget reforms by, 49, 55, 63-64, 70, 249; Constitutional powers, 15; decision making by, 222, 231, 245-51; decline of, 46-50; emergency powers delegated by, 93-98; executive functions increased by, 234; fiscal powers, 70-73; foreign combat authorization by, 100-1; in foreign relations, 41, 246-49; intelligence needs, 79-93, 249; interim president elected by, 275; legislative role of, 54-61; news media and, 126-27; popularity in Nixon removal, 124; presidential power versus, 21, 46-48, 69, 71, 176, 234; and presidential war making power, 99-100, 103-4; reforms of suggested, 229; revolt of 1975, 48; seniority in, 48; televising sessions of, 237-38, 250; treaty-making role, 14, 81; veto override by, 102; war-making powers of, 101; watchdog committees of, 247; White House liaison with, 77-78; see also House of Representatives; Senate
Congressional Budget Office, 63
Congressional committee(s): closed sessions of, 81; drawbacks of, 49, 59; and executive agencies, 187; in the legislative process, 60; revolt against seniority system, 48; structure of, 48-50, 59

Connally, John, 182, 205
Connelly, Matt, 199
Constitution: Article II, 9; emergency violations of, 93-94; fiscal controls mandated by, 61, 64; impoundment of appropriations justified by, 68; on personal testimony, 92; on presidential response to legislation, 73; provisions pertaining to presidency, 271-77; revisions proposed, 227; war powers intended by, 101
Constitutional Convention, 8, 12, 81, 222
Coolidge, Calvin, 28, 35, 55-56
Cooper, Chester, 204
Cordtz, Dan, 166, 170, 172
Corporation for Public Broadcasting, 250
Corruption of precedents, 65
Corwin, Edward, 192, 230, 248
Council of Economic Advisers, 62, 198, 207, 233
Council on Environmental Quality, 207, 233
Council on Science and Technology, proposed, 234
Cox, Archibald, 190, 208, 239, 242
Creel Committee, 26
Cronin, Thomas, 31, 74-75, 80, 207, 217, 234, 249
Cuban missile crisis, 22, 43-46, 120, 231
Cunliffe, Marcus, 245

Daugherty, Harry, 240
Dawes, Charles G., 191
Dean, John, 85-86, 91, 140, 208, 212, 241
Debs, Eugene, 27
Defense, Department of, 71, 79
de Grazia, Alfred, 217, 252-55
Dennis, Jack, 149-50
Dent, Frederick, 206
Documents, classification of, 80-88
Domestic Council, 58, 91, 205, 233
Drew, Elizabeth, 235, 236
Dulles, John Foster, 199

Eagleton, Thomas, 103
Eastland, James, 48
Easton, David, 111-13, 149, 150
Economic policy, 62
Education programs, 235
Egger, Rowland, 48

Ehrlichman, John, 58, 87, 91, 170, 183, 206, 209, 241
Eisenhower, Dwight D., 6, 29, 33, 66, 89, 118–22; administrative technique, 199; election, 174; and Congress, 174; press conferences, 133; staff activities, 77; television use, 129
Elections, presidential, reforms of, 222
Electoral College, 272, 274
Electoral results, 114
Ellsberg, Daniel, 82–87
Energy Policy Office, 233
Environmental improvement, 49–50, 59
Environmental Protection Agency, 50, 68
Ervin, Sam J., 241, 247
Espionage Act (1917), 26
Evans, Daniel, 261
Evans, Roland, Jr., 78
Ex Com, 43–46, 182
Executive agencies, reform of, 233–38
Executive agreements, in circumvention of the Senate, 246
Executive assistants: see White House staff
Executive branch(es): American and British compared, 232; congressional legislation versus, 49–50; growth under F. D. Roosevelt, 56; reorganization of, 232, 238; testimony of personnel barred Congress, 91; see also Cabinet; White House staff
Executive departments and agencies: appropriations for, 55; career professionals in, 188–90; establishment of, 13; legislative positions of, 55, 58; lobbying by, 78; presidential controls of, 186; public client relations in, 187; White House ex-staffers in, 192
Executive Office of the President, 56, 194, 207, 232; see also White House staff
Executive privilege, 14, 20–21, 88–93

Fairlie, Henry, 183, 258
Farm organizations, national, 186
Farmers' interests, 33
Federal Bureau of Investigation (FBI), 82, 141
Federal Communications Commission

(FCC), 136, 140, 243
Federal Elections Commission, 244
Federal Energy Administration, 97
Federalist, The, 8, 10, 12
Federalist Party, 13
Federal Register, 98
Federal Reserve System, 24
Federal Trade Commission, 24
Feldman, Jacob, 117
Fillmore, Millard, 28
Finch, Robert, 189
Finer, Herman, 227
Florida, legislature broadcasts, 250
Ford, Gerald R., 1, 6, 138, 152; administrative technique, 214; cabinet rapport, 58; Cambodian intervention by, 100, 104; congressional relations reform, 78; on foreign affairs, 246; government by veto, 59, 74; impoundment of housing appropriation, 70; Mayaguez affair, 120, 246; on the presidency, 253; press relations, 137; public image of, 120, 176; reactions to public opinion, 215; on staff ethics, 210; vice-presidential designation, 146; vetoes by, 59, 74
Foreign affairs and policy: Congress' role in, 41, 246–49; as presidential domain, 16, 40–46, 98–105, 245–46, 254; presidential popularity and, 118, 120–23, 248; see also Treaty-making process; War powers
Fourteenth Amendment, 244
Frankel, Charles, 179
Freedom of Information Act, 249
Freeman, Orville, 183
Friendly, Fred, 143
Fulbright, William, 42, 247

Gallup Poll, 102, 251
Garfield, John, 29
Genet, "Citizen" Edmond Charles, 16
Gesell, Gerhardt, 87
Goldberg, Arthur J., 241
Goldman, Eric, 131–32
Goldwater, Barry, 130, 173
Grant, Ulysses S., 28, 65
Great Society program, 66
Greenberg, Bradley, 250
Greenstein, Fred, 113, 115, 148, 151, 176
Gulf of Tonkin Resolution, 100–4

Gurney, Edward, Jr., 208
Guthman, Edwin, 257

Habeas corpus, presidential suspension of, 20
Haig, Alexander, 190, 205, 208, 254
Halberstam, David, 158
Haldeman, H. R., 85, 86, 91, 134, 141, 183, 205, 209, 211
Halperin, Morton, 141
Hamilton, Alexander, 10–13, 16, 41
Harding, Warren G., 28, 55, 240
Harlow, Bryce, 78
Harrison, Benjamin, 28, 193
Harrison, William Henry, 29
Hartman, Robert T., 183, 214
Hatfield, Mark, 97
Hayden, Carl, 201
Hayes, Rutherford B., 28
Health, Education, and Welfare, Department of, 74–75
Hebert, F. Edward, 48
Henry, Patrick, 10
Hess, Robert, 111–13
Hickel, Walter, 182, 186, 205, 237
Higby, Larry, 136
Hoffa, James R., 240
Holtzman, Elizabeth, 103
Hoover, Herbert, 28, 33, 193, 256
Hoover, J. Edgar, 180
House Appropriations Committee, 71
House Judiciary Committee, 136, 251
House of Representatives, 14, 63, 92; see also Congress
Hughes, Emmet John, 31
Humphrey, Hubert, 131, 143
Hunt, E. Howard, 70, 85–86
Huntington, Samuel P., 59
Huntley, Chet, 135

Impeachment: articles against Nixon, 92, 136; presidential, 28, 91, 136, 271, 273
Impoundment of appropriations, 49, 59, 64–70
Inflation, 66–69, 123
Ingram, Timothy, 71
Internal Revenue Service, 136, 170
Intelligence, presidential resources, 79–93, 179–80, 249
Interstate Commerce Commission, 33

Jackson, Andrew, 17, 28, 54, 89, 254
Jackson, Robert H., 96

Jackson, William, 192
Jacob, Charles E., 207
Janis, Irvin, 216–17
Jaworski, Leon, 242
Jay, John, 14, 81
Jefferson, Thomas, 13, 16, 28, 89, 98, 264; on foreign affairs role, 41, 64; on legislation, 54; on unlimited reelection, 10
Johnson, Andrew, 21, 28
Johnson, Lyndon B., 2, 4, 6, 58, 252, 256, 263; administrative technique, 175, 183, 203; Cambodian intervention, 99; candidacy, 157; capital outlay on, 170; congressional relations, 175; executive privilege under, 90; impounding by, 66; press relations, 133, 138, 140; on television, 130; vetoes by, 73; Vietnam intervention, 100, 123, 157
Joint Legislative Council, 230
Jones, Charles O., 47, 79
Jones, John, 140
Judiciary, 126–27, 240
Justice, Department of, 188–89; reforms proposed for, 239–45

Katzenbach, Nicholas, 101, 247
Kefauver, Estes, 77
Kehrli, Bruce, 211
Kelly, Stanley, Jr., 75
Kennedy, Edward, 73–74
Kennedy, John F., 6, 58, 122, 162, 167, 169; administrative technique, 201; assassination, 116, 167; Cambodia, 99; Cuban crisis, 43, 157; executive privilege, 90; expenses, 169; impoundment, 66; news controls, 144; popularity, 113, 173; on the presidency, 252; press conferences, 133; staff efficiency, 175; on television, 129; vetoes by, 73
Kennedy, Robert, 44, 182, 202, 240
Kennerly, David, 137
Khrushchev, Nikita, 6, 45
King, Martin Luther, Jr., 240
Kissinger, Henry, 81, 91, 124, 191, 206, 209, 214
Kistiakowsky, George B., 234
Klein, Herbert, 134–37, 214
Kleindienst, Richard, 91, 92, 239
Knox, Henry, 13
Koenig, Louis, 14, 40, 50, 231
Kohlberg, Lawrence, 150

Krogh, Egil, Jr., 87, 192, 211
Kubitschek, Juscelino, 171

Laird, Melvin, 217
Lame duck problem, 225
Larson, Arthur, 256–57
Laski, Harold, 30
League of Nations, 27, 41
Legislative process: congressional-executive rapport, 57–60; executive liaison, 77–79; intelligence in, 79–80; presidential role in, 54–58, 271–72
Lewis, Howell, 192
Liaison Office for Personnel Management, 194
Lincoln, Abraham, 28, 39; arrogation of war powers, 20, 43, 93, 101; presidential activities, 16–19
Lippmann, Walter, 176
Lloyd George, David, 232
Locke, John, 17, 94
Lost Crusade, The, 204
Louisiana Purchase, 16, 64
Lowell, A. Lawrence, 228
Lynn, James T., 206, 214

MacArthur, Douglas S., 43
McCarthy, Joseph R., 243
McClellan, George Brinton, 43
McGinniss, Joe, 131
McGovern, George, 139, 143, 173
McGrath, Howard, 240
McKinley, William, 22, 28, 100, 193
McLane, Jamie, 141
McLaughlin, John, 183
McLuhan, Marshall, 131
McNamara, Robert, 83
Madison, James, 8–9, 14, 16, 28
Magruder, Jeb Stuart, 134, 136, 191, 211, 212
Making of the President, The, 174
Malek, Fred, 183, 191, 213
Mansfield, Mike, 69, 224
Mardian, Robert, 191, 239
Maroon, Hoke T., 173n
Marsh, John O., Jr., 183, 214
Mayaguez incident, 100, 104, 120, 246
Mason, George, 10
Meir, Golda, 171
Merton, Robert, 32–33
Military affairs: see War powers
Miller, Warren, 75
Mills, Wilbur, 48
Mitchell, John, 189, 205, 211, 239, 244

Mollenhoff, Clark, 261
Monarchical tendencies in presidency, 8–12, 17
Mondale, Walter, 79, 237, 238
Monroe, James, 10, 28, 89
Monroe Doctrine, 22, 89
Montgomery, Robert, 129
Morgan, Edward, 192
Morton, Rogers, 185
Moyers, Bill, 184, 203, 204
Mueller, John, 120–22
Muskie, Edmund, 141, 143

Nader, Ralph, 264
National Academy of Public Administration, 238, 241
National Academy of Sciences, 234
National Opinion Research Center, 116
National Park Service, 161
National security, and presidential power, 40, 95, 101, 254
National Security Council, 91, 140, 198, 199, 205, 207, 233
Negative government, 33
Nessen, Ron, 137, 214
Neustadt, Richard E., 187, 198, 200, 237, 252, 255
Neutrality Act (1794), 15
New Deal, 35, 96
New Jersey Plan, 229
News leaks, unauthorized, 140
News media, presidents' relations with, 126–44, 147
Nixon, Richard M., 1, 4, 6, 263; administrative technique, 5, 91, 176, 191, 205, 207–9; broadcast media and, 134–36; and cabinet, 182, 206; campaign promises, 252; candidacy, 157; congressional liaison under, 77; contempt for political tradition, 93; on Ellsberg break-in, 85; and foreign affairs, 191; identification with office by, 170, 173n, 255, 259; on information requests from Congress, 90; intelligence withholding, 89–93; isolation, 5, 207, 211; judiciary, 240; on Lincoln, 29; military intervention by, 43; national emergencies declared by, 95; opinion of electorate, 5; personal outlays by, 167; popularity, 119, 123, 174; press relations, 132–36, 139, 143, 156; science advisors and, 234; separation of powers claim, 89; "six crises," 156; support after ouster,

169; Supreme Court nominations, 157; on television, 129, 132–34, 143–46; transfer authority by, 71; veto actions, 59, 73–74; vice presidential papers, 179; Vietnam war secrecy, 82; War Powers Resolution veto, 102; White House formalities, 162; wiretapping under, 140–42; *see also* Impeachment; Watergate; White House staff

Nixon v. Sirica and Cox, 89

North Vietnam, 81, 101, 120

Novak, Michael, 262

Novak, Robert, 78

O'Brien, Larry, 77, 202

O'Donnell, Kenneth, 190, 202

Office of Communications, 134, 137

Office of Economic Opportunity, 67

Office of Government Reports, 194

Office of Management and Budget (OMB), 57, 62, 172, 207, 236, 238, 249

Office of Public Attorney, 242

Office of Science and Technology, 234

Office of Technological Assessment, 249

Office of Telecommunications Policy, 134, 207, 233

Ombudsman, 242

Organization of American States (OAS), 45

Pardons and reprieves, presidential, 9

Party politics, 98, 114; in cabinet selection, 185; and Nixon removal, 124; restoration of, 264

Patronage, presidential, 74–77

Pensions, presidential, 169

Pentagon Papers, 82, 85, 87

People's Republic of China, 95, 143

Petersen, Henry, 86, 188, 240

Pierce, Franklin, 28, 59

"Plumbers," the, 70, 84–87, 140

Plural executive, proposed, 229

Pocket veto, 73

Political socialization of youth, 111–16, 147–48

Polk, James K., 20, 28, 100

Pompidou, Georges, 171

Porter, Bart, 212

Powers of the presidency, 3–8, 12–16; appointment of officers, 273; in budgetary matters, 55–58, 61; centralization of, 39–41; ceremonial versus executive, 262; constitutional provisions for, 9–10, 271–77; checking, 97, 263; criticisms of, 222; in emergency conditions, 20, 39–46, 247; fiscal nonconstitutional, 64–73; in foreign affairs, 41–46, 98–105; increases in, 3–4, 30–31; in legislation, 58; Lincoln's concept of, 20; Nixon's presumptions of, 67–68; personal basis of, 110, 248; popular view of, 118; reforms in, 223; secrecy and, 81–84; scope and limits of, 256, 263; stewardship theory of, 23, 30; *see also* Executive privilege; Impoundment of appropriations; Veto

Presidency, the: absolutistic tendencies in, 258; bureaucratic collectivism of, 253; candidates, 156–58, 173; ceremonial roles, 262; costs to maintain, 167–70, 173; criteria for, 28–31; disability of, 273; election to, 272–76; eligibility for, 273; Finer plan for, 228; as head of government and state, 3, 42, 112, 115–16; historical development of, 12–16, 32–41, 54, 160; image of, 1–2, 111–16, 147–50; impact on man elected, 177–79; incumbent versus office, 170–73, 177, 216, 222; isolation of, 172–81; myths about, 251–63; national constituency, 47; national symbolism, 115–16, 257–58; operational parameters, 216; perquisites of office, 160–62; popular attitudes toward, 115; political blunders, 157; political limitations, 222; politics and, 225–26; positive role of, 31–32, 50; and professional bureaucracy, 189; protocol of office, 159; as public advocate, 253; reforms proposed, 222–26; removal of, 273; responsibility in, 254; remuneration, 160; tenure, 119, 223, 275 travel in, 158, 163–68; virtues inherent in, 93; *see also* Powers of the Presidency; Presidents; *and names of specific incumbents*

Presidential assistants: *see* White House staff

Presidential Power, 201

Presidential Science Advisory Committee, 234

Presidents: on broadcast media, 250; comparative rating of, 28–31; death of, 117–18; effects of office on,

178-79; popularity of, 118-23; staff loyalty, 182; television's effects on, 129-35, 142-47
Press relations, presidential, 23, 127, 133, 139-40, 261-62
Proclamation of Neutrality, 15
Progressive movement, 24, 48

Randolph, Edmund, 13, 229
Ranney, Austin, 228
Rather, Dan, 261
Rayburn, Sam, 48
Reedy, George, 84, 158, 225, 256
Rehnquist, William, 67
Reprieves and pardons, presidential, 9, 273
Richardson, Elliot, 190, 208, 239, 244, 254
Rivers, Mendel, 48
Rockefeller, Nelson, 185
Rogers, Will, 46
Rogers, William, 91
Romney, George W., 185-86
Roosevelt, Eleanor, 196
Roosevelt, Franklin D., 4, 6, 27, 28, 36, 81, 98, 133; administration of, 35-39; administrative technique, 193-97; Congress and, 174; emergency powers, 94; "fireside chats," 37-38, 128; impoundment of funds by, 65; Japanese-American removal, 96; legislative program, 38, 55; performance rating, 122; on presidential power, 4; public image of, 37; staff needs, 193-94; Supreme Court packing, 157; vetoes by, 54
Roosevelt, Theodore, 28, 39, 254; administration, 21-24; on executive power, 23; press relations, 22, 127
Roosevelt Corollary, 22
Rossiter, Clinton, 19, 30, 263
Ruckelshaus, William, 208, 239
Rumsfeld, Donald, 214
Rusk, Dean, 180, 183
Russell, Richard, 48

Safire, William, 141, 210
Sallinger, Pierre, 190, 202
Saxbe, William, 158
Schlesinger, Arthur, Sr., 28
Schlesinger, Arthur, Jr., 41, 65, 105, 194, 202, 246
Schoolchildren's image of the presidency, 111-16, 147-51

Sears, John, 141
Second Bank of the United States, 18
Secrecy, in government, 80-89, 93-94
Secret Service, 160, 164-67, 178
Security: clearance, 83-84; document classification, 80-81; presidential, 165, 167, 169
Sedition Act (1918), 27
Seidman, William, 214
Senate: abdication of power by, 6; advice and consent role, 13, 273; circumvention of, 246; in foreign affairs, 41-42, 246; in treaty making, 15; see also Congress
Senate Foreign Relations Committee, 83
Senate Select Committee on Presidential Campaign Activities, 238; see also Watergate affair
Senate Watergate Committee, 242; broadcast hearings, 251
Separation of powers, 8-9, 89
Sheatsley, Paul, 117
Sigel, Roberta, 118
Smith, Howard, 48
Sneed, Joseph T., 68
Sorensen, Ted, 183, 185, 190, 202
Special Committee on the Termination of the National Emergency, 96
Special prosecutor, 158, 189, 240-44; see also Watergate affair
"Spoils system," 18-19
State, Department of, 41, 91
"State of the Union," proviso and message, 9, 14, 274
Steelman, John, 198
Stennis, John, 48
Stokes, Donald, 75
Strachan, Gordon, 191-92, 211
Supreme Court, 38, 69, 85, 92, 96, 103, 127

Taft, William Howard, 28
Taft-Hartley Act, 59
Talmadge, Herman, 87
Tanaka, Kakuei, 171
Taylor, Zachary, 28
Television, in politics, 129-35, 142-47
terHorst, Jerald F., 138, 183, 215, 261
Terms of office, presidential, 2, 119, 223, 275-76
Timmons, William, 78
Tolley, Howard, 148
Train, Russell, 50, 68

Transfer of funds, 72
Treasury, Department of, 56, 62
Treaty-making process, 14, 15, 246, 273; see also Foreign affairs
Truman, Harry S, 6, 29, 178, 254; administrative technique, 197–98; budget office under, 56; Congress and, 174; impoundment of funds, 66; Korean intervention, 100, 123; legislative decisions, 57; MacArthur firing, 123; popularity, 120, 123; press relations, 133, 139; secrecy under, 81; state of emergency, 95; steel industry seizure, 96, 157; wartime powers, 43
Tuchman, Barbara, 229
Tugwell, Rexford G., 225, 227, 245
Twain, Mark, 46
Twentieth Century Fund, 250
Twenty-second Amendment, 223, 226
Tyler, John, 28

Udall, Stewart, 183
United States v. *Nixon*, 92
Urban Affairs Council, 205
Urban government, growth of, 32

Valenti, Jack, 204, 224
Van Buren, Martin, 28
Veto, presidential, 9, 18, 64, 73, 90, 97, 102, 247, 271
Vice-president, 227, 272, 275
Vietnam war, 50, 61, 82, 85, 99, 100, 104, 119, 203–4
Virginia Plan, 223
Volpe, John, A., 186

Wallace, George, 143
War powers, presidential, 40, 42–43, 98–105; constitutional intent, 101; impoundment of funds and, 66; Lincoln's assumption of, 20–21; sought by Wilson, 26
War Powers Act, 59, 101–5
Warren, Gerald, 141
Washington, George, 1, 54, 28; administration of, 12–16; aides, 192; executive privileges asserted by, 14; protocol instituted by, 158–59; tenure precedent, 16
Watchdog committees, 247

Watergate affair, 2, 6, 47, 85, 87, 139, 147, 208, 224; cover-up, 241; financing of, 70; potential effects, 6, 50; public opinion on, 121, 148, 150; Senate hearings on, 87, 146, 238, 241–42, 250; see also Special prosecutor
Webster, Daniel, 16
Weinberger, Caspar, 68
Wheeler, Harvey, 229
Whig Party, 17
Whiskey Rebellion, 14
Whitaker, John, 192
White, Byron R., 69–70
White, Leonard D., 194–5
White, Theodore H., 174
Whitehead, Clay, 134, 136
White House, 161–66, 171, 178
White House staff, 56; cabinet and, 181–92; Congress and, 77–78; costs of, 195; in executive agency positions, 191–92; functions of, 195; growth of, 207, 235; Hatch Act and, 238; history of, 192; under Johnson, 204; under Kennedy, 175; limitation and reform of, 232, 238; under Nixon, 91, 134–37, 195, 207–14; policy initiation by, 57–58; presidential deference of, 181–82, 211–13; rapport and loyalty, 182–83; rights and prerogatives, 184; selection, 185, 211; Senate confirmation proposed, 238; wire taps on, 85, 89, 141, 240
Wildavsky, Aaron, 39–40, 55
Wilhelmsen, Frederick, 142
Wilson, Harold, 233
Wilson, Woodrow, 15, 28, 39, 98, 254; administration of, 24–27; emergency powers, 94; legislative initiative, 54; precedents made by, 25–27, 54; on presidential powers, 25; on presidential persuasion, 99
Wiretapping, in the White House, 85, 89, 140–42, 240
Wirtz, Willard, 183
Wise, David, 83, 137
Wobblies (IWW), 27
Woodward, Bob, 261

Ziegler, Ron, 134, 137–38, 141, 166, 182–83, 211